I0820343

BEYOND THE OUTPOST

An Army Cavalry Officer's War Diary on the Frontlines of Afghanistan, 2003–2007

ROSS A. BERKOFF

Savas Beatie
California

First edition, first printing

Names: Berkoff, Ross A., 1980- author
Title: Beyond the Outpost: An Army Cavalry Officer's War Diary on the Frontlines of Afghanistan, 2003-2007 / by Ross A Berkoff.
Description: El Dorado Hills, CA : Savas Beatie, [2025] | Summary: "This is the first and only raw daily chronicle from the perspective of a junior officer covering this delicate and hostile early period of the U.S. Army's 20-year campaign against the Taliban. Berkoff's diary-raw and unscripted-carries us along the bumpy ride as Army operations roil in its counter-insurgency mission designed to destroy pockets of extremists and separate them from the beleaguered Afghan people. As this records the early years of America's Afghanistan Conflict, this book offers unique clarity and detail of the common soldier's perspective, the evolution of tactics of the Taliban insurgency, and how the U.S. Army Cavalry fought to defeat it. Berkoff's stories of courage, sacrifice, adaptability, resilience, and leadership, enhanced with original maps, illustrations, and previously unpublished photographs, help carry the weight of the collective experiences of our Afghanistan veterans"-- Provided by publisher.
Identifiers: LCCN 2025023289 | ISBN 9781611217629 hardcover | ISBN 9781954547704 ebook
Subjects: LCSH: Berkoff, Ross A., 1980- | United States. Army. Mountain Division, 10th | Afghan War, 2001-2021--Personal narratives, American | Counterinsurgency--Afghanistan | Soldiers--United States--Biography | LCGFT: Autobiographies
Classification: LCC DS371.413 .B43 2025
LC record available at https://lccn.loc.gov/2025023289

SB
Savas Beatie
989 Governor Drive, Suite 101
El Dorado Hills, CA 95762
916-941-6896 / sales@savasbeatie.com / www.savasbeatie.com

All of our titles are available at special discount rates for bulk purchases in the United States. Contact us for information.

Printed and bound in the United Kingdom

Dedicated to the men of the 10th Mountain Division, 3-17 CAV and 3-71 CAV,
with whom I served during Operation Enduring Freedom,
and who are no longer with us today.

PFC Brian Bradbury

SPC Armer N. Burkart

SGT Matthew J. Chadbourne

LTC Joseph Fenty

SGT Daniel H. Granica

Captain Ben Keating

SSG Patrick Lybert

SFC Jared Monti

PFC Brian M. Moquin Jr.

Major James D. Mullin

Specialist Justin L. O'Donohoe

Specialist Anthony "Nick" Pilozzi

1st Sgt. Billy J. Siercks

SPC David N. Timmons

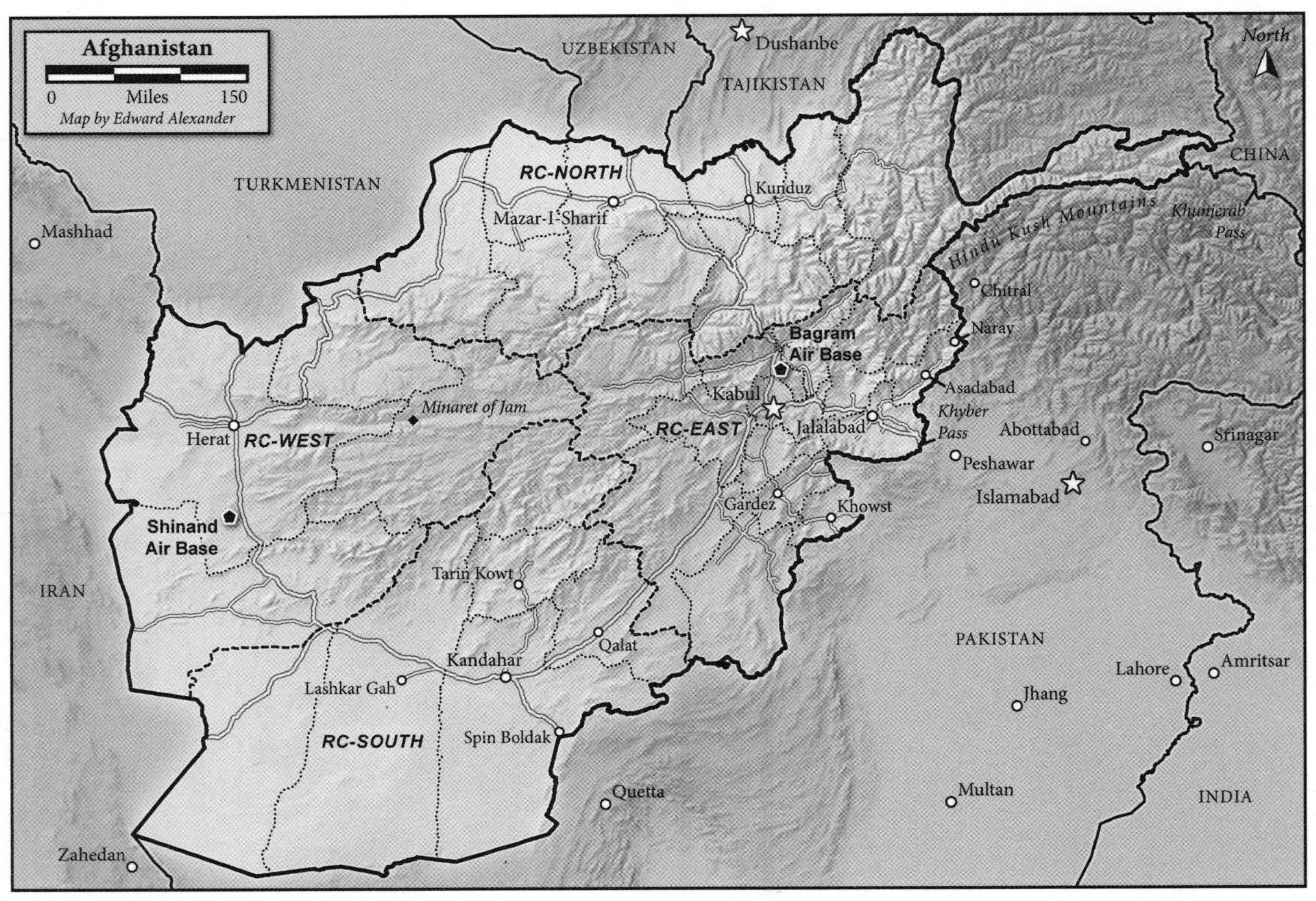
Afghanistan
0
Miles
150
Map by Edward Alexander
North
UZBEKISTAN
Dushanbe
TAJIKISTAN
CHINA
TURKMENISTAN
RC-NORTH
Kunduz
Mazar-I-Sharif
Mashhad
Hindu Kush Mountains
Khunjerab Pass
Chitral
Naray
Bagram Air Base
Kabul
Asadabad
Khyber Pass
Minaret of Jam
Herat
RC-WEST
RC-EAST
Jalalabad
Abottabad
Srinagar
Peshawar
Islamabad
Gardez
Khowst
Shinand Air Base
IRAN
Tarin Kowt
Qalat
PAKISTAN
Kandahar
Lashkar Gah
Lahore
Amritsar
Jhang
RC-SOUTH
Spin Boldak
Quetta
Multan
INDIA
Zahedan

TABLE OF CONTENTS

TABLE OF CONTENTS (continued)

LIST OF MAPS

by Edward Alexander

Photos have been added throughout for the convenience of the reader.

GLOSSARY

ACM: Anti Coalition Militia

Air Assault: To seize an objective through helicopter transport and aerial deployment

AO: Area of Operation

AOBC/OBC: Armor Officer's Basic Course/Officer's Basic Course

AMF: Afghan Militia Force

ANA: Afghanistan National Army

AQAM: Al Qaeda and Associated Militia

Article 15: A non-judicial punishment allowing a commander to discipline service members for minor offenses without a formal court-martial.

ASP: Ammo Supply Point

B1 Bomber: A long-range supersonic heavy bomber aircraft used by the U.S. Air Force

BAF: Bagram Airfield

BCT: Brigade Combat Team

BDA: Battle Damage Assessment

BDU: Battle Dress Uniform

BN: Battalion

Boonie cap: A wide-brimmed soft hat issued to soldiers in hot or jungle environments for added sun protection and camouflage

BTR APC: Soviet series armored personnel carrier vehicle used to transport troops across a battlefield

BTR-80: Most widely used Soviet-era troop transport vehicle, equipped with a 14.5mm machine gun and 7.62mm coaxial.

C-130: U.S. Air Force fixed wing aircraft used to carry troops and vehicles and airdrop supplies.

C-17: Larger U.S. Air Force strategic airlifter designed to carry tanks, helicopters, and over 100 troops at a time.

CH-47 Chinook: Heavy lift U.S. Army helicopter with two large tandem-rotors for heavy lifting of troop and cargo transport

Chalk: A specific group of soldiers or equipment assigned for a load onto a single aircraft for an air-assault, airborne drop, or other air movement operation.

Class A Uniform: Formal service dress uniform used for ceremonial or official duties

CO: Commanding Officer

DAB: Dansk Automobil Byggeri is a Denmark-base company that produced military vehicles for European/NATO allies.

DCU: Desert Combat Uniform

DFAC: Dining Facility

DoD: Department of Defense

EOD: Explosives Ordinance

FARP: Forward Area Resupply Point

Fires NCO: Non-Commissioned Officer responsible for deploying indirect fire (artillery sections or mortars teams)

FM 17-98: Field Manual for Cavalry Scout Platoon Tactics focused on reconnaissance and security missions

FOB: Forward Operating Base

Full Battle Rattle: Soldier slang for donning all gear needed for a combat mission including Kevlar, body-armor, load-bearing equipment (ammunition, canteen)

GAC: Ground Attack Convoy

HHC: Headquarters and Headquarters Company

HIG: Hezb-e-Islami Guldbuddin, or "Party of Islam," is a political and paramilitary organization in Afghanistan founded in 1976 by former Afghan prime minister Gulbuddin Hekmatyar.

HUMINT: Human Intelligence

IED: Improvised Explosive Device

ITAS: Improved Target Acquisition System

JAF: Jalalabad Airfield

JAG: Judge Advocate General

KAF: Kandahar Airfield

KBR: Kellogg Brown & Root

KIA: Killed in Action

LMTV: Light Medium Tactical Vehicle

MGRS: Military Grid Reference System

MOS: Military Occupation Specialty

MOUT: Military Operations on Urban Terrain

MP: Military Police

NAIs: Named Area of Interest

NCO: Non-Commissioned Officer

NCOER: Non-Commissioned Officer Evaluation Report

NDS: National Directorate of Security was Afghanistan's national intelligence and security service

ODA: Operational Detachment-Alpha (a 12-person U.S. Army Special Forces team)

OEF IV/VII: Operation Enduring Freedom

OIC: Officer in Charge

OP: Observation Post

Order of Battle (OB): Order of Battle is a structured listing of military units and command relationships for a specific campaign or operation

PA: Physician Assistant

PIR: Priority Intelligence Requirement

PRT: Provincial Reconstruction Team

PSG: Platoon Sergeant

PUC: Person Under Custody

PX: Post Exchange

R&R: Rest and Recuperation

RC: Regional Command

RDF: Rapid Deployment Facility

RIP: Relief in Place

ROTC: Reserve Officer's Training Corps

RPG: Rocket Propelled Grenade

RSTA: Reconnaissance, Surveillance, and Target Acquisition

S3 Shop: Operations and Planning Team for a U.S. Army command headquarters (battalion, brigade, division)

SF: Special Forces

SOP: Standard Operating Procedure

SPC: Specialist

SRC: Soldier Readiness Center provides the administrative and medical support to soldiers preparing for a deployment

TAC: Tactical Action Center

TOC: Tactical Operations Center

Troop: A U.S. Cavalry Troop consists of about 60-80 Troopers

UCMJ: Uniformed Code of Military Justice

UXO: Unexploded Ordinance

VCP: Vehicle Checkpoint

WIA: Wounded in Action

ACKNOWLEDGMENTS

I have been a passionate consumer of American soldier diaries ever since I was a young teen in the 1990s, when I first heard the documentarian, Ken Burns, present the reflections of Confederate Private Sam R. Watkins from Tennessee, alongside the Union officer, Elisha H. Rhodes, from Rhode Island. I had imagined that one day, I might collect my deployment journals into a literary publication for posterity. But in the years following my separation from the U.S. Army, a time marked by a whirlwind of adult responsibility—marriage, raising children, intense career ambition—the prospect of publishing my war journals seemed like a project more fit for retirement.

In 2023, I made a new addition to my library of soldier diaries: *One Of Custer's Wolverines: The Civil War Letters of Brevet Brigadier General James H. Kidd, 6th Michigan Cavalry*. I reached out to the author, Eric J. Wittenberg, who also happened to be deeply integrated into the American Civil War history community. I offered Eric my gratitude for delivering Kidd's personal letters to new generations of history buffs, especially those interested in the U.S. Cavalry. I casually mentioned to Eric a few of the things that James Kidd and I had in common. We both had served as cavalry officers during an American war. We had both journaled our combat experiences. We both possessed an irrational attraction to all-things George Armstrong Custer. Kidd and I had both been involuntarily extended in our combat service—mine, through an extended tour that dragged on for several additional months fighting the Nuristani insurgents, Kidd's, after the final surrender of the Confederate armies, by a seven-month detour to the Great Plains fighting the Sioux and Cheyenne Indians (a strikingly similar adversary to that of the Nuristani).

The connections struck Eric as well. Only seconds after mentioning my handwritten war journals, and my interest in publishing them, Eric offered his assistance. His early endorsement, his encouragement, and his introduction to Ted Savas and Savas Beatie Publishing was not merely helpful—it was essential. Thank you, Eric Wittenberg, for graciously opening the door toward publication. *Beyond the Outpost*, is a tribute to the soldiers who both participated in and bore witness to America's wars, like James Kidd and Elisha Rhodes. I am grateful that Eric was there to help me contribute to that noble tradition.

Thank you to all the wonderful people at Savas Beatie who took a risk on me and nurtured this book from idea to reality, especially Ted Savas, Sarah Closson, and Veronica Kane. Sarah Keeney and Ian Hughes quickly accepted my cover design proposal and turned it into a final image that truly captures the essence of the book's narrative—blending the old with the new. I could not have done this without copyeditor, David Snyder, who has a remarkable mind and style that captured my unique voice. Thanks to Derrick Lindow for indexing the book. Many thanks to cartographer Edward Alexander for his geospatial precision, fusing science with a touch of artistic clarity.

To the men and women of the 10th Mountain Division that I served with, named and unnamed in the chapters that follow, I hope this book does justice to their hearts, their spirits, and their fierce devotion to duty. Chief among them, I wish to acknowledge the coterie of men that was 2nd Platoon, Apache Troop, 3-17 Cavalry, 2003-2004. Thank you for helping write the opening chapters of America's Longest War: Platoon Sergeant Jason White, Senior Scouts George Elsaesser and Bill Letunic, along with David Stricker, Shane Colby, Tristian Mortensen, Jason Goff, Ryan Fleming, Dominik Melite, Daniel Priego, Darom Kounlavong, Brent Learnard, Timothy Gossett, James Callaway, Brandon Casper, Austin Burke, and Everest Brooks.

To my 3-71 Cavalry S2 section, an unrivaled team of field analysts and data collectors who displayed iron discipline and analytical precision, I am confident their quiet bravery and intellectual rigor saved American lives on the battlefield: Clay Huffman, Ward Yoder, John Tierney, Neil Chemplavil, Patrick Wasik, Daniel Butler, Daniel Gonzalez, Adam Boulio, and Jessica Saenz.

To my fellow 3-71 Cavalry founding officers, their mentorship and companionship kept me philosophically and emotionally grounded. Many continued to fight on with new Army units long after our deployment, but all acknowledge the rare and enduring bond that we forged: Rich Timmons, Paul Garcia, Thomas Sutton, Andrew Ornelas, Dennis Sugrue, Todd Polk, Matthew Cannon, Peter Stambersky, Matthew Gooding, Frank Brooks, Mike Schmidt, Joe Hansen, Matt Winters, Aaron Swain, Doug Weaver, Roy Chiquitucto, Will

Hammond, and Tim Dillon. And to the founding non-commissioned officers of 3-71 CAV, who never failed to offer candid guidance and taught me how to earn the respect of my soldiers: Delbert Byers, James Reese, Donnie Little, Ralph DeLosa, Mike Laclair, Gary Hunsucker, Jeffrey Hackett, Aaron Jongeneel, Brendan Kearns, Milt Yagel, Chris Cunningham, John Hawes, John Garner, Steven Brock, Charles McNeill, and Donald Kernan. I thank them all.

I am forever grateful for the mentorship and support that came from John "Mick" Nicholson, General, U.S. Army, Retired, a true gentlemen-officer whose life exemplifies servant leadership. Thank you to Jake Tapper, for his authentic pursuit of truth and his trust in me for helping him attain it. I'm indebted to the great author, Jon Krakauer, who risked much in the name of accuracy and authenticity by placing himself with us in Konar province. Jon encouraged me to broaden this book into a memoir-novel, which perhaps someday I will do. He also taught me that clarity and patience in good writing is hard earned.

Thank you, Jeb Ridgeway, former 3-71 Cavalry scout, for allowing me to show the world the beauty and pain of Afghanistan which he captured on his personal camera during our deployment.

To my family—my parents and my siblings, Todd, Sari, Damian, Stacie—and to my closest friends— Mike DeMarco, Mike Gourgues, David Floyd, Nate Duncan, Peter Benninger, Ian Watt, Chris Morrison, Brian Taylor, Scott Shanksy, Scott Polirstok. Mark Burshteyn, and Adam Turkel—who offered me the rarest kind of support, not just cheerleading but patience and understanding in my absence, and also the willingness to carry me through every high and hollow of my Afghanistan journey, I remain forever grateful.

Finally, and most importantly, throughout the long, uneven terrain of this book's creation, I leaned on the quiet but strong compass provided by my wife, Rebekah, whose patience and counsel steadied me in moments of doubt. Indeed, throughout my 2006–2007 deployment to Afghanistan, it was her presence that my letters home sought and my physical being craved. This book bears her touch in ways that are both subtle and profound. To my children, Eliana and Aaron, I hope this book teaches you that hardship reveals true character, being a leader means responsibility and not privilege, holding onto hope is a form of discipline, and listening to stories of the past will help charter a better future.

FOREWORD

I served alongside Captain Ross Berkoff in combat for 16 months in Afghanistan. He's an incredible officer with an important untold story, and he has done us all a great service by writing and sharing his combat diaries of two deployments to Afghanistan early in the war. While the young men and women who served there were all volunteers, in retrospect, they bore a disproportionate share of the burden of protecting our nation and the American people from another 9/11. While the vast majority of Americans are deeply grateful for their service, it's fair to say that most Americans don't fully understand what combat service entailed or the enduring impact on the lives of those who served.

Ross's diaries provide an unfiltered view into that world. His contemporaneous account of experience as a junior officer leading a cavalry scout platoon in Kandahar, the heartland of the Taliban, and again as the intelligence officer for a cavalry squadron fighting insurgents in the Hindu Kush Mountains, offers first-hand insights the reader won't find elsewhere. Ross's candor, strong character, faith, and values come through as he relates how he dealt with the challenges and emotions of combat: love of comrades developed through shared hardship and trust; the uncertainty and fear of the unknown; the deep shock of losing people who you love; the sense of futility when trying to console their families; frustration over higher level decisions which abruptly and significantly impact lives at the lowest level; and the satisfaction of doing one's duty juxtaposed with lifelong grief for those who didn't return.

And then . . . it's over, and he transitions to civilian life forever shaped by events and emotions to which few can relate.

I'm personally very familiar with Ross's story because it was my honor and privilege to be his Brigade Commander in the 3rd Brigade Combat Team "Spartans" of the 10th Mountain Division, both building the brigade and leading it in combat. Having served alongside Ross and his unit in action in Konar and Nuristan provinces, the scene of some of the heaviest fighting and incredible displays of valor by American Soldiers in this war, I can personally attest to the difficulty of the conditions under which the 3rd Squadron, 71st Cavalry fought. Ross's personal humility is on display throughout his narrative, but the reader should know that this was one the toughest missions given to any unit in Afghanistan during the entire war.

America's longest war was fought by the smallest percentage of our population of any major conflict in our nation's history. On 9/11, there were 480,000 soldiers in a 1.42 million active-duty force serving an American population of over 300 million. In 2004, Congress increased the size of the Army by 30,000 active-duty troops and added three BCTs, one of which was 3d Brigade Combat Team, 10th Mountain Division—"The Spartans" in which Ross served as S2 of 3-71 Cavalry on his second deployment. In May 2004, I was redirected from another assignment to Fort Drum, NY. The officer who sent my orders from the Department of the Army was named LTC Joe Fenty. A few weeks later, Joe himself was reassigned to Ft Drum to take command of 3-71 Cavalry. It was my honor to command the 3d BCT, 10th Mountain Division, from July 2004 to June 2007. Together, with our exceptional team of NCOs and officers, which included CPT Ross Berkoff, we built the brigade in 18 months and deployed for 16 months.

In 2006 the disparity between the number of service members in Afghanistan versus Iraq was pronounced. Iraq had 130–140,000 U.S. service members, whereas Afghanistan had only 30–40,000 troops. Yet Afghanistan was physically larger and had roughly the same population as Iraq. The population in Iraq was concentrated around urban areas whereas the Afghan population was distributed across a vast and austere landscape from the high deserts of Kandahar to the 15,000-foot peaks of the Hindu Kush in Nuristan.

Over 20 years of war, a total of 775,000 U.S. personnel served in Afghanistan; 244,000 did multiple tours. 2,461 were killed and over 20,000 were wounded. The total number represents one quarter of one percent of the nation's population. A third of them served multiple deployments. For two decades, they prevented another 9/11. Churchill's quote comes to mind: "Never has so much been owed by so many to so few."

Policy decisions at the highest levels have a direct and enduring impact on the lives of soldiers and their families at the tip of the spear. Ross's account relates the impact of those decisions, such as the unprecedented extension of our brigade's deployment from 12 to 16 months. The effect of the U.S. decision to focus on Iraq over Afghanistan, perhaps best articulated by Chairman of Joint Chiefs of Staff Michael Mullen when he said, "In Iraq we do what we must, in Afghanistan we do what we can," comes through in Ross's account. Following the rapid collapse of the Taliban in 2001, the U.S. excluded them from the December 2001 Bonn Conference on Afghanistan which charted the reconstruction of Afghanistan. At this point, the Pakistanis had agreed to support the U.S. effort. However, 15 months later in March of 2003, the U.S.-led invasion of Iraq began. The campaign in Iraq became the main effort, taking focus and resources away from Afghanistan. It also took pressure off the Taliban and caused Pakistan to doubt America's commitment to the theater. The Pakistanis feared a united Pashtun resistance to their rule and by backing a Taliban insurgency in Afghanistan they would "divide and conquer," fighting the Tehreki Taliban Pakistan (TTP) while supporting the Afghan Taliban.

Ross's 2003 nine-month deployment to Kandahar was very challenging but ended fortunately, as he put it: "I've led my platoon over 12,000 miles, conducted over 200 missions and everyone is coming home . . . truly remarkable." In retrospect, it reflected the calm before the storm which began in early 2006 when a resurgent Pakistan-backed Taliban intensified the fight in Afghanistan. Ross's second deployment in 2006/7 with 3-71 Cavalry and 3d BCT, 10th Mountain Division, met that resurgent Taliban effort head on.

The U.S. decision to simultaneously fight two wars without significantly increasing the size of the U.S. Army meant extension of units for longer and longer tours. The Spartans of 3/10th Mountain Division were the first Brigade Combat Team in the Army to be extended from 12 to 16 months. That extension was ordered after they had begun their redeployment home, which had a significant impact on families back at Fort Drum. By mid-2007, all Army combat deployments were extended from 12 to 15 months. Other services retained unit deployments of a year or less. The Afghan war was fought on the backs of the 244,000 soldiers and their families who served two or more tours in Afghanistan. Units had 12 to 18 months to reset and retrain before deploying back to Iraq or Afghanistan.

The abrupt manner in which America withdrew from Afghanistan in 2021 contributed to the rapid defeat of the Afghan armed forces and imposed a horrendous cost on the Afghan people, many of whom were abandoned despite their long-time support of the United States. It also exacted a significant toll on those who fought in Afghanistan, as tragically illustrated by the suicide of 3-71 Cavalry Specialist Anthony "Nick" Pilozzi for whom the chaotic withdrawal meant that he increasingly saw the sacrifices of his friends killed in Afghanistan as "meaningless." He joins a growing list of veterans who have taken their own lives.

Ross Berkoff was one of the few Americans who served multiple tours in Afghanistan. He has done us a great service by sharing his unfiltered experiences and emotions as a young leader in combat. In particular, several themes common to men and women undergoing the stresses of combat, and which are rarely made visible to those who do not serve, are apparent in his journal:

- *Love*: The human dimension of war includes the strong bonds that grow between soldiers and between leaders and led. These bonds are a form of love, *Philios* or brotherly love, as the Spartans of ancient Greece called it. Ross's love for his comrades and for his Squadron Commander, LTC Joe Fenty, come through in his words on the days immediately following their loss. What Ross leaves unstated is that he and his entire unit continued the mission despite the emotional shock to them as individuals and as a unit. This resiliency is a hallmark of a highly professional and well-trained unit, another legacy of Joe Fenty's outstanding leadership.
- *Loss, regret, and survivor's guilt*: Losing anyone in your charge is gut-wrenching but losing people whom you love means you will be grieving the rest of your life. Ross's grieving for his fellow soldiers such as Joe Fenty, Ben Keating, and Nick Pilozzi gives the reader an insight into what it means to be a combat veteran.
- *Elation and frustration*: The end of Ross's first tour in Kandahar ended with the satisfaction that they had accomplished all missions and were bringing everyone home alive. The end of his second deployment was quite different and intensely frustrating as his unit was extended with no warning and then continued to sustain casualties.
- *Lessons in training and combat effectiveness*: Ross also shares experiences of losing people through the dangerous conditions on the battlefield in the Hindu Kush where bad weather, poor roads, and uncertain conditions are as dangerous as a cunning enemy who can prepare in sanctuary across the nearby border before attacking. Leaders must be at the top of their game, they must know they did everything they possibly could for the success and survival of their soldiers because even when you do everything right, the enemy can still get lucky, a piece of equipment can fail, or bad weather can prevent an operation. This is why tough realistic training was so essential to 3-71 Cavalry's success in Nuristan. They were a highly trained and well-led

unit placed in the toughest conditions imaginable. And they accomplished their mission.

Ross Berkoff and a relatively small number of Americans in uniform with him made the honorable and selfless decision to step up and serve their country in our longest war, protecting America for 20 years from radical factions who enjoyed sanctuary in Afghanistan. By doing so, they've earned the eternal gratitude and respect of all Americans.

John W. Nicholson Jr.
General, U.S. Army, Retired
Four-Star Commander of the Afghanistan War, 2016-2018

PROLOGUE

I woke to the sound of a fist pounding against my bedroom door and a loud voice commanding: "Berkoff, get your butt out of bed and come check this out on the news. Something about the World Trade Center on fire."

It was a few minutes after 8:00 a.m. in New Orleans, Louisiana, on September 11, 2001. I was a senior at Tulane University and a fourth-year cadet in the Army ROTC program, under contract to begin four years of active-duty service the following May. Upon graduation from Tulane, I would be commissioned as a second lieutenant and begin my life-long goal of serving in the military as an Army officer.

I was living in a cramped, on-campus apartment with some great friends, mostly other Army ROTC cadets. For the rest of the morning, we sat in front of the television wondering what this day meant for us.

My stepdad, Bill, worked for the Port Authority of New York and New Jersey, and he often conducted meetings in the World Trade Center; he was scheduled to have a meeting that very day. I called home and was relieved to learn he was still in his Weehawken, New Jersey office.

A moment later, the television showed a Boeing 767 slamming into the second tower. Reports started to trickle in of the Pentagon burning. Slowly, we began to grasp what it all meant: We would be starting active duty in just nine months, and when we did, we would be going to war.

Two months later, I was asked by my professor of military science, an active-duty Army major with a strong Alabama accent, to come to his office. When I entered, I inquired, "Sir, you wished to see me?"

"Stand at ease, Berkoff," he replied. "I wouldn't be surprised if you're sent to Afghanistan, and you probably want to think twice about wearing your dog tags. I mean, you're Jewish, right? I strongly encourage you to get some new tags. Mark 'em 'no preference' or something, but wipe 'em clean, Berkoff. If they get their hands on you, a Jew, it would be a bad day. Know what I mean?"

There was a long, awkward pause before I answered, "Yes, sir. I appreciate the advice, sir."

When I walked out of his office I was roiled by conflicting emotions. I was angry at this officer, whom I generally respected, for calling me out like that. But part of me was also thankful for the heads up. What if he was right?

A few months later, I submitted my request for an Army branch assignment and got my first pick: Armor and Military Intelligence. I was intrigued by a special program in the Army that allowed newly minted lieutenants to begin their service in a combat arms branch for 36 months (in my case, Armor) and upon completion, transfer to a combat-support "Basic Branch" (in my case, Military Intelligence). Such officers would then continue their remaining years of service in their Basic Branch—potentially all the way through retirement. I felt strongly that there would be no better way for me to become an excellent career intelligence officer than first getting experience as a combat-arms officer on an actual battlefield.

A few weeks before I began active duty, the Army notified me I would be posted at Fort Drum, home of the storied 10th Mountain Division, about 30 miles from the Canadian border. I was assigned to 3rd Squadron of the 17th Cavalry Regiment (3-17 CAV), which consisted of four troops of about 80 men each (troops are known as "companies" in non-cavalry units).

One of the troops was a unique elite unit: Alpha Troop—better known by its call sign "Apache Troop." Apache was the only *ground* cavalry unit in the entire 10th Mountain Division. No tanks and no helicopters here. Apache Troop consisted of three light-cavalry scout platoons—each led by an Armor Branch second lieutenant.

Each platoon was comprised of eighteen cavalry scouts manning six Humvees. Apache Troop's headquarters section included a few support personnel (supply clerks, armorers, etc.) and an eight-man, 81mm mortar section to provide close-up, indirect fire on the enemy when necessary.

I started to get excited. I was going to an elite cavalry unit, and an utterly unique one, as well. I grew up watching Horse Soldiers on the big screen. I was accustomed to yelling things in my backyard like "Bring up the Cavalry!" while playing Army with my childhood friends. As a teenager, I took my obsession with military history to a whole new level of nerd-dom. I was an American Civil

War Union solider reenactor by age 15. I stared at photos of General George Armstrong Custer for hours, with his knee-high cavalry boots, his long saber, his colorful, non-regulation red scarf and customized uniforms. The kids I went to high school with would catch me in class sketching Custer in various poses, with varying styles of mustache and goatee, and with his slouchy Stetson hat tilted here or there. As a teen in the mid-1990s, I was fascinated with the cavalry's 1870s campaigns on the Great Plains, and I knew more about the musical notes of Custer's favorite regimental march, "Garry Owen," then I did about some band named Hootie and the Blowfish. To say that I was excited to become a real Army cavalry officer would barely begin to capture my colossal enthusiasm.

On May 17th, 2002, I raised my right hand and declared:

> I solemnly swear that I will support and defend the Constitution of the United States against all enemies, foreign and domestic; that I will bear true faith and allegiance to the same; that I take this obligation freely, without any mental reservation or purpose of evasion; and that I will well and faithfully discharge the duties of the office on which I am about to enter. So, help me God.

But wearing a "butter bar" on my uniform did not yet grant me the privilege of leading soldiers. First, I needed to become even more qualified. Every newly commissioned armor officer must complete the Armor Officer's Basic Course (AOBC or OBC), which at that time was located at Fort Knox, Kentucky. It was a four-month course that certified officers to "successfully lead a tank platoon in an operational environment." Throughout my Armor OBC experience, instructors and peers would see the 10th Mountain Division patch on my left shoulder and immediately ask me, "10th Mountain?! They've got tank platoons?"

"Nope," I'd reply. "I'm going Light Cav."

"Damn, that's hardcore man," was the usual reply. I liked the sound of that.

When I graduated from Armor OBC, I had my sights set on completing a specialty school at Fort Knox that focused on leadership in light cavalry tactics called the Scout Leaders Course (SLC). I thought SLC would be the perfect capstone to prepare me for being a real cavalry platoon leader.

"Where do I sign up?" I asked.

The response I got was not what I was expecting: "You're in the 10th Mountain Division, Berkoff, remember? You're supposed to be hardcore. You really should become Ranger-qualified first."

To wear the coveted Ranger Tab on your left shoulder, which indicates you're "Ranger qualified," requires you to survive—and graduate from—the Army's notoriously grueling Ranger School. But attending Ranger School was never part of my plan. Indeed, I had avoided the Infantry Branch largely to dodge anything resembling Ranger School. I'd been forced to train like an infantryman for four years as a cadet, and I was over it. I had no interest in experiencing the intense physical and mental pain that Ranger School dishes out.

I spent that entire Fall immersed in all things related to the M1 Abrams main battle tank. Armor OBC culminated with four straight weeks of tank gunnery, tank driving, and tank platoon situational training exercises, all while mired in northern Kentucky's clay-rich and weathered mud-hills. So, when I abruptly received orders to report to Ranger School with two weeks of notice, I quickly realized my body was woefully ill-prepared to operate as a ruck-toting infantryman.

None of that mattered, however, because orders were orders.

In late November 2002, I drove 500 miles south to Fort Benning, Georgia, and reported for Ranger School to begin the first phase of what I expected to be a punishing, 61-day trial. Phase One of Ranger School is when they beat you down to a pulp, and if you make it through that, your leadership abilities are tested against advanced infantry tactics under duress, in the cold mountains of north Georgia and in the wet jungles of Florida.

I never made it past Phase One. In late December, with a torn medial-collateral ligament, I drove back to Fort Knox and tried desperately to get a slot in the next SLC course. When I found out that it wouldn't be available until February 2003, I called my personnel officer at 3-17 CAV at Fort Drum. "February, Berkoff?" he asked. "Are you fucking kidding me?" He explained that there was a platoon in Apache Troop—2nd Platoon—that needed a platoon leader right away because it would soon be deployed overseas. The personnel officer bellowed, "I'm amending your orders. Get your ass up here! Right! Now! And dress warm. Out."

In January 2003, I reported for duty at Fort Drum with the 10th Mountain Division, 10th Aviation Brigade, 3-17 Cavalry, A Troop, 2nd Platoon. One of my first tasks was to sign for 2nd Platoon's entire equipment inventory, including all weapons. Essentially, my signature meant that if anything was lost or damaged, my ass would be on the line. Night-vision goggles, M4 carbines, various machine guns, and two dozen infrared laser illuminators that we'd bolt onto our weapons for aiming in the dark—it was a very long list, worth several millions of dollars. It made me a little queasy, but I knew it was part of the job.

The soldiers of 2nd Platoon were a representative cross-section of American society, in a lot of ways. I had rednecks, California surfers, hard-drinking Irishmen from the Rustbelt, inner-city kids who'd barely escaped gang life, god-fearing Christian Midwesterners, even some first-generation American

Buddhists. My platoon sergeant (the most senior non-commissioned officer in the platoon, and essentially my right-hand man) was Sergeant First Class Jason White. About ten years my senior, SFC White had already deployed to Iraq during the first Gulf War. My two "Senior Scouts" were Staff Sergeant George Elsaesser, a fellow Garden-Stater who'd in-processed at Fort Drum the same week as me; and Staff Sergeant Bill Letunic, a soft-spoken, Ranger-tabbed scout who'd recently deployed with Apache Troop to Kosovo where he'd earned the respect of everyone around him. All three men were masterfully proficient in their technical skills, offered solid leadership, and were superb subordinate NCOs.

During the winter and early spring of 2003, we trained together in the frozen tundra that comprised Fort Drum's vast, flat training areas and weapons ranges. We conducted live-fire exercises with our machine guns, automatic grenade launchers, and shoulder-based Javelin missile launchers, all from the ground, while coordinating fire and surveillance with our sister troops, Kiowa helicopter pilots, in the air just above us.

On 11 March 2003, our platoon was called upon for its first "real-world" mission, when reports came in of a Blackhawk helicopter that went down hard in a snowy, wooded area near Fort Drum. We sped our trucks out to the crash site and set up a security zone while bodies were pulled from the wreckage. Eleven soldiers died that day, including four aviation soldiers from our own brigade, and seven infantrymen from Charlie Company, 4-31 Infantry. We didn't know these men. But such a tragic loss sunk in quickly for all of us, regardless. How easily could that have happened to any of us? It was an eye-opener for sure, especially for some of the new guys (including myself) who had never seen so much death hit so close to home. I had no idea at the time that it would not be my last close call with a deadly helicopter crash, grieving for men taken from us so abruptly and so tragically.

My troop commander during this period was Captain Frederick Gilliand, but he was a short timer. In June, just as we were firming up deployment dates for Afghanistan, his command time expired. He was replaced by Captain Thomas Barnes. A few years older than most of his peers due to his prior service as an enlisted soldier, CPT Barnes had been patiently waiting to take command of Apache Troop. Bear in mind, there is only one company-level command slot for Armor Officers in the entire 10th Mountain Division, so 3-17 CAV's squadron staff included several young Armor captains, eagerly waiting in a line of succession for their moment.

Before he took command, CPT Barnes was a staff officer at Squadron HQ in the Operations (S3) Shop, and as I recall, he was the one who was usually the brunt of other officers' jokes and pranks. For some reason, he was not well-liked by his peers. I knew this was not a good sign for things to come.

Soldiers can tell quickly if their leaders are authentic or not. They can tell if their leaders are genuinely motivated to ensure their soldiers have everything they need to be successful. Or not. They can surmise quickly which leaders are merely going through the motions of looking after their soldiers' best interests and which officers are concerned primarily with optics and show just enough care and compassion to be duly noticed by higher headquarters.

CPT Barnes was an Optics Guy. The best officers and consequently the best leaders are those whose soldiers not only follow their orders implicitly and with celerity, but also willingly go above and beyond the mission because they want to make their leadership proud of them. Soldiers do this out of respect for their leaders, and, to a large degree, to earn the trust and respect of their peers. Under the leadership of Captain Barnes, however, soldiers followed orders because they were afraid of the consequences of not doing so.

The best senior officers that I ever served with always called me by my first name. With Captain Barnes, I was addressed strictly as "Lieutenant Berkoff" or "LT" (pronounced "El-Tee"). He wanted everyone to know he was in charge. As Peter Gibbons once said in the classic movie, *Office Space*, "My only real motivation is not to be hassled; that, and the fear of losing my job. But you know, Bob, that will only make someone work just hard enough not to get fired." This sums up Apache Troop perfectly. There was a toxic leadership cloud that hung over the troop during our pre-deployment months and continued to exist throughout Captain Barnes's command.

I tried my best to create a bubble around 2nd Platoon to block the toxicity, and I think, for the most part, it worked. I don't think a similar bubble protected the other two platoons in the Troop, unfortunately.

Just before Apache Troop deployed to Afghanistan in August 2003, we were briefed on how we were to fit into the Order of Battle for the deployment. Apache Troop was technically part of 10th Mountain's Aviation Brigade, but the primary mission of the deployment was the responsibility of its 1st Brigade—specifically, the 1st Brigade Combat Team (1BCT). 1BCT was composed of three Infantry Battalions, one of which was the 2nd Battalion, 22nd Infantry Regiment, otherwise known as 2-22 IN, or "Triple Deuce."

Triple Deuce was going to be based out of Kandahar Airfield (KAF) in Afghanistan's southern desert, while the other two infantry battalions would operate in the more mountainous central and eastern provinces. Probably due to the flatter terrain, which is more conducive to mounted reconnaissance and screening operations, Apache Troop was assigned to operate in support of Triple

Deuce. There were rumors, however, of Apache Troop eventually being split three ways and dispersed all over the country, with each platoon supporting one of the three 1BCT infantry battalions.

We had mixed feelings about this. The three platoons of Apache Troop had trained together and formed strong bonds together, for some soldiers going back all the way to Apache Troop's deployment to Operation Joint Guardian-Kosovo in 2001. Most of the men wanted to fight together once again in Afghanistan as a complete Troop. But I believe that desire was tempered by the no-love-lost feelings for our Troop commander.

Regardless of whether Apache Troop was split up or not, we believed we brought a unique and lethal capability to the battlefield, one that an infantry battalion did not yet possess organically, nor did they yet fully appreciate. The latter was going to change when we arrived in Afghanistan.

During the entire 20-year war in Afghanistan, approximately 800,000 U.S. troops would deploy to forward operating bases across the volatile countryside. Now in hindsight, modern critics of U.S. military strategy are quick to point out (and perhaps they're not wrong) that the Afghanistan War was fought in twenty, disparate, one-year engagements, and the Army consequently failed to iteratively share and implement valuable lessons learned over time, a practice much needed to effectively prosecute a unified and sustained campaign. In truth, this was felt not only by our soldiers who served multiple tours but also felt deeply by the static and beleaguered Afghan people. Especially during and leading up to the Obama administration's troop surge in 2009, U.S. soldiers completed months of intense pre-deployment certification and training, including Afghan village simulations, Military Operations in Urban Training (MOUT), and in-depth cultural, tribal, and language familiarization. None of that existed in 2003 while I was packing our weapons and equipment at Fort Drum into huge metal shipping containers bound for Kandahar. At that time, less than 10,000 U.S. troops had set foot into the country. There was no memory store yet, no lessons learned. We lacked the "wisdom" that benefited the troops that came after us, including my own unit when I deployed again in 2006. In mid-2003, with the nation's attention and military resources focused on Iraq, we felt wholly unready for what awaited us in Afghanistan.

I first started keeping journals when I left for my first big adventure as a 15-year-old Boy Scout. I documented my 110-mile backpacking trek across the Cimmaron Mountains of New Mexico at the Philmont Scout Ranch. Despite the exhaustion that set in during each night of the trek, I found comfort in the practice of preserving my memories and experiences in detail. Looking back on the entries later, I gained new insight into my own personal growth and was able to see just how and when my behavior changed—both for better and for worse—when faced with adversity. So, in August 2003, as I packed my gear for my first deployment to Afghanistan (we were told to be prepared to be gone for at least six months, but possibly twelve), I decided I would try my best to document my daily experiences. During one of my last errands before I deployed, I purchased a small gray notebook from a Rite Aid in Watertown, New York. It was barely small enough to fit into the cargo pocket of my brand-new Desert Combat Uniform. But it did. Those experiences are captured in Tour One. After that first deployment I wished I had purchased a larger notebook. I made sure to do exactly that when I returned to Afghanistan with the 10th Mountain Division in 2006, this time as an Intelligence Officer in a brand-new cavalry squadron, 3-71 Cavalry. Those experiences are captured in Tour Two.

During my first deployment to Afghanistan as a young lieutenant in Apache Troop, I was constantly maneuvering my platoon between the dusty outposts of Kandahar and the arid slopes of the central provinces. For weeks at a time, there would no internet, no phones—no way to send a letter home. My family back home had very few electronic updates—only the hope that no news was good news. Consequently, my pocket journal became more than just paper and ink, it was where I laid down what I couldn't say out loud—not just my fear and anger, though those came out too, but the quiet things like the way the people and villages were suspended in bygone centuries. During my second deployment, as a senior staff officer with 3-71 Cavalry, my duties required long hours in the Tactical Operations Center (our squadron's command and control node) which afforded me ample access to the internet. Thus, Tour Two includes many of those letters sent home. Those emails had a dual-purpose—they notified my friends and family that I was still alive, while also attempting to describe what I was witnessing, without divulging too many details over email that could compromise operational security. In truth, and over time, I think the act of writing letters home became a form of therapy. They became a meaningful outlet to share my combat experience with the home front, while simultaneously allowing me to process and release emotional tension, oftentimes laced with intentional levity and sarcasm. My journal entries, on the other hand, are grittier, unfiltered, unredacted and in some cases offer the reader graphic accounts of the war happening around me in real time.

During both deployments, I lacked the time and energy to enter daily accounts into my journals, but the reader will recognize my attempts to capture everything that had happened to me since my last dated entry. Through each time-stamped account, the reader will also come to understand the use of military time and its 24-hour clock that starts at 0000 hours (midnight) and runs all the way to 2359 hours (11:59 p.m.). The journal entries that you will read are virtually the same, word-for-word, as the hand-written notes that I logged into these notebooks during my 25 months in Afghanistan from 2003 to 2007. The only corrections or edits that I made in the production of this book was to correct misspelled words, or to apply needed grammatical rules, for which the substance of the thought would not be easily conveyed otherwise. In a few places, bracketed editorial insertions have been made to aid clarity. In addition, I've supplied footnotes and an exhaustive glossary to help lay readers and civilians unfamiliar with military terminology, and our profligate use of acronyms, better understand organization, equipment, and missions. The contents of this book have been approved for publication by the U.S. Department of Defense, Office of Prepublication and Security Review.

TOUR ONE:

RIDING INTO THE UNKNOWN

CHAPTER 1

HERE IN RESPONSE

6 August 2003. 0200 hrs. Wheeler Sack Airfield, Fort Drum NY.

The waiting has begun. I thought the waiting around for "The Big Day" (our deployment date) was excruciating enough. This evening, we were bused from the Troop HQ and corralled into the RDF building for a weigh-in and chow. Each trooper needs to be weighed in carrying all of the equipment they intend to board with. We are now hearing that there is too much weight for the plane to carry. The men are asleep, side by side, on the cold cement floor, their rifles resting between their legs, and under their arms. It's a strange feeling to now be a "real soldier"—always attached to his gun. I signed for my M4 carbine tonight and made the pledge to keep it within arm's reach for what could be a yearlong deployment.

I've got so many new faces in my platoon. Only a small percentage of the men with me now actually trained with me and the rest of the platoon and I during the spring. Moreover, the soldiers in their current positions as gunners and truck commanders are being tested for their first time, not to mention in a combat zone. I'm no grizzled veteran but I know that I've also grown with the platoon over the past seven months. I'm very lucky to have the platoon sergeant that I have. SFC Jason White has made my job so easy. It's literally a bore most of the time. So, I have an untested platoon. Our greenness is balanced, however, with our excellent noncommissioned officers and seemingly well-disciplined and dedicated "Joes." Easy Company of the 506th PIR from World War II were also green and untested on June 6th. Look what they accomplished with good leaders and even better followers. We will do it right too. I'm still waiting here.

7 August 2003. 0700 hrs. Flying over Kazakhstan.

At approximately 0430 hrs., I led a chalk of 20 soldiers on the tarmac and boarded a B-777 Continental on route to central Asia. After a seven-hour flight, we landed in Milan, Italy and sat on the runway for two hours. We then took off again bound for Manas Air Force Base, near Bishkek, Kyrgyzstan. As I am writing this in the plane, I'm looking out to a land of nothingness, a barren desert of cracks and rivers and dotted habitats, which is southern Kazakhstan for now. It was an eerie feeling to step off the airfield at Fort Drum, knowing that my feet will not touch American soil again for possibly a year. From space, the ground below looks so calm and undaunting. I know that's not the reality of the case however, and sooner rather than later, I will find out just how brutal this landscape can be. We are not really sure what the next few days has in store for us. I assume we will board a C-130 and move to Kandahar Airfield (KAF).

We're about to land in Kyrgyzstan.

8 August 2003. 1250 hrs. Kandahar Airfield, Afghanistan.

Technically, the time is 0850 Zulu, but I am not sure how I feel about using the Zulu time system for this journal.[1] We are finally here. Yesterday morning, we landed at Manas International Airport, which is really nothing more than an old Soviet airbase near Bishkek. The airbase was converted for United States Air Force, Dutch, German, and Kyrgyzstani military forces. Our troop was bused into a hanger and told to wait for the next available C-130 transport to Kandahar. 14 hours later we were alerted to be ready. I spent most of the day sleeping on the hanger floor with my head resting on my flack vest. Just before we left, I walked behind the hanger to what I thought was an abandoned Russian villa. I was looking for a quiet place to shave, and a little exploration. After my shave under the villa porch, I walked around the building and found a Kyrgyzstani armed forces fire fighting unit, washing their fire truck. I introduced myself to a young soldier with a mouth full of gold teeth and overwhelming body odor. He showed me a few of the firetrucks. I thanked him, and I went on my way.

When I returned, 2nd Platoon was in "full battle rattle" and we left on a C-130 soon thereafter. The flight into Afghanistan was uneventful. We touched down around 0230 hours and we were brought into a tent for a welcome briefing. I made contact with 2-22 Infantry (Triple Deuce) personnel who escorted my

1 Zulu time, also known as Greenwich Mean Time, is the standard time used by global military units to aid in the synchronization of operations, regardless of time zones.

platoon to our living quarters. Two 10-man tents equipped with new cots, and an air-cooling fan system. I made my home in the rear corner of the first tent with the rest of 2nd Platoon's Alpha section. KAF is an unassuming place. It's flat and dusty with very few trees to offer escape from the scorching sun. Our tents are less than a kilometer from the very active airfield runway, and we're reminded of the Air Force's presence just about 24 hours a day.

Today I took a walk to the PX, which was surprisingly well stocked. I made a credit card call home and spoke to my mother very briefly. There are all sorts of soldiers walking around this place—Romanians, Germans, British, 82nd Airborne soldiers (outgoing), and Special Operations Soldiers, who are usually easy to identify with their uncropped beards and desert uniforms absent name tapes.

Today is the day to relax and recover from the 60-hour journey from Fort Drum. Tomorrow we will have our first formation with Triple Deuce. We still have no idea when our trucks will get here, and when containers will arrive with our equipment. We should be grateful that all our personnel and gear made it right to our tent without really breaking a sweat.

I can see a considerable amount of time passing without seeing any action. Idleness only leads to problems, and it makes a deployment feel much longer than it really is. I hope we will be busy or else it will definitely affect morale. The men are hydrating obsessively with nothing but bottled water, and we were told to drink nothing else. Even the shower water is not safe for drinking. The men are playing cards, listening to music, and sleeping. A guard roster was established to have at least one man in the tent, guarding our gear every hour of the day. This did not make the men happy but it's necessary because unfortunately we can't trust some of the soldiers around here from taking our supplies. There's a brand-new church built a few hundred yards from our camp. It seems very nice but according to the welcome brief, the church offers services for just about every religion here except for my own, including Mormons, Muslims, Roman orthodox and Protestants. I think I'll make an inquiry.

It's hard to know how to feel. I've only been here a day and I'm already getting the sense that this deployment is going to own me. It's going to rattle my unconscious yearning for routine and introduce a whole new concept of an Army "workday." I've quickly been plucked from my "cush life" of working at Fort Drum from 0600 to 1800; all relative of course, if you can call a 12-hour workday cush. Still though, my weekends at Fort Drum were normally spent traveling, barhopping, internet dating, and playing video games on the couch. Although my Army garrison job at Drum had its difficulties, it was just a day job for me. I could close the front door of my Watertown, NY studio apartment at the end of the day and enjoy creature comforts and privacy. I now must leave all that behind me and accept a whole new way of life. Discomfort, inconvenience, stress will be daily hurdles for me here in Afghanistan. Combine all that with the anxiety that I'm always outnumbered by my soldiers, constantly being watched by them. Oh, and don't forget that I'm just one operations order away from getting dropped into a firefight.

Still though, I have to remember "the big picture" when I question what I'm doing here. Men have had these same wonders and feelings about soldiering for thousands of years . . . why should I be any different? September 11, 2001, is a day that will live in infamy and the fact that Afghanistan became a new place for U.S. soldiers to deploy is directly tied to that infamous day. Now, enter 2nd Platoon, Apache Troop, 3rd Squadron 17th Cavalry, LT Berkoff and SFC White. 23 months after the towers fell and the Pentagon burned, here we are. It's no coincidence, but rather a response. I have to keep thinking on that. I am here to respond. We're here in response. My country is sending me to kick down a few doors because ours were kicked down first. It's a lot of political and patriotic rhetoric perhaps. I also sometimes think I am here for an adventure. I kind of like that one better.

11 August 2003. 1830 hrs. Kandahar Airfield.

I'm starting to get into a routine now. 1200 wake up (Zulu time) which is 0400 local time and fall in for PT formation.[2] PT from 1230 to 0130. Not many places for running on this airfield except a foot trail which circles a huge pond of burning shit and fuel. Then chow and personal hygiene from 0200–0300, followed by whatever training is on the schedule for the day which takes priority. We spent the past few days getting settled in here.

On Saturday we were told to move a new set of tents about 100 feet of way. I was pretty content in my original set of quarters, but this new tent suits me fine. My men have been busy building a fine wooden door and entranceway to the tent. They laid out corduroy wooden planks in the entranceway to keep our boots out of the sand and occasional mud. They also nailed our platoon cavalry guidon on to my tent door.[3] They have also set up a camouflaged hooch over our Bravo Section tent and placed picnic tables underneath.

2 PT is "physical training."

3 The cavalry guidon, the military version of a team banner, is a small, swallow-tailed flag used by Army cavalry units to identify the unit.

I think I'll be comfortable here, but the heat is unbearable right now. It reached 115 degrees today. I also haven't been sleeping very regularly at night. During the hottest part of the late afternoons, we cease training and seek refuge in our cooled tents, and while sitting in our bunks there is little to do at that point except rack-out on the cot and nod off. That has made it more difficult for me to fall asleep later, and I also wake up in the middle the night.

On Sunday, August 10th, SGT Dave Stricker, one of my truck commanders, and I met up with the Triple Deuce dismounted scout platoon and we hiked about 2 km to a small bunker on the side of the airfield. Here we waited for a couple of hours in the ungodly, warm sun for the mortars to do their work—our training mission was to practice observing and adjusting fire. The mortars never fired a shot, something about safety reasons, and we had to walk back to the camp. I met a Fires NCO named SSG Sheaffer, who told me he's a Messianic Jew, and he liked to refer to himself as a Redneck Jew. I introduced myself and we talked about the Jewish people's resolve, their history and his experiences in the Army as a Jew. Apparently, they had Friday night Shabbat services here at KAF, and I'll look forward to attending.

Today, we went to the rifle range to confirm our zeros on our M4 carbines.[4] The rest of Apache Troop was there as well. I learned today that the rest of Apache Troop will be moving about 500km to the northeast, to a place called Firebase Salerno[5] and this will include our Troop HQ Section, our Mortars Section, and the entirety of 3rd Platoon. They will support 1-87 Infantry BN at that location. So, at least for now, it appears that Apache Troop will in fact be split up across the BCT, leaving my 2nd Platoon here in KAF with the bulk of 2-22 IN.

We're going to do a night fire at the range tonight. I'm very anxious about getting our vehicles and our weapons together to start missions. We've been training as dismounts for far too long, and we need to start focusing on being Cavalrymen, and that means vehicle movement drills, mounted crew serve weapons drills, and gunnery. And this all depends on the arrival of our containers and our vehicles.

I do confess that nothing scares me more than taking my platoon out for a reconnaissance mission, or a convoy operation, and getting trapped in an ambush from the hills by Al Qaeda, hiding in the cracks and caves. I feel like we're going up against guerrilla warfare out here. My job will be to protect the main effort and our supply convoys from the local bad guys. It's not too unlike

4 To confirm a "zero" on a rifle means to make sure it's accurately sighted, ensuring your aiming device is a match to where the bullets hit the target.

5 Located in Khowst Province along the Pakistani border.

the Army of the Potomac supply line in northern Virginia in Mosby's Raider country. Not a very desirable place to be.

All of the troops that we "replaced" here in Kandahar Province have appeared to have already re-deployed back to the States. I didn't meet any of them. No left-seat-right-seat, transition, or relief-in-place conducted, at least not from my perspective. No one around me, equal to or superior in rank, seems to know what exactly we're going to be doing. That scares me and my senior NCOs. We're the Cav. We're supposed to be Eyes and Ears for the main effort, for 1st BCT and Triple Deuce. How can we be any good at reconnaissance if we're this unfamiliar with the landscape (and the local population) around us? I feel burdened by this, by the wildness of this unmapped and untamed land. I feel the weight and strain of this notion that we are starting something really hard, from complete-fucking-scratch. Nevertheless, I would love to get a chance to kill some of these bastards. It's a tough game to balance, but good training will make us win.

15 August 2003. 0600 hrs. Kandahar Airfield.

We're still killing time here while we wait for our equipment and vehicles to arrive. Yesterday, I jumped in a truck convoy out to a place called Tarnak Farms, which is about 10 km south of Kandahar Airfield. We were escorted out by some Romanian soldiers, in their BTR-80s and DABs, since we don't even have enough of our own vehicles to protect ourselves. I'm told that Tarnak Farms was once Osama Bin Laden's family compound and an Al Qaeda training camp. It was a suspected chemical and biological warfare munitions camp according to the CIA. And it was targeted by the CIA in the 1990s and then destroyed between October and December 2001.

The land south of the airfield is flat and desolate with nothing on the horizon but dirt and sand. Tarnak Farms is nothing more than a collection of crumbling, sunbaked, mudbrick huts made of dirt and straw. It was recognizable from the post-911 footage on CNN of AQ terrorists training on monkey bars. The compound today is abandoned, and all that's left are the scars of battles, including mines, unexploded ordinance, shell fragments and bones. I was told even full human skeletons are still being found. Last year, we heard a bunch of Canadian soldiers were accidentally killed at Tarnak. Apparently, they were firing their rifles on the range just like we were—but an F-16 mistook them for bad guys and dropped a bomb. Pretty awful. Today, we used the area for a sniper rifle range and an AT-4 firing range. I observed from a Humvee for about two hours and then came back to Kandahar.

The platoon had some light indoor classes today for a few hours in the morning, and then had the afternoon off, followed by an afternoon PT session, then dinner and then sleep. Very little we can do but just repeat the same hip-pocket training until our vehicles get here. On a personal note, I've been here for two weeks, and I wouldn't say I miss my family much, but I do miss my luxuries like privacy, television, a couch, fast food, women, and beer. I suppose it's natural to long for these things under present conditions but if I were also missing a wife and children, I cannot imagine how hard that would be. There will be a Shabbat prayer service tonight at 1730 hrs and I'm curious who might attend.

I'm still working on some kinks in the relationship between my platoon sergeant and me. I think there will always be some strain and disagreement on how things are done. I've got some of my own opinions and he has his. This morning during the last stretch of a 4-mile PT run, I ran to the front of the formation, and I asked SFC White where he planned to stop the formation. His response to me was curt: "wherever I feel like it, sir." After PT, I said to him that "I respect that he runs the formation, but I'm at least entitled to a less sarcastic remark." He agreed that I was correct in that assumption. I think I need to continue to speak up with SFC White when he speaks to me like I'm an enlisted man. I think if I do so, respectfully, he will see that I am a good man and I've earned it.

17 August 2003. KAF.

Sundays, at least for now, are days off here. Not to say that we accomplish less on a Sunday than we do on another day since we are really getting all used up here without any of our equipment, but at least there's no scheduled training on Sundays, and no early morning formations. On Friday, I had a very unique Shabbat service in Afghanistan. I met up with three other participants in the congregation and we had a Shabbat prayer meeting like I've never had before. I've volunteered to lead the service which I did mostly in English. We said the Amida, Adona-Lom, La-Cha Dodi, and some other blessings over a zippo lighter. Two of those in attendance were Messianic Jews. The other soldier was a Blackhawk pilot named CW2 Levin. Afterwords, we all went to the DFAC for a Shabbat dinner of barbecue ribs.

So, I completed my first 10 days on KAF and it feels like it's been months. The weirdest thing is that I couldn't wait to leave Ft Drum, leave the Apache Troop monotony, and the formations, and the PT, but now I feel like, "holy shit, am I really here for six months . . . what the hell did I get in to?" Back at Drum, even though the work got monotonous, at least there was always something tangible for me to look forward to . . . like seeing friends or family on weekends, or going out to dinner, or having some beers with my buddies, or just relaxing in my apartment with some Taco Bell and a movie. There were always those distractions to make me keep my sanity. But there are no distractions here. So far, the highlight of my day is eating a good meal in the DFAC. There's just too much time to ponder and read letters and count the days on the calendar. Of course, there is the looming expectation of a mission outside the wire any day now to break up the monotony and make the time go faster but then again, there is a catch there: people might be trying to kill us in the process, or there will be mines on the road to blow us up into small pieces. I guess I should feel lucky that I'm getting bored here in a tent when I could be in active combat. But isn't that why I came here . . . to be in combat? No, I didn't come here looking to get shot at. . . . I did come here to accomplish a mission and if I can do that without killing anyone or getting any of my men killed, then I feel like I've done my job, right. I just have to keep remembering the big picture and keep the long-term rewards on my mind for when I return.

This place is not so bad. It could be a lot worse. The first month of adjustment has got to be the hardest. Tomorrow, I'm going into Kandahar city with some Civil Affairs patrol and psychological operations unit. I am not exactly sure what I'm doing, but I'm excited to converse with the locals and see the city. I guess what it comes down to is that Army life is monotonous at times, and soldiers have complained about the dullness of camp life for hundreds of years. We will get through this together.

It was about one year ago today that I finished my tank gunnery training at Fort Knox. The hardest part of Armor OBC was behind me. It was a good time at Fort Knox, in retrospect. Strange . . . that I recall those days so fondly now. I guess maybe one day I'll reminisce fondly about my time in Afghanistan?

23 August 2003. 2000 hrs. Kandahar Airfield.

Another week has passed by here in Kandahar and rather quickly at that. I guess it's because I have been pretty busy lately. On Monday, I traveled out to a few villages south of Kandahar City with a team of civil affair patrols and psychological operations soldiers. The depravity and poor state of conditions in these villages are beyond anything I've ever seen in person. I listened as we used interpreters to help "win the hearts and minds" of the local villagers and village leadership.

On Wednesday morning I took a Blackhawk helicopter out to an Army Special Forces base near Spin Boldak along the Pakistani border. It was the first time some of my NCOs got outside the wire, so I'm glad we all went. But it was really nothing more than a joyride yesterday and a chance to see the desert terrain. Yesterday, Bravo Section completed its first real mission, which was to provide security escort for a scout platoon and medics to a rifle range about 7 km away. Nothing eventful, but we had to beg for a Humvee to complete the mission, which was borrowed from an MP unit and an anti-tank platoon.

This morning I jumped in a Psychological Operations patrol Humvee and rode out in a convoy led by the Romanians in their BTRs, to set up a traffic control checkpoint between Highway 4 and Spin Boldak. It took us almost 3 hours to travel 30 miles, which was only one way. The novelty of seeing the countryside is beginning to wear off. But I still do enjoy conversing with the locals through my interpreters. I'm starting to get a sense of the utter duality of the common Afghan citizen: stuck once again, between a foreign army and a localized insurgency. I spoke to dozens of them at my traffic checkpoint today and most were agreeable and obliging, but I get a sense, when they go back into their cars and keep driving, that with just a small bit of persuasion they would turn violent against us without warning.

Things are picking up towards operations in the Sami Gowhr mountains, east of here and nearer the Pakistan border. Operation Mountain Viper is the big mission kicking off soon in early September. We're still not sure how they will use us as a cavalry platoon in the fight upcoming. And it's quite possible they will air assault our trucks into the AO rather than allow us to convoy in. At least we finally have some trucks. We just received three new up-armored Humvees. *Our* trucks that we trained on back at Fort Drum are still stuck in customs/processing somewhere in Qatar, but should be here any day. Those trucks, however, are all "light-skin" Humvees. We're now being told we need to get ready to fill the light-skin trucks with sandbags under our feet to withstand the blast of an IED. Why we can't get all up-armored trucks is another story. Probably all headed to Iraq right now which seems to be our country's focus at the moment.

I just passed my five-year anniversary since starting college and Army ROTC. It's been five years since I first donned the battle dress uniform, and now I practically live in it.

CHAPTER 2

BECOMING SABER 1

30 August 2003. 1520 hrs. KAF Airfield.

Another week down and although they have stopped tasking me on leader recon missions, things have been no way boring. This culminated on Thursday night, August 28, when we were almost dropped into a hot landing zone. As the platoon trained and worked on our new up-armored Humvees, I attended hours of mission analysis, planning briefing, and operations orders development regarding a 2-22 search and destroy mission in the Towr Ghar/Sami Ghar mountain ranges. On Tuesday night I gave my first real combat warning order to my NCOs, and explained to them that we were being used as the only mounted force in the upcoming battle. Our mission was to be dropped in, air-assault, by Chinook helicopter into the town of Lowy Kariz and set up blocking positions. This was supposed to be the beginning of a larger battle in other villages to the northeast. The men were excited to be involved and their spirits were high. I'll get back to that in a second.

One of my soldiers, Specialist Austin Burke, acted clearly unexcited and outright depressed when he heard the news of our pending mission. The past few days he's been walking around with a photograph of his wife, his gaze constantly fixed on it. He sleeps little and talks to almost no one. He is also seen carrying around and obsessively sharpening his bayonet with him everywhere he goes. I can read the signs. So, I called him over to my bunk to find out what was wrong. He began to tear up and speak of his wife and family and his fear being killed and leaving them without a provider. After offering him whatever limited encouragement I could, I sent him to the battalion chaplain, Captain

Stewart, for consultation. His spirits have since lifted, and he will pull through this just fine.

Apache Troop is understrength in our 19D-Cav Scouts, and Burke is one of a handful of aviation mechanics from 3-17 CAV's Kiowa helicopter troops who volunteered to join Apache Troop on this deployment. They were told they would be our truck drivers, but I think we can see how this deployment will soon be converting everyone into a combined scout-gunner-driver-mechanic and why not just include infantryman too while we're at it. When you volunteer for a combat-arms MOS, like 19D/cavalry scout, you've made some degree of peace with the prospect that you're signing up to get into a gun fight. Burke and the other Kiowa mechanics that filled 2nd Platoon's ranks just weeks ago will need some time to come to grips for what they signed up for. I'm damn proud to serve alongside each one of them.

My truck driver is Specialist James Callaway. He's from central Missouri, I think. He speaks with his native drawl and he's probably a few years older than me. He's white, over six feet tall, and comes from a blue-collar family, but I guess just about everyone from central Missouri does. He only listens to Tim McGraw and Toby Keith, and he politely asks my permission if he can play it out aloud in our tent or in the truck. He's a mechanic by trade, so he's good with his hands and he can pry open just about anything you hand him (he's got utterly huge hands). He already taught me a trick which will come in handy once we're out on extended operations: if you pry a few bolts from the chairs of the truck commander seat in the Humvee, the chair folds down almost full horizontal and makes a nice bed. Beats sleeping outside. My gunner is a 19-Delta Cav scout by the name of Tristan Mortensen. He's a sharp kid, probably not much younger than I. He was one that stayed out of trouble in the barracks on the weekends before we deployed. He's also Caucasian, tall, lean, and with a chiseled jawline, he looks a bit like Prince William of England.

Okay, back to the hot landing zone . . . at chow hall a few nights ago, along with my NCOs, we watched a group of aviators suddenly react to their radios and all leave the mess hall in a sprint. Something was up. I reported to the BN operations center only to find out from my commander that an Army Special Operations team was in contact with hostile forces in large numbers and Mullah Omar, the leader of the Taliban, was reportedly at the scene. Triple-Deuce was immediately tasked to react in force. I was told to have 2nd Platoon ready for combat in three hours. This meant we would have to borrow essential equipment and weapons from the 2-22 Anti-Tank (AT) Platoon. The AT Platoon was the only other element in 2-22 IN that trucked-mounted heavy weapons similar to our own. It was a task that I ordered to make happen, but I learned thereafter that our heavier, up-armored trucks might not be suitable to sling load onto Chinook at the altitude we were going into—which exceeded 10,000 feet. We nevertheless prepared for combat and stood by all night, wanting and waiting to go. At about midnight, the order was countermanded, and the men were allowed to get sleep. We then learned our mission was handed off completely to the Triple-Deuce AT platoon (the only other mounted force in KAF, aside from the MPs), since their trucks are lighter without any armor, and could better handle the air lift in that elevation.

This morning, two infantry rifle companies along with some scouts, mortars artillery, and engineers were air-assaulted into a hot landing zone. We watched them take-off from our tents. For the most part, we were pissed, but we understood. . . . It was an odd feeling. I really wanted to go knowing full well that the enemy was reported to be aggressive, well-trained and hiding in the mountains, amongst the villagers. Moreover, the mountainous terrain made mounted maneuvering very difficult and the likelihood of ambush very good. I thought "I could just stay here and not worry about being hurt" or I could go in and very well get hurt. Common sense says stay put. But I know that I came here to see some action, among other things, and it's a frustrating paradox. I want to see action, but I also don't want my men and myself to get hurt in the process. These two concepts rarely go hand-in-hand. Therein lies the conflict. I have to remember, however, that sooner or later, our equipment will arrive in country, and 2-22 will call us to do our duty. I'm still here for another five months at least. A lot can happen in five months.

One thing is for sure the days are passing by faster now and the money that I'm making is raking in. So far, I've been able to put $3,000 into my savings account and I've only been here for a month. I received some mail today from my family including magazines, food, and music, which all greatly lifted my spirits.

3 September 2003. KAF.

To be honest with myself right now, I have no fucking clue what I'm doing here most days. I feel like I'm completely winging it. Every one of us is doing this for the first time. Sure, we trained for a few weeks here and there on the flat tundras of northern New York, but our training was hardly designed for this shit. SFC White talks about his time in Desert Storm, but that was Kuwait and that was 12 years ago. Some of my guys, including SSG Bill Letunic, recently completed a deployment to Kosovo but that environment and the rules of engagement couldn't be more different. So, we are all green, but despite that,

2nd Platoon has some very technically proficient NCOs and I need to keep learning from them.

I had a conversation with SFC White this morning. I pulled him aside and asked him to "help protect me from myself out here." I told him that I'm a fast learner, but I could use his help running some technical drills. I don't want to mess up catastrophically while out on a mission and lose the respect of my truck crew, or worse, the rest of the platoon. I told him that I felt my primary technical weakness in the platoon was knowledge of the crew-served weapons. It was my intention to refresh the procedures for assembly and disassembly, clearing and loading, crew-served skills training, whenever we get our weapons in country. He agreed that it's something I need to work on. I can't be too vulnerable in front of SFC White. I need to lead, but I also need to show him that I'm curious and humble enough to ask him these questions.

While on the subject, I asked him how he felt the men viewed my leadership style. Apparently, they want to see me training with them more frequently during the day. I have no problem with that but lately I've been tied up in the battalion and company headquarters in meetings, and that could take all day. But I will make it a point to train with the men and lead from the front more often. It is, however, absolutely exhausting to be the focus of an entire platoon's watchful eye, 24 hours a day. I need to continue to commit myself to the learning process and be humble enough to seek counsel, advice, and mentorship. I need to continue to try and earn my men's trust and respect as a Cav Scout first, in all the technical tradecraft, and then I think they will respect and follow me with more confidence as their platoon leader.

Earlier this week, I took my platoon back to Tarnak Farms for crew-served weapons shooting. It was the first time that my entire platoon left KAF at the same time. No more than 20 minutes after we began firing, one of our gunners, PFC Darom Kounlavong, experienced mechanical malfunction on his .50 caliber machine gun. A round exploded prematurely in the chamber and his legs were sprayed with shrapnel. I watched him exclaim and slump over the gun. We laid him out and administered first aid. We stopped the bleeding and loaded him into a truck bound for the hospital at KAF. It was a scene that was eerily familiar from hundreds of war movies I watched. The blood, the call for medics, cutting the uniform to get to the wound, etc. I escorted him back to base and I think he'll be fine. He'll have some shrapnel in his leg, maybe forever, but other than that he's OK.

PFC Kounlavong is affectionately known as "Buddha" by all the guys in 2nd Platoon. I'm not sure if he's a practicing Buddhist, and I don't think he was born in Laos because he speaks good English without an accent. He and his family settled in a tight Laotian-American community in the suburbs of Nashville and if anything, he may have a slight east Tennessee twang. Like most southeastern Asians, he's slight and wiry, but strong. He's conscientious, reliable, and respectful to all those around him, and likely due to his disciplined demeanor, he's managed to steer clear of the UCMJ infractions that beset many in our Apache Troop barracks earlier this year. He consistently demonstrates a strong work ethic and that's earned him respect from everyone around him. During my one-on-one interactions with him, in addition to my observing him engage with other senior leaders in the Troop, he's exceedingly formal, quiet, and reserved. I can only assume his culture and his upbringing emphasize the importance of deference and humility when interacting with people in leadership and authority. It has not been easy to get him to talk, but in all our down time this month he did confess to me his love for Eminem. Not just the music, but the story behind the man, and his respect for the hustle and grind to build something from nothing.

I attended another Shabbat service recently and I met an army dentist there named Captain Albert Sohnen. He said one thing that I liked. He said he was putting a mezuzah on the door post of his operating room so that all his Afghan patients can see that "a heathen" was fixing him. I thought that was pretty amusing.

5 September 2003. KAF. Letter Home.

Dear Family,

I am happy to report that my soldiers and I are in good spirits and health, passing the time dutifully within the confines of Kandahar airfield. We continue to live in close quarters within a venerable city of tents, stretched out along the sand dunes parallel with the airfield strip. The mornings here come earlier than ever—before the sun rises so that physical training can be conducted in the pre-dawn chill. Once the sun rises however there is scant shelter from its murderous blaze. Temperatures hit 100° plus by 8 AM. This evening my men have been busy building an entranceway to the tent, with a corduroy wooden plank to cover the sand on the ground. They decorated the entrance with the sign saying "You took our Towers. Now we are taking your country." It has a background sketch of the New York City skyline.

The soldiers continually show me much respect and consideration and guaranteeing my satisfaction of their work. I, in turn, make a tangible effort in making sure they're getting enough food and mail, phone and computer access, and information regarding possible missions. It is my silent vow to make sure everyone comes home with us in the spring.

It might be hard for you to all grasp the concept, but as each day passes here, the lucidity of my responsibilities becomes more evident. We came here in response. I have to keep remembering that. I think I would unconditionally lay down my life for any of these guys in my platoon, if it means were helping get rid of one more jihadist in this country bent on terror, injustice and cruelty. These tactics have been practiced against the peaceful citizens of Afghanistan and of course they made their mark on September 11. Especially as that anniversary soon arrives, our soldiers here feel all the more committed to the cause. And they could not be more eager to be placed in harms way, and allow our training to take over our instincts.

We had a sad affair yesterday. The regimental chaplains all gathered for a memorial service in honor of two young soldiers recently killed in action—a 21-year-old and a 24-year-old from Missouri, and from New York, both from 1-87 Infantry. Their dusty boots were presented with their rifles pointed down into the soles, with their dog tags dangling from the rifle stocks. After psalms and amazing grace was sung, their names were called in vain for a roll call by their Company 1st SGT. This is known as Military Honors. Afterwards, all the soldiers exited the church in silent respect. And that was that. Another couple of soldiers KIA, in defense of their country. The unusual part of this event occurred later: none of my soldiers seem very emotionally affected by the service (including me). We were decidedly stoic, but maybe with a clearer sense why we were here.

I'll close the letter here as it's getting late in the evening and that morning nudge from SGT Stricker, "Sir, are you awake?" is not too far off. I will try to call or email as often as I can but please know that I'm doing fine. I am honored with a great responsibility, and I'm trying to make my family proud. I love you.

Affectionately Yours,

Ross

6 September 2003. KAF.

Another week down here. Exactly one month since we left Fort Drum. This week passed without too much excitement. On Saturday night of last week SSG George Elsaesser finally arrived at KAF from Qatar. SSG Elsaesser is the leader of Alpha Section, 2nd Platoon, but had spent the past month in Qatar making sure our trucks, weapons, and equipment were processed correctly through logistical channels to reach our destination. We had been anxiously waiting for his arrival, because it meant we'd finally be fully mission capable. With SSG E's arrival, our equipment finally began rolling in off the C-17s. So, most of the week was spent unloading the containers and cleaning our weapons.

I spent way too much time this week dealing with my soldiers' disciplinary actions, in CPT Barnes's tent. I was going through Article 15 readings for Private Everest Brooks—he mouthed off to an NCO again and he will be punished with a pay cut, extra duty, and restrictions. Brooks is my platoon problem child. He can't be much older than 18 and he's talked to me about how he barely escaped gang-life growing up in Los Angeles. He's got a bad temper and he's quick to show his disdain for authority, especially if he feels like he's being singled out for something. He's also prone to inciting physical disputes with fellow enlisted men. As part of his "additional training," SSG Letunic has been making him dig foxholes in the sunbaked mud near our tent.

Specialist Shane Colby's Article 15[1] is also now complete. Colby is one of my gunners and he lost his promotable status to sergeant for disrespecting an NCO and will remain specialist a little longer. Colby is a hard-drinking Irishman, and former high-school wrestler from a small coal mine town along the Susquehanna called Towanda, in northern Pennsylvania. He's about four years older than me, which means as an enlisted man he's known as "grandpa" around here. He reminds me of SGT Don Malarkey from *Band of Brothers*. He's undoubtedly the most popular guy in all of Apache Troop and probably one of the smartest soldiers in my platoon, but you need to study him closely to realize it. He's also our platoon prankster, quick to mimic a voice or mannerism of some junior officer that he'd like to poke fun at, but all good fun and with the best of intentions. As he's a bit older than his peers, his age must also bring with it some wisdom. Back at Drum this past spring, he found me in the troop HQ office studying my dog-eared FM 17-98 before the Squadron Spur Ride.[2] Colby said to me: "Sir, knowledge is power . . . so, if you want the power, just show us you know your shit." That really stuck with me. I respect him more than he probably knows, so processing this Article 15 has been very difficult for me personally.

2-22 IN has been gone all week doing missions from the sound of it that led to little results. They returned to KAF yesterday and the next operation is planned for this week. I'm told to expect to go in as part of the security force for

1 Minor disciplinary action taken in the field, short of a court martial.

2 A rigorous mental and physical challenge that tests soldiers' cavalry skills to earn the privilege of wearing spurs.

the Tactical Action Center, but rumors and possible courses of actions are flying around like flies. Last Sunday, two scouts from 1-87 infantry were killed—PFC Adams and Specialist Fuller were both shot by hostile Taliban.[3] These are the first KIA that we know of so far from our brigade, 1st Brigade Combat Team, 10th Mountain.

Apache Troop HQ, including my CO, has been more of a pain than a friend to 2nd Platoon since we got in country. So I am not too upset to hear they're moving out. Apache Troop HQ, the mortar section and 3rd Platoon all leave for Gardez (430 kilometers to the northeast) in a few days to support 1-87 Infantry. 1st Platoon is also supposed to leave soon for the north somewhere, in support of 2-87 Infantry. With CPT Barnes moving north with the rest of the troop, my platoon will fall under the command of HHC/2-22. My platoon is being treated as another "specialty platoon" within HHC. Infantry battalions typically consist of specialty platoons such as Mortars, Snipers, Anti-Tank, and Medical. These platoons, or sections of them, are essentially loaned out to the maneuver companies as needed, in a la carte fashion for operations. They've never had a light cavalry scout platoon before, however. So, we're trying to educate them on what we bring to the fight.

Captain Joel Cunningham is the commanding officer of HHC 2-22 Infantry, so he's technically my commanding officer for the time being. He's a West Pointer—and it shows in many ways. He's much smarter than I am, for one. Unlike CPT Barnes, he does not have a chip on his shoulder and doesn't come across as needing to prove anything to anyone. He's also much more affable and modest than my previous company commanders, so he's just a likable guy. CPT Cunningham has named me the "Training and Resources officer," so consequently, my time has begun to fill up with lots of paperwork and preparation for training meetings. That sounds like a nice and fancy title if I were working in garrison,[4] but I'm not. I'm in Kandahar. So, I'm not sure what he expects from me. I guess we need the mission tempo to pick up before these captains will dispense with the bullshit.

I am now getting closer to having a fully-mission capable scout platoon of six Humvees. CPT Cunningham asked me what our call sign is. Technically, we are "Apache White." As per SOP in light infantry divisions, there is a Red, White and Blue custom going back to WWII. 1st Platoon is "Red Platoon," 2nd Platoon is "White Platoon," and 3rd Platoon is "Blue Platoon." But CPT

3 I later learned their names were Adam Thomas and Chad Fuller.

4 A term used to describe a soldier in a training environment while working on an Army installation.

Cunningham balked at "Apache White." "Really, Berkoff? That's the best you could come up with? C'mon, you can get creative with me." I thought about this for a few minutes. I knew my guys in 2nd Platoon really wanted to be known as the "Saber Platoon." That was it, and Cunningham loved it. Although CPT Barnes got wind of it and told me not to get used to the new call sign. Once Apache Troop was back together again, we'd be back under his call sign, he said. But for now, we're known as Saber Platoon.

Saber Platoon would be divided into two, three-truck sections: Alpha Section (led by SSG Elsaesser) and a Bravo Section (led by SSG Letunic). Saber 1, part of Alpha Section, is my vehicle's call-sign, which is the second in the order of march on operations. Only two of our six vehicles are up-armored. So, we've been very busy this week filling up sandbags and placing them under the feet of our drivers, truck commanders, and underneath the gunner position. With our containers emptied out, each truck now has its fitted weapons system in the turret. Two trucks, including mine, have .50 caliber machine guns, while the other four trucks [have] M240B machine guns, two of which are also fitted with MK19 grenade launchers.

There's already talk of redeployment dates and talk about going to Iraq after this. All rumors, as things could change at any time but there's a scenario floating around that goes: A troop will redeploy back to Drum with our respective infantry battalions starting in mid-January through February. When we return, they might send A Troop HQ and one scout platoon to Iraq. Since I am the ranking lieutenant in the troop, that could leave me as the commanding officer of Apache Troop . . . hell maybe even the rear detachment commander for 3-17 Cavalry.[5] Bottom line is Fort Drum will be a very different place and different work experience next year than it was for me during these past eight months. And that is fine by me because I welcome the change and new challenges.

5 The rest of 3-17 Cavalry Squadron was made up of air cavalry/Kiowa helicopter scout troops and were getting ready to deploy to Iraq at this time.

CHAPTER 3

SEARCHING FOR POO

18 September 2003. Kandahar Airfield.

On Saturday I was sitting in the chow hall for breakfast, and I heard a deafening explosion. We all ran out to see what happened. I found out later than an RPG was shot into our camp. The POO, or Point of Origin, was triangulated by somebody, and early Monday morning of September 15th, I was alerted to have 2nd Platoon ready for a mission to go out there and find it. This was going to be our first real combat operation, and my guys could not restrain their laughter when I repeated our orders: we need to go find the POO. What exactly happens after we find the POO, we weren't exactly sure yet.

That day began as any other—I had a morning shave, followed by PT. SFC White led us on one of his lovely five-mile runs while carrying our M4 carbines[1] around KAF's "shit pond."[2]

After I was thoroughly exhausted, and eating breakfast, word came about this POO mission, and then a very long day began of operations orders, map rehearsals, reconnaissance, and preparation of vehicles and equipment. I next jumped in a Blackhawk helicopter with LTC Joseph Dichairo, commander of 2-22 IN, along with two other lieutenants for a leader's recon of the village. One of the lieutenants was an infantry platoon leader, Will Swenson.[3]

1 5.56 mm caliber assault-rifle weighing about 8 pounds.

2 Our affectionate term for the drainage ditch where all of the camp's porta-potties are dumped. In this case, it was literally a pond of shit, garbage, and fuel about half the size of a football field.

3 Will Swenson earned the Medal of Honor in 2009 while fighting in Konar province and is one of the few living Army soldier recipients of the Medal of Honor from wartime service in Afghanistan.

I like LTC Dichairo. He wears his M9 sort of low on his hip, like a gunslinger. He also walks with this swaggering gait that exudes confidence. I'm not sure what his company commanders think of him, but I see an extremely knowledgeable and competent officer, and I'm glad to serve under him.

From our vantage point in the Blackhawk, we assumed the shooters of the RPG were hiding in certain caves and mountains and we got a good view of the POO. I stayed up until after midnight with the rest of the 2-22 leaders who came up with a plan of attack. Finally, about 2 AM, I bedded down to sleep for about three hours. The next morning, I lined up all of our vehicles in a convoy of about 13 trucks and I gave a convoy briefing and then led us out of Kandahar airfield for my first real "combat mission."

As we approached the village of Zakar Sharif, I had my lead A section scout truck set up an observation post looking into the village as the 2-22 infantrymen got on the ground. Then we heard the crack of a rifle and observed a round land in front of my truck. It caused a little bit of excitement but nothing to get worried over. Soon after this though, I saw a boy approach me with something in his hands and I was a little overcautious, so I ordered him to "stop and put up his hands" (I said this in Pashto). He dropped the watermelons in an instant and ran away.

After linking up with the rest of my platoon, we moved to establish a blocking position north and west of the village. We had considerable trouble negotiating the terrain as we moved to set these positions. The ground was crisscrossed with irrigation canals, which bottlenecked us into a position well north of where we needed to be. So, we basically went back to where we started, and we used the town itself as a compass to get us to the western and northern routes leaving the village. Eventually we got it all set up.

The traffic control point in which I was located was very active with passing vehicles and civilians. Around 4 PM we closed down our positions and linked up with the infantry east of the town. I took Alpha section out on an area reconnaissance of the mountain valley, looking for signs of enemy activity. We searched a few caves and marked them but other than that it was lacking in much result. The large 25 vehicle convoy of almost 200 soldiers meandered past our position and we took up rear guard security on the route home to KAF. It was a good first mission: no one got hurt, nothing was lost, and no one committed any major tactical errors. We all worked well together. Best of all, we returned to Kandahar airfield to find a hot meal waiting for us at the DFAC, a shower, and a full night's rest. We should be lucky if all missions allow us such luxuries. The following day was spent in recovery and maintenance. It looks like we may be stuck in Kandahar for a while because I don't see any major operations for us on the horizon, unless some unforeseen event engenders a new mission like this recent RPG attack.

On an unrelated note, I woke up Monday morning with a bad stomachache, diarrhea, and fever. The fever went away, but my bowels have not given up. I assume it's normal to constant exposure to non-potable water, and the choking dust in the air, but nevertheless, it was quite uncomfortable. Lately I've been thinking more about coming home. Oh, all the money I'm gonna blow! But home is all still so far away.

There is so much poverty in this country and it pains my heart to pass through these villages with our Humvees filled with rations enough to last weeks, most of which we probably won't even eat. But here we see these malnourished four-year boys run up to us motioning over their lips for food. They're hungry, but I'm not allowed to feed them. If the kids expect us to hand out food, this causes unwanted behavior, makes for crowds around our trucks, making it more difficult to employ our target acquisition systems, and utilize lethal means if necessary. We're not supposed to be humanitarians here. The last thing we need is for kids swarming our vehicles looking for handouts when we're trying to locate and find Al Qaeda. This is a tough pill to swallow, but it's a rule that I have to enforce.

With my first combat mission complete, I can reflect on my feelings of the day. Even if I didn't actually see real combat today . . . I felt comfortable in command. I liked the power of it all—the adrenaline rush. I liked the sound of myself when I gave a quick, clear and authoritative order to my soldiers and NCOs. After all, I've only been training for days like today for the past five years! I tried to remain cool and collected throughout the day. I talked softly most of the time unless the situation called for a louder tone. If I can relay my orders to my soldiers in a casual and nonchalant manner, I think it might put them at greater ease and allow them to execute the mission more efficiently. These are all the things I'm working to perfect. In no way did I master the art of levelheaded confidence 100 percent of the time. It's quite possible not even the best officers can do this, but it is a goal that I want to reach for.

30 September 2003. 1730 hrs. Kandahar.

It's been a while since my last entry. I guess due to a general lack of activity here at KAF. Last week 2-22 executed their second "village reconnaissance" mission of which our unit was held back in reserve as a reactionary force. Actually, the intelligence that led them out to the village (called Shur Andam) was based on my personal tipoff. On our mission on 16 September, I gathered some intel from some local farmers that "strangers" had recently left their village and fled to a town called "Shur." I reported this to our intelligence officers and, low and behold, 2-22 is now gone for a town name "Shur" a few days later.

Anyways, we've been busy with PT and mission recovery and preparation over the past 12 days. However, the past 24 hours have been the most active since 16 September. Tomorrow morning, I'm leading the platoon out as the reconnaissance element for another large village security operation. Today, I went through the troop leading procedures by the book—as drilled into me during four years of Tulane Army ROTC and Armor OBC. I think I gave a damn good operations order. We shall see how it actually turns out, as I fear land navigation may prove more dangerous than the slim likelihood of encountering Taliban. Nevertheless, it will be a challenging mission, or at least it has a potential to be challenging with all the minefields and the crisscrossing goat trails out there.

On an unrelated note, I had a little verbal conflict yesterday morning with SSG Elsaesser, my A section leader. He was running the PT formation, and I was in the front setting the pace. During the third mile of a six-mile run, I decided to pick up the pace and initiated a 100m sprint. I guess I failed to make that clear to SSG E, because he told the formation to stop running so fast. I said "c'mon, let's do a sprint" and he said "No, sir. This is my formation." He then told the Joes "Do not listen to the LT." I then ordered SSG E. that "we will do the sprint" (wrong or not, to back out at his point would show weakness). He eventually did comply, but he was pissed. As was I. Whether or not he runs the formation, I'm still the platoon leader, and he asked me to set the pace for this run, and then he outright negated my order and he was arguing about it in front of the soldiers. I think that's where he went wrong. After PT we talked it over and I admitted my fault by not being clear . . . which made it look like he didn't know what he was doing. I should've said something like "Hey Sarge, I think we should do a 100m sprint when we get to that pole or something" and he probably would have still been a little annoyed that I was modifying his PT plan but at least I would have respected his stripes by informing him of it first. SSG E admitted his fault in arguing with me and his insubordination. SSG E does have a temper—he blew up at me once before back at Fort Drum. He gets frustrated when he thinks the LT is being too pushy and then he loses his composure. One more time, and I think I'll write him up. OK that's my NCO-LT leadership relations lesson for the day.

Rosh Hashanah passed this weekend here in KAF with a short service. My mother sent me a challah in the mail, with honey, which was quickly devoured. Now approaching my two-month mark which means 1/3 of the deployment is already down. It seems that "village operations" in this general vicinity is going to continue for the next few weeks, and a large operation to the northeast near FOB Shkin will commence in late October or early November. We will get through the rest of November and December and then boom: January means redeployment of equipment and vehicles. February of course means we get to go home.

I'm excited to take on a new role as a 3-17 Cav officer when we return, especially if the bulk of the squadron is deployed to Iraq (including part of A Troop?). This means I go from a combat LT and Platoon Leader, to a Garrison Troop Executive Officer (XO), and then maybe to a Rear Detachment Commander for A Troop. By the time 3-17 Cav returns home from Iraq in October 2004, and completes their recovery and leave, CPT Barnes will be relieved of command by Captain Mullin.[4] And by that time, I'll be only six months away from transferring to military intelligence. And, most likely I will head into a staff position at that point. This is all interesting stuff to try and portend.

2 October 2003. 0100 hrs. KAF.

We returned to KAF last night after a 12-hour mission in the "suburbs" of Kandahar City's northeast. Apparently, last week, a U.S. ordinance vehicle was struck by an IED near the town of Safdar Kalay on the outskirts of Kandahar City. This was an obvious indication of enemy presence, so a mission was put together to send 2-22 HHC into the area for mounted security patrols. After a full day of operations orders and vehicle preparation, we were staged early on the morning of 1 October to leave.

We woke at 2 AM and we left two hours later with a team of engineers and forward observers as support. My 2nd Platoon was the advanced guard for the rest of the company. As we approached our route to the bridge, which was our first objective to secure, my Humvee's power steering box "shit the bed" and it caused our truck to become immobile. I reported this to SFC White. Much to his discontent, I told him that I needed to take over his vehicle, and he needed to recover the deadlined[5] truck and move it back to our last major checkpoint with another truck for security. While he was doing this, I would lead a three-truck

4 Captain James D. Mullin never had the chance to assume command of A Troop due to the Army Brigade Re-Organization Plan that occurred in 2004. He took his own life in 2014, not long after a deployment to Iraq.

5 Refers to a military vehicle that sustained too many mechanical or maintenance failures to be operated safely or effectively.

section to the next bridge and complete our reconnaissance objectives, so that the rest of the company could follow on and complete the battalion's mission.

SFC White tried to take over things and he asked me to go back with the recovery team, so that he could go forward. I quickly (and tactfully) changed his mind and reminded him that I needed to be with the main effort and he needed to oversee maintenance, which was the primary responsibility of the platoon sergeant on a combat mission. So, I jumped in his truck, and I went forward. We reached the bridge. We cleared it for traffic-ability, and we pressed on to set up an outer cordon for the vehicle checkpoint. We remained at the base of the mountain range for the rest of the day, the recovery team eventually joined the fight, and after securing my deadlined truck at a checkpoint, they moved to set up similar type cordon positions south of the town while I stayed in the northwest with the forward observers.

At our checkpoint, we were ordered to stop vehicles that looked suspicious throughout the day. Most of the "suspicious" vehicles belong to the local Afghan militia forces or AMF, who patrolled this area, and chose their sides quite liberally. I did meet the local AMF company commander who passed through my checkpoint, and after a long talk with my interpreter about the presence of the Taliban and Al Qaeda, and of Afghanistan's politics, I thought we established good relations. He invited my soldiers and I to have tea, goat, and bread with him at his dwelling. His offer was tempting as I had eaten very little this day, yet I had to decline. I cannot leave my post, and I did not want to distract my soldiers from the mission or be put in a position where I would have to return the favor (i.e., we were not allowed to give the locals our food or supplies).

Eventually, I linked up with the rest of my platoon, and we led the convoy in its return to KAF. Although in the early morning hours things seemed to keep going wrong during today's mission . . . i.e., we missed an important route, then our truck deadlined (mine of all of them), then we got bottlenecked in a dense village . . . and finally we had to split up our recovery team and a bridge team. But in the end, we overcame these obstacles, and I think we did very well. Again, no one got hurt, nothing got lost. No one had any weapon accidents, and we learned valuable lessons in land navigation, vehicle maintenance, and teamwork. We got back to KAF with a hot meal waiting, a shower, and seven straight hours of sleep, so all in all it was a good mission.

We might need to go back to the same area in the next few days to secure an ammunition supply point that might belong to the enemy. Notice all of the "mights" in that sentence. Nothing is ever certain here. This morning, I went on a 90-minute Blackhawk helo "leader's aerial recon" with LTC Dichairo looking at the next major objective area. It's about 40 km to the east and south of here

2nd Platoon establishes a checkpoint near Safdar Kalay, outside of Kandahar City.
George Elsaesser

and it's a more backward and uncivilized area than I've ever seen. I saw many nomadic tribes, roving bands of wild camel, and clay-hut igloos used to make up towns. Part of this terrain is very scenic, with some lush, agriculture, oases, and canyons and mountains with intermittent streams and lakes. Looks like good country for a two- or three-day operation. We shall see maybe next week we'll get to go.

It's October now and the weather is very fine. I believe we are finally finished with the triple digit degree days. Quite the contrary, the evenings and mornings have become quite chilly; the afternoons, however much filled with dust, are still very pleasant.

One year ago today, I was leading my OBC class platoon on a graded and evaluated leadership mission in the mud of northern Kentucky. Although I feel like I've come a long way since my days at Fort Knox, I still feel somewhat technically incompetent when it comes to more advanced 19 Delta MOS skills that I am supposed to be an "expert" in. Each time I get into my vehicle, and I go somewhere I encounter technical issues that I should be able to overcome like a radio frequency loading, or plugger operations,[6] yet I still stumble. I need to swallow my pride and ask more questions when we have downtime because the delay on the battlefield might prove deadly if I'm stumbling to perform a task that my gunner or driver would normally do.

Thinking back, it was about nine months ago today that I was getting ready to move to Fort Drum. Man, I've done a lot since then! Moving to Fort Drum

6 Plugger or PLGR (Precision Lightweight GPS Receiver) supports our vehicle's radio operations with time synchronization, GPS coordination, and navigational mission planning.

was a major point of transition in my life. For all intents and purposes, I was just a glorified cadet at that time, with no real responsibility yet except for myself. Now, on the other hand, I'm in a combat zone in southwest Asia with millions of dollars of equipment and the lives of 18 soldiers to take responsibility for.

I sometimes think about comparing my 4-year Army commitment to my four years as a student and cadet at Tulane. My Army "Freshman Year" was completing AOBC, not-completing Ranger School, meeting 2nd Platoon and freezing my balls off training with 3-17 CAV earlier this winter, earning my Spurs, and getting ready for this deployment. I'm in the middle of my "sophomore year" right now. Two more years to go.

I love this job. Most of the time it's a very tough position to be in with so many eyes watching you to do the right thing. But when it's time for me to really "play platoon leader"—like I did the past couple days—this job is a major rush. I know one day I will read over these journal entries and think to myself "Was it all not real? Did I really do those things?" It will seem impossible that I led a platoon of Cavalry trucks in combat operations, and I will miss the adrenaline rush. I will forget what it feels like. I will want to do it again, that I am sure of. Hell, I bet that even when I'm a staff officer in a year or two, I will look back on my combat time as immeasurable. Still, though, here I am. This dust-filled, desolate landscape, cut off from the rest of the civilized western world. And it's hard to believe that this experience will be placed in high regard after I return home. The passage of time can yield unexpected results, I think, when it comes to experiences like this.

CHAPTER 4

BABYSITTING A BUNKER

5 October 2003. 1300 hrs. Northeast of Kandahar City.

Well, this is my first journal entry from the "frontlines"—although I understand all too well that there are no real frontlines on this kind of battlefield. Still though, we're taking our turn out here, away from the relative safety afforded by the KAF perimeter. I write this now from the seat of my Humvee in the middle of a barren and desolate valley to the northeast of Kandahar City. Yesterday morning we left KAF en route to an old ammunition supply point (ASP), a compound of munitions buried into the side of a mountain through a series of underground caches and bunkers. I'm told some of this ordnance is 100 years old left over from the British colonies in Afghanistan . . . artifacts of a forgotten piece of history, and another sign that this land has been ravaged by foreign armies for far too long.

On Friday night, I was given a hasty operations order to take command of an infantry squad, plus four infantrymen, plus one of my Cav sections of three vehicles, and to lead them all to this ammo site in order to provide protection for the US State Department contractors that are being tasked to dig out the ordnance and destroy them. We were told to plan on babysitting this bunker for at least three days. Apparently, the locals (enemy or not) have been pilfering this ammo site for their own personal stop-shop, and many rockets have disappeared during the night over the past few months . . . and lo and behold KAF has been in numerous rocket attacks recently as well. Most of these UXO can be modified into IED explosives or mines. So, we made it to the ammo hill yesterday at about 10 AM, and we relieved the US Army MPs that had been here for three days. Just as I completed my leader's recon of the ammo site, the chief political officer of the 2nd Corps AMF dropped in to visit the ammo site. He requested that our contractors cease destruction. I intervened with my interpreter, and I ordered him to leave the area and that ammo destruction would continue unless I received orders otherwise. He left and we had no similar interventions as of yet. Not sure how to feel about this mission. Incredibly boring. Combined with an October heat wave, and field-living conditions here that are not very sanitary.

I deployed my ITAS gun truck to cover the northside of the mountain. My #2 truck to cover the west, supported by the infantry squad. My vehicle covers the southern approach, supported by the second infantry team on the east. This is a pretty decent position to prevent theft of any munitions. However, there are small patrols of AMF that have also been assigned to protect this hill and it's hard to be sure of their loyalties. They have been exceedingly cooperative, even making a run into the town market and purchasing chickens, flatbread, and potatoes and melons for all of six US dollars. They are very friendly but nonetheless they make me nervous—many AMF are former Taliban. Some still sympathize, while others are effective at masquerading themselves on both sides.

The good thing is that progress is being made: over 5,000 pounds of 107 mm rockets were destroyed in the last 24 hours alone. I want to believe we had something to do with that. We're told not to expect relief until Thursday, which is five days away—a long time to babysit ammo. But I guess we've been living the "cushy life" on KAF with air-conditioned tents, with TVs and showers, and hot meals, for long enough already. Our Bravo Section 2nd platoon leaves soon for a ground attack convoy into the east—the same area where I did the aerial reconnaissance recently. We are expected to return to KAF around the same time as them.

Yesterday there were reports of ACM attacking Afghan diggers (like our contractors here) about 25 miles away. We will be on our watch, but no one really expects to make much contact. We are here in response to the ammo caches that were found during our mission on October 1. In fact, my old position from that day is just off the distance about 2.5 km. What's different about this mission—apart from any other that I've encountered (even at Fort Drum), is that out here I am the OIC. I've got 26 soldiers on this mountain, and I report back to the operation center at KAF. So other than that, I can make all the decisions on this hill, with authorization over not only my own soldiers, but the local AMF as well. It's certainly more liberating of a leadership lesson, and it allows me to arrange for food exchange between our soldiers and the AMF (which I was hesitant to do during my previous mission). I'm also making simple uniform modifications like no BDU-top needed during the hottest part of the day. Flak vests and Kevlar helmets must remain on. We will be watching this line for a few days longer.

10 October 2003. Back at KAF.

After six days guarding the ammo supply point, we returned to KAF and we're presently recovering on sleep and performing maintenance before we go right back out to the same spot tomorrow. I shall call this past week "Guard shift ASP #1" because we can expect at least two more rotations in the next couple of weeks until all the ammo is destroyed. For 48 hours during this past week's shift, my section conducted reconnaissance in the valleys and mountains around the ASP, which resulted in our discovery of 47 tank rounds that were recently stolen from the ammo site and left in a creek bed about 5 km north. We set up an OP around the site and we waited for Ronco (the demolition team hired by the State Department). Eventually Ronco destroyed the tank rounds and we returned to our posts on the ASP. Time went by a little faster out there and we are not too disappointed about going back out. Things have certainly picked up and this new tempo is a welcome change.

16 October 2003. KAF.

Another week spent guarding the ammo supply point, and we returned to KAF last night. This past week was really no different than the first mission on the line. I left on Saturday with a four-vehicle section composed of Alpha Section/2nd Platoon, two Avenger[1] teams, and a squad of infantry, totaling 34 men under my command. On 12 October, I took the platoon out on an area reconnaissance of some of the mountain passes a little further north than we traveled last week. We heard we might find some more weapons caches, and we did. We came across two separate caches: one cut into the side of a mountain filled with several hundred mortars, and another one lying in a pile of rocks. This one was much larger. I would say several thousand mortar rounds and many of them brand new. We marked the grid coordinate and reported it to HQ.

While we were setting up [our] patrol base for the night, we came across an abandoned Taliban palace and stronghold at the top of the mountain. I think this was probably built by the Russians, given the villa's architecture and construction and seemed too grand for Islamic fundamentalists. In any case, it was covered with Taliban graffiti and anti-America propaganda, at least

1 Humvee-mounted air defense systems designed defend against low-flying air threats.

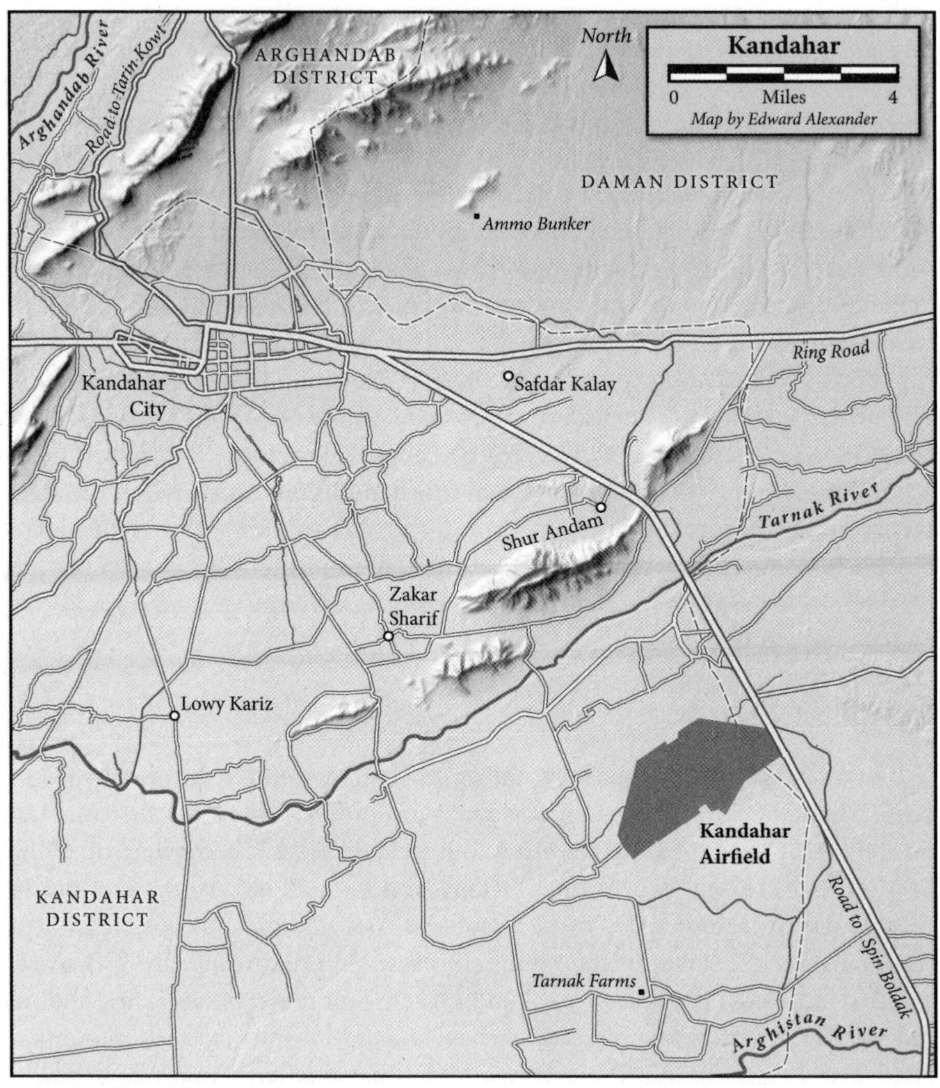

according to my interpreter. As only a true Garden Stater would, I ordered my men to empty their bowels in each room of the house before we left. This order was promptly obeyed as we had not had a chance to relieve ourselves indoors in quite some time. Several of the soldiers might've gotten sick from the local chicken and flatbread that we've been dining on, and they took full advantage to relieve themselves. One of the gunners, Private Ryan Fleming, decided to follow the order exceptionally well, until I realized he was probably suffering from a severe case of dysentery. He looked severely dehydrated and his condition started to worsen, so I had him medevac'd back to KAF the next day.

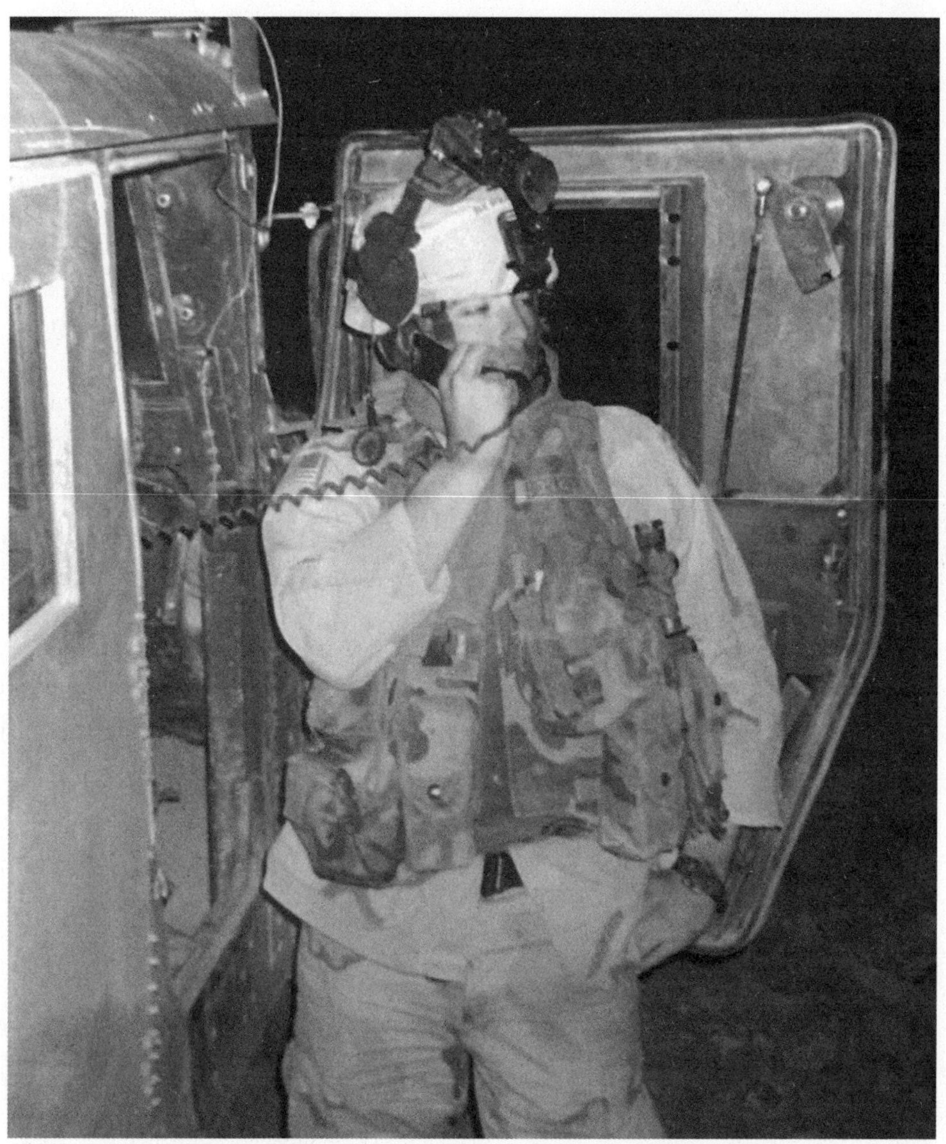

LT Berkoff calls back to the TOC at KAF while guarding the ammo bunker on the outskirts of Kandahar City. *Author Collection*

Ryan Fleming comes from a very small town in southwest Virginia Appalachia, near the tri-border of Kentucky and Tennessee. He speaks with a thick southern drawl, including rich vernacular, and I've never heard anything like it. He's the type of kid that were it not for the Army, he'd probably be a drunk or an addict living under a bridge right now. But he made the decision to serve, and he escaped that future. He came from a broken childhood, and I think he realizes his life up until now has not benefited from any socio-economic advantages, nor has he many natural gifts, but he is physically strong and technically proficient (in weapons, radios, etc.), and he takes that as far as he can. He's a workhorse, in fact. When you give him a task, either in the training fields of Fort Drum or out here at the bunker, he works harder than anyone I've seen to get it done. In the field, he's one of the best privates in Apache Troop, but when offered distractions or temptations on weekends in the barracks at Drum, Fleming too easily gets in trouble. Always one-step ahead, and then two-steps back. I hope I have enough time out here to help him straighten out.

We spent many nights at the ammo point with the local AMF, who shared this guard-post with us. I'm not impressed with the appearance of most Afghans, but there was one militia soldier who [was] much more suitable to the eye. His name was Mohammed Akhtar, and he had a long and full black beard. He was tall and slim with very straight white teeth (which was a rarity here). He sat next to us with some other AMF soldiers, and we all partook in chicken and rice. We had purchased the food prior to Fleming's illness, and afterwards, I ordered the men to avoid additional local food from this market. Anyways, these Afghans are very animated speakers. Their Pashto language is almost hypnotic and mesmerizing to hear. At dusk, we sat around a small fire, while Mohammed told us stories of Taliban cruelty.

On our last day at the ASP, and only hours before we were scheduled to be relieved, Ronco told me about a weapons bunker that was being pilfered by the locals. I took two trucks over to the bunker and I found the AMF loading their vehicle with RPG rounds. After a long negotiation between the AMF commander, and after receiving piecemeal instructions from our TOC over the radio in KAF, I eventually ordered the RPGs to be returned to the bunker and I sent the AMF away. AMF was not happy about this (if that's who they really were).

We're not sure what missions the future will hold for us now. Technically there's only two more months of campaigning left here before we begin to re-deploy critical equipment. I saw some photos of my friend's wedding the other day, and it hurt to see my buds gathered together on such an occasion without being able to participate. I also just saw photos of my youngest newborn niece Sophia. I know this Thanksgiving they will all get together for a feast—this year with many new babies. Another holiday celebration missed, thanks to my Army service. I'm feeling very ill today I hope my morale will improve when my health does.

20 October 2003. KAF.

I'm getting over being ill, but I had a very relaxing weekend which I think replenished my body enough with energy and nutrition to allow for another mission to come this Wednesday. I woke up on October 17 with an illness, terrible stomach pains, feeling of nausea, and a fever. I struggled through the morning only to vomit violently by midday. Then I spent the next 24 hours sleeping it off and drugged up.

On Saturday morning, my platoon received orders to deploy to Kandahar City for a 24-hour mission. I had to stay back and recuperate. At first the plan was for only about 3/4 of the platoon to deploy on this mission, but my NCOs wanted to bring the whole platoon out so they would have enough soldiers to pull guard shift. I did not have the energy to debate the issue with them. They were content on taking this mission without my help, which actually allowed for a nice break for me to get better. What resulted next was a 24-hour period of sheer bliss—at least the closest thing to bliss in Afghanistan. My health improved pretty much 100 percent by Saturday morning, and I woke up to a completely empty tent, with all my soldiers out on mission. So, I had full access to their DVDs, to extra sleeping, to snacks, and to some privacy. This turned out to be the best day of the deployment so far and unless my soldiers leave without me again or if I get a chance to take R&R in Qatar, I do not see another day that will match October 18th. It was almost like I could be home watching a movie and drinking beer (well, we drink "near-beer" in KAF called O'Douls) in the privacy of my own apartment in Watertown, New York. At least that's what it felt like.

The good times had to end and we're now back to the routine. Today was my first PT session in three weeks. We sort of thought life would feel like garrison here for the next couple of weeks but tonight I was told to get ready for another big mission on 22 October. We're going to leave for a 24-hour mission in northern Kandahar City to set up vehicle checkpoints. Unfortunately, this looks like the same terrain that we covered during the past few weeks . . . but what do I know? Higher says they want us to do it again so we will.

CHAPTER 5

THE ROUTE RECON . . . FROM HELL

1 November 2003. Back at KAF.

Nothing ever remains constant here. The only constant is uncertainty and surprise. This was my feeling when I received orders to execute a 300-mile route reconnaissance through the central provinces of Afghanistan beginning on 24 October. Brigade HQ ordered us to assess the trafficability of several routes connecting Kandahar Airfield to Oruzgan Province—a central, more mountainous location that would possibly become a Forward Area Resupply Point —or FARP—to be used for future operations. We were given about 72 hours' notice, and that time was spent wisely on vehicle preparation and route analysis.

On 23 October, I took a Blackhawk out on an aerial reconnaissance of a portion of the route, which turned out to help very little. HQ wanted us to determine if LMTVs could maneuver through these routes and it appeared to me the variance for LMTV route-trafficability could be measured in inches in this region's non-existent roads. It was impossible for me to assess the route from a Blackhawk moving at 140 knots. It became a very high-profile mission within the brigade, and my 2nd Platoon had everyone's attention. Lots of attached personnel were coming with me, including U.S. Air Force communication technicians, mechanics, medics, interpreters, engineers, and artillerymen. CPT Cunningham sent his company executive officer, 1LT Nat Wilson, who was overall officer in charge of the convoy. I remained in charge of my platoon, and the overall maneuver and security elements of the convoy. We left on early Friday morning with seven vehicles bound for Oruzgan. The first 48 hours of the

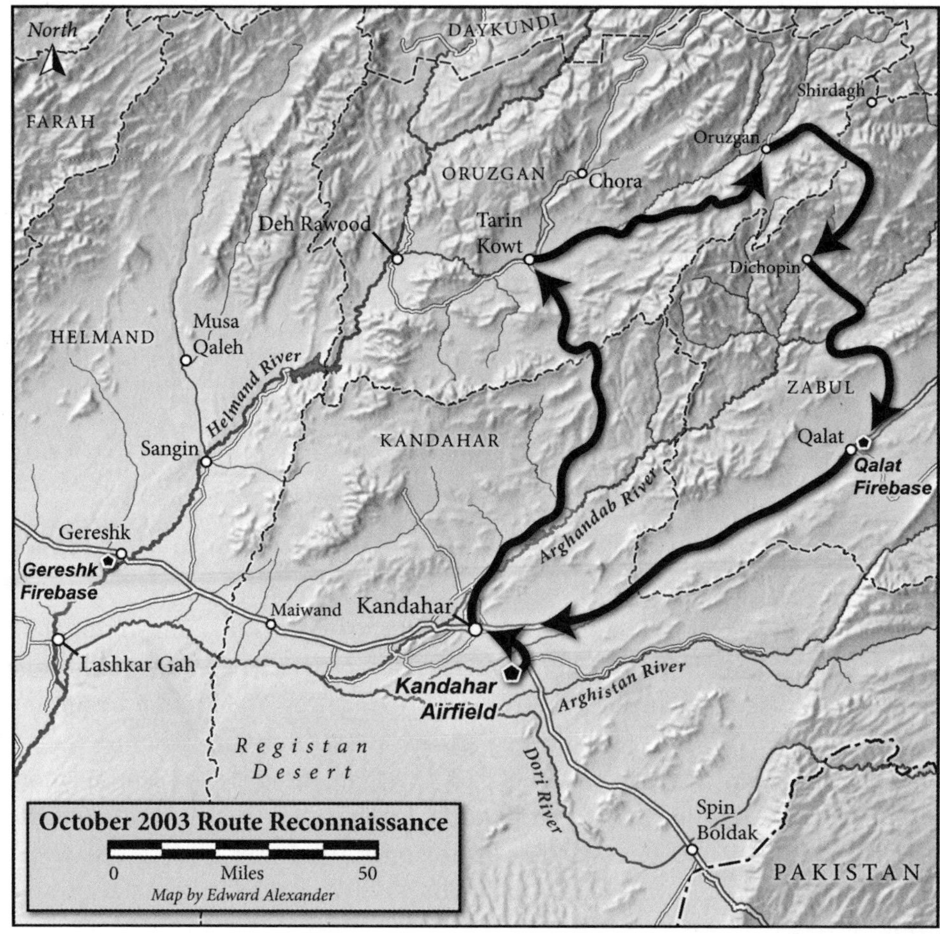

mission went incredibly well. We covered almost 90 km the first day, classifying terrain features and bridges along the way for LMTV truck trafficability which remained passable. Best of all, no personnel or vehicles were damaged. Our first day ended with our travel through a particularly nasty mountain pass that was once frequented by Taliban guerrillas. But we made no enemy contact.

I had to control the temper of one of my lead scout NCOs. As we were moving to set up a patrol base after 12 straight hours of reconnaissance, he complained he was tired of all of this, and he became very disrespectful and irritable. I tried to remind him that we were all very tired, but we still had work to do. This time I went to SFC White. He and I straightened out the attitude.

Day 2. The route became much more difficult. Not suitable for LMTVs (which we knew was a priority for HQ and planning) but at least it remained Humvee-passable. At one point along the route Saber 2 and Saber 4 vehicles both went down with major malfunctions, and we needed a Chinook to air-drop resupply parts to get the trucks going again. At the end of day two, we reached the Oruzgan airfield (a lone dirt strip in a field) and we set up a camp. We had reached our objective, and we sized up the area for a future FARP. The big question next: do we go back to KAF along the same route we just used, when we already determined that it was not trafficable for LMTVs? We were experiencing vehicle deadlines, and no one wanted to go back the same way we had just come. There had to be a better way back. We set up a patrol base for the night.

Day 3. We were authorized by HQ to conduct a map recon to identify a new route back to KAF, which would connect us to Afghanistan's Highway 1—which is essentially the only paved highway that circles the country, and it leads directly to KAF. We thought we had a good route picked out and we moved out by the mid-morning. We got about 15 km into this route when the "road" became so dangerous to travel over that I actually needed to bail out my entire crew for fear of a rollover. I got on the radio and ordered the rest of [the] platoon to bypass this route, allowing the lead scout to recon an alternate that led into a nearby creek bed. The creek bed was so filled with boulders, we conducted another halt and spoke to a local civilian who told us it was not passable ahead. Several hours of good daylight had passed since we left the FARP area, but it was no good. I ordered the entire convoy to turn around and travel back to where we started. As much as we wanted to reach Highway 1, we did not have enough knowledge of the local terrain to determine the best route to make it there, and the maps offered little reassurance. Turning around was a difficult decision to make, but I think it was the right one.

After turning everyone around to head back to the FARP, 2 km into our route, Saber 4 broke down again with a destroyed hub. The mechanic worked on it for many hours, and finally did make it drivable, but there was no way it could make it back to KAF without another resupply of parts. So, we went back to old patrol base near Oruzgan of the previous night, and we waited for another resupply which would come the next morning. HQ also told us they would drop in a new map with a better route connecting to the highway, but it meant going directly through the Dichopin district. This village and the chokepoints around it were infamous for heavy contact in the past few months. The positive thing was that if we can get through Dichopin quickly, Highway 1 was not far off.

Day 4 was about to begin. After receiving new maps, new graphics, and a new hub for Saber 4, we left on October 27 on a new and circuitous route which would take us right through Dichopin. We started out making good progress, traveling until sunset and getting within 15 km of the village. Just as we were passing through a village in a very narrow valley, Saber 4 died again, and we knew that new parts were necessary for us to continue the march. So, we set up observation posts along the valley, dispersing them along a kilometer stretch of the valley floor. During the night, we observed two possible ACM burying supplies, and what looked like ammunition and rifles. Although, technically, we are approved to engage them, I did not want to start a hornet's nest in this valley, especially with a truck down and our platoon spread so thin.

Day 5. The next morning, we drove to that spot, and we dug up the ammunition and took it with us. We couldn't move much this day, waiting on the birds, which finally arrived but with barely enough day light time for the mechanic to fix the truck and still make any forward movement progress. We traveled for about two hours, and this was probably the worst route we had seen thus far. The terrain wasn't so terrible, but the road simply failed to exist. Instead of a road there were just huge boulders strewn about. We conducted a halt in another valley or gorge about 5 km from Dichopin, and we set up positions for the night. It was a cold night, and I had two squads move into dismounted, observation posts on mountain tops to observe some of the dead space around us.

Day 6—29 Oct—Somehow this operation continued to only get worse. We made it to a narrow mountain pass about 4 km long. The pass was the scene of heavy Taliban ambushes against Army special operations forces in August and September. Halfway through the pass—known as "Ambush Alley"—there was a boulder directly on the road in a perfect place to block us. This sent up our pucker factor. We first tried to assess the practicability of demolishing the boulder with C4 explosives, but it was decided that that would probably just destroy the road. There was a bypass we could have taken into an adjacent valley that would have only left our vehicles at the mercy of another impossible creek bed with large enough rocks to cause more trucks to go down. So, we were forced to take another bypass—a longer route around Dichopin. Of course, only about 2 km into this route, 1LT Wilson's truck went down and the Saber 6 truck was on its last leg. We then made the request to HQ at KAF: Sling us out or we are not moving! HQ agreed to sling out the two dead trucks, along with unessential personnel via Chinook lift. Of course, this took all day to coordinate and left us again with only a couple hours of daylight to push into Dichopin. Say nothing of the fact that we knew this was a Taliban staging area. With now a much smaller force, we executed our "Line of Departure" or LD, and about 1 KM into the route, the road ran out again! We had to use a local civilian to direct us on which way to go and this proved to be very effective. It allowed us to push into southern Dichopin and set up patrol bases in a beautiful apple

2nd Platoon cautiously moves through the village of Dichopin, Oruzgan Province, October 2003. *Author Collection*

orchard. This was a nice setting for a rest overnight, however, we were just a couple hundred meters from an armed, AMF compound and all sorts of signs that war had ripped through this village recently.

Day 7. We left early in the morning, 30 October, and we set off for the flat desert terrain we were all waiting for. This was the final ground connection between us and Highway 1. We were making great progress, covering 20 km in less than two hours but then Saber 4 vehicle decided it had enough. The half shaft blew off, and even if we had all the parts to fix it (we didn't), it would have taken all day to make it mobile again. It took eight precious hours to coordinate another Chinook sling load with HQ. The staffers back in KAF could not decide on a course of action. Finally, the bird arrived, and Saber 4 was lifted out with its crew. The rest of us—only four trucks left (we started with seven), pushed on as far as dusk would allow. As the sun set over the oasis, flat desert ground, we saw wide lanes of trafficability. I ordered "white lights on" and a fast push to Highway 1. Everyone knew that this meant we were going "home" for certain. It's funny how we kept calling KAF "home."

We hit real desert around nightfall, and the moon dust[1] caused major dustouts. Dustouts were just huge dust storms that precipitated zero visibility, even just a few meters away. This route during the daytime would be too easy. But at night, dustouts make tactical mounted movement very dangerous.

1 A fine, powdery, talc-like dust that kicks up into clouds causing low-visibility.

(Top) 2nd Platoon navigates the mountains in Oruzgan Province, October 2003. (Bottom) CH-47 Chinook drops supplies for 2nd Platoon during the October 2003 route reconnaissance. *Author Collection*

There were already several close collisions between our trucks, and some were offloading into ditches deep enough to cause another mission stop deadline. After this went on for about 90 minutes, we took a short halt in the desert to catch our breath and regroup. How much more of this could we take? I huddled in with all the NCOs. Our biggest concern was taking unnecessary risks. It was late at night, so we decided we would find one last suitable patrol base for the night, and we'd leave for KAF at sunrise (which was only about four hours away).

We mounted up and continued about 1 km when suddenly the moon dust disappeared, and gravel roads were now a site to be welcomed. This route took us safely to Highway 1, dumped us out on a paved road not far from the city of Qalat, and the rest was smooth sailing to KAF. No one wanted to stop for the night if we didn't really have to. For the past week, our trucks slowly crept up jagged switchbacks, barely moving, as if we were living in a perpetual school zone. Once our drivers felt the safety of paved roads however, our convoy moved like a freight train. KAF's bright lights in the distance was the most welcome sight. After some vehicle cleansing, everyone went to sleep around 1 am. It was a very long day, and the end of our most stressful mission to date. Miraculously, no one was hurt and not a single shot was fired in anger.

7 November 2003. KAF.

Little rest for the weary. We came in response. I must keep remembering that.

Since we returned from our route recon, we've conducted two Kandahar City patrol missions. Our first patrol included the 2-22 Anti-Tank platoon plus an air defense artillery unit, plus a squad of Romanian soldiers. I was the patrol leader. I dispatched two vehicles to help establish vehicle checkpoints on the busiest routes into the city. I took my vehicle, along with the Romanian convoy of five BTR APCs, to establish a checkpoint at another location. I served as the liaison officer and reported our situation reports back to the TOC at 2-22 HQ in KAF. On 6 November, my platoon rode through downtown Kandahar City as "a show of force" amongst the UN and Afghan government offices. This past week has seen the majority of 2-22 forces moving into the 2-87 IN area of operations, which is near Asadabad east of Bagram Airfield.

We had a little scare earlier this week. Reports came in that our own 1st Platoon from Apache Troop (which is operating near Asadabad in the northeast) was hit hard by an ambush. It turns out that their convoy was hit and lost one vehicle, but no one was wounded. With 2-22 IN all out on an operation, my Cav platoon is the last remaining mounted force in KAF right now able to conduct large missions.

Rumors keep flying around regarding our deployment possibly being extended to 12 months. That's a real long time and it sounded exciting and adventurous to be gone that long while I was back at Fort Drum, but now I'm not so sure. The one positive result of this would be I could save a lot more money. Plus, I would totally miss the upstate New York winter.

I am beginning to miss my family, especially with the holidays coming up. My family has two new additions, my nieces, Sophia and Batya. I think if it's determined that I am here until July or August, then the first thing I need to do is change some quality-of-life elements here. I really don't own a single thing that's good for distractions other than a few books and music on my CD player. And that's not enough to hold me off for a whole year. I just purchased a portable DVD player (thanks mom) which will be a start. I need a video game. Maybe I'll buy my own TV and I'll start using Amazon.com to have things shipped here. I've heard some guys are doing that.

With most of 2-22 out on missions, things might be quiet here for a little while. No complaints if the mission tempo slackens.

16 November 2003. KAF.

Enemy tactics have shifted towards our camp over the past week, and in Kandahar City. We've been doing these UN security patrols and driving by Afghan government offices during the week, but earlier this week a sniper took a shot at our Romanians, who were riding on the top of their BTRs. The sniper got lucky and killed two of them while it was moving down Highway 4 only a few kilometers from KAF. It was the first small-arms, close-range combat this close to KAF in the time that we've been here. So later that night, I was up late in brigade HQ, helping plan a new mission that was supposed to take us out west to Gereshk, which is a large village about 70 km west of here in Helmand province. Intelligence reports are telling us that the sniper responsible for the killing resided in a town near Gereshk, so a follow up mission was planned to locate this guy. We were supposed to be waking up at 1230 hrs. in order to leave by 0200. While I was sleeping, we were all awoken by a rocket attack which impacted a few hundred meters away.

This event was enough for brigade HQ to scrub our Helmand mission, and instead, decided that our efforts should remain focused on the near. We left early on the next morning with some EOD teams to investigate the point of origin for the rocket attack. It was suspected to be located about a kilometer north of the Tarnak River, which is just a few kilometers north of KAF. We've had a good deal of rain lately and the usual fording point we use to cross over and through the Tarnak looked to be much angrier on this day. As my truck is the second in the platoon's order of march, I watched as our lead scout, SSG Elsaesser, almost got his truck stuck in a very deep section of the river that appeared to bottom-out. As we approached, I yelled out to my driver, SPC James Callaway, to avoid that spot. "Try going out that way," I said, pointing down river. Callaway maneuvered our truck into an even deeper chasm on the bottom of the Tarnak riverbed and we were in trouble. We felt the river currents start to take control of our truck, and then we started taking on water quickly. We were sinking. I ordered everyone to bail out and grab sensitive items and weapons and swim for the banks. Once we accounted for all our gear and made sure we spit all the river water out of our mouths, we tried, unsuccessfully, to hitch our truck to the Saber 3 truck behind us (still on land) to get pulled out, but to no avail. Eventually, a farmer on a very large tractor approached the river and we paid him in MREs to pull us out. Which he did!

We finally made it out to the proposed POO site, we talked to some of the locals and militia soldiers, and everyone played deaf, dumb, and blind. A few hours later, lo and behold, came reports that rockets were found near the same spot, so we had to go back out there and pick them up. This time, we used a local bridge to cross the Tarnak. Always good to remain unpredictable and change up our routes, as it is.

CHAPTER 6

APACHE WHITE, ONCE AGAIN

27 November 2003. Thanksgiving Day. KAF.

Daily patrols now through Kandahar City over the past 10 days. My call sign is back to "Apache White." We are "Saber" no more. Bummer. Every day I send out a six-hour patrol to ride around and set up vehicle checkpoints where needed. 22 November, CPT Barnes returned from Gardez with 3rd Platoon and our HQ and mortar sections. Ever since they returned, morale has gone down steadily, and I feel like I'm walking on eggs every day and everywhere I go. I should not feel this way. I know I'm doing a good job out here and even our seasoned NCOs are counted in the numbers of those who are unhappy with our troop commander's leadership. He has nothing positive to say. He's super critical and more concerned about doing what looks good for his own image as opposed to how it might affect the morale of our troops. Today he reversed the evaluations I wrote up for SFC White for his NCOER. By the regulations, he's not allowed to do that. It shows his ineptness to rely on and trust his subordinates and their judgment. In addition to his own ignorance.

It will be a new adjustment for life here at KAF. The days working for HHC 2-22 and CPT Cunningham are over. CPT Barnes is my new boss again and I need to find a way to get used to it without feeling paranoid all the time. The division among our platoons is at an all-time high, with particular animosity between 3rd Platoon soldiers and 2nd Platoon soldiers. We think they feel like they're better than us for doing missions in the wild lands of Gardez, while we've been enjoying the "comforts" of KAF all this time. Hardly the case. It shouldn't be this way. I'm just going to need to speak my mind more often with CPT B in a professional matter. I will potentially be his XO for six months after we return to Fort Drum, until CPT Mullin takes over command. That seems like a long time to put up with these bastards, but I have to find a way. For the first time ever, I considered applying for the "Lieutenants to Knox" program when I redeploy home, depending on how bad it gets once I settle in at Drum.[1]

The most important thing is that I have a strong platoon here that supports me. I also have the agreement with LT John Torrealba (3rd Platoon) that CPT B's leadership sucks—and someone to complain to. I guess in a way I had it too good while I was attached to CPT Cunningham. No one bothered my platoon with anything unless it was about a mission. Now we're back to the bullshit inspections, equipment layouts, formations, meetings, new procedures and protocols for missions that I previously called my own shots on.

All of this hits home hard right now on this holiday that I normally spend with my family (except last year at this time I was hating life in Ranger school). This is an even more special Thanksgiving for us . . . . right now as I write this my family is together for the first time with our two new babies (my nieces). This is a real hallmark date for us. I would love to be home with them in Fair Lawn. Five more months until I'm home. I sometimes think of it more like a prison sentence than time spent serving my country overseas and in combat. Lieutenants throughout history have served under shitty commanders. Think about what LT Winters had to endure under Captain Sobel, from Easy Company, WWII. I can deal with Captain Barnes.

I will be promoted to first lieutenant on Monday, 1 December. We just learned it's official that we're going to be here until at least May. My DVD player and computer games are now set up so that's a nice diversion. I sometimes compare my four-year Army career to my college years, in terms of years of service, and I've said this is the middle of my sophomore year . . . well, it's proving to be a really tough one.

31 December 2003. 2030 hrs. KAF.

No longer a butter bar. On 1 Dec., our brigade commander (1st BCT/Task Force Warrior), COL Burke Garrett and LTC Joe Dichairo pinned a black bar on my collar in a brief ceremony in front of the 2-22 TOC. There were a few others with me that also commissioned 18 months ago (the time in grade for a 2LT). I was also recognized by the commanders for a job-well done ensuring the munitions were destroyed at the bunker, and for October's route recon to

1 This is a program that allows 1st lieutenants to return to Fort Knox in a training capacity.

Oruzgan. I have no use for a black bar pin until I get stateside and don my class-As. So, my first act as 1LT was to steal a black sharpie marker from the S3 shop and color-in my yellow butter bars on my boonie cap and on my DCU collar.[2]

This past month has been one of adjustment, transition, and "get used to it" mentality. Early December consisted of the final merger of 3rd Platoon/Apache Troop into daily operations in the Kandahar area. Occasionally, I was attached to a 2-22 rifle platoon to help set up a vehicle checkpoint or conduct a cordon operation, which was actually a nice break from working with CPT B. Physical training has picked up the pace immensely—with long early morning runs, with weapons and gear on, around shit pond—and we're back to the way it was in the beginning of August and September. Mostly due to CPT B's new SOPs.

The Christmas holiday came and went with a nice meal and some celebrities visited us on a USO tour. I had my picture taken with General Richard Myers, the chairman of the Joint Chiefs of Staff. I watched Robin Williams do a live comic stand up. I also saw Al Franken drive by and wave to me on the base.

From 27-29 December, we conducted our first joint mission with 3rd Platoon/Apache. I set up my platoon in several observation posts facing south to the Registan Desert, watching the southern sand dunes for ACM movement. Nothing much turned up but we are all going back out there in the next couple of days, hopefully to find indications of enemy activity.

Today, on this last day of 2003, we had a bit of excitement which may have resulted in the best set of actual results in our five months out here so far. Apparently, the AMF was holding a Pakistani Taliban officer prisoner in their compound, only a few miles away. Intel said the AMF made a deal with Pakistan to turn him over for a nice cash reward. But we were ordered to move in and intercept. 3rd Platoon and 2nd Platoon rushed out of the gate and we sped towards the AMF compound. We surrounded the compound while our MPs moved inside to make the grab. After a two-hour search that was going nowhere, my own PFC Kounlavong reported to me that he had positive identification of a local in the compound that matched the description and face-card we had received. I reported this up to Captain Barnes who moved the MPs into position to make the arrest. It was a nice way to end the year.

This has been one very long year. It began with processing at Fort Drum and my move into my first ever apartment, in Watertown, NY. Followed by taking over 2nd Platoon for a seven-month period on post. Field training in April and

2 My desert combat uniform collar, cap and Kevlar, each displayed a tightly sewn yellow bar denoting the rank of second lieutenant. Without proper supplies to sew on a black bar, the rank of a first lieutenant, the black sharpie marker sufficed.

LT Berkoff in the Registan Desert, December 2003. *Author Collection*

May, followed by the arrival of John Torrealba and Justin Stenner.3 Followed by the change of command ceremony with CPT Barnes in mid-June. In July, I took block leave and said final goodbyes to friends and family. We arrived in country on 8 August and started the days of working for HHC and CPT Cunningham through mid-November. Now, the reintegration of Apache Troop in KAF. The entire troop has reconsolidated here, with 1st Platoon finally returning from Asadabad on 29 December. It appears operations will last another 90 days with Apache Troop working together out of KAF. I think this could be a good change—I like that I have more lieutenants for my company.

I have many options to consider when we return to Fort Drum. The "Lieutenants to Knox" program is a possibility, but I'd like to know exactly what type of positions are open for me there. There's something called the FLEP program which allow me entrance into the Army's JAG Corps—which sounds interesting. I complete my term of service in 2006, and I'd like to go for my master's degree through the National Guard, I suppose. It's been a challenging

3 3rd and 1st platoon leaders—finally giving me some officers to socialize with.

time out here and I miss the happy distractions that were so frequent and available back at home. This deployment will end soon enough and for the rest of my life I'll be sick of saying "When I was in Afghanistan . . ." This time will serve as a very small imprint on the much larger picture of my life. There are times here where I feel like I'm doing great things, for a noble cause. We are helping rid the world of terrorists, however indirectly.

So may God grant my platoon and I the same amount of good health and success that we have seen in 2003. Goodbye, 2003. Your departure is not regretted, for it brings us ever closer to the end of this deployment and very welcomed homebound preparation. It will be a quiet New Year's Eve for me here. Certainly the calmest of my life. So, Happy New Year! I trust 2004 will bring peace to our country's many front lines, and hopefully quieter days for me.

1 January 2004. KAF.

Just another day in KAF, like any other. Tomorrow morning, we leave for a mission southwest of Kandahar City. It's a pretty large operation involving all Apache Troop plus up to three rifle platoons from 2-22 IN, and all sorts of attachments. There is a good possibility of making contact with the enemy on one of these fronts. I will write again when we return home in a few days.

29 January 2004. KAF.

I regret that I have not logged more frequent entries into this journal as of late but constant movement has precluded much rest or time to sit and ponder. Apache Troop left for another big mission in early January. Jan. 4–8. My platoon set up a VCP that was continually run for 80 straight hours. Very little resulted from this mission, except that we managed to anger and piss off many of the locals. I was ordered to put under custody all armed individuals that moved through my sector. Not sure that headquarters fully understands that everyone in this damn country is armed. So, I detained many respected Kandahar City officials—unbeknownst to me at the time, of course. We began by tying their hands and placing them behind a barbed wire cell that we constructed, but we lightened up our tactics when we realized the lack of ACM in this area. We returned to Kandahar Airfield to refit and get some rest in time for our next mission.

For the next operation, I was assigned to Charlie Company/2-22 IN for a two-week operation that would be based out of a new outpost/firebase being constructed in Qalat village, in Zabul Province—about 100 miles northeast of here. We were somewhat familiar with this region from our miserable route-reconnaissance operation from October. Our new Qalat firebase was in visual range of Alexander's Castle—or so it's called—an earthen fortification apparently built by Alexander the Great's army as he moved through this region to expand his empire. Interesting that this little village still bears strategic importance, which is about halfway between Kandahar (named after Alexander the Great) and Kabul. The activities during those two weeks were nothing much to speak of other than I got a chance to work closely with U.S. Navy Seal teams for the first time. Always reports of some High Value Target for us to chase down, but always turned up empty-handed. Every hole we dug up, turned out to be a dry one. The expected enemy contact never materialized. In fact, all the action was going on back in KAF.

On 17 January, LTC Dichairo, who is with us at the firebase, called me over and asked me to bring my platoon together for a huddle. This was unusual for him, and I suspected the news wouldn't be good. My initial thought was that our deployment was going to be extended. Instead, he told us that a soldier from 3rd Platoon, Apache Troop accidentally shot PFC Kenny Adams (another Cav Scout in 3rd Platoon) in the head, and it was not going to be a hopeful recovery. He went on to tell us that 2-22 IN's Deh-Rah-Wud (DRW) firebase in a central province, which is currently housing our Apache mortar teams, was just attacked and there were three casualties. At the time, this news was very frightful, but it turns out no one from the Apache mortar section was hurt. Then, the next day I found out that 1LT Stenner, my friend and the 1st Platoon leader, was being relieved of his position due to accusations of drinking, excessive force against locals, and even his own soldiers. His case is now under investigation, and meanwhile, he is being reassigned to the 2-22 battalion S3 shop as an assistant plans officer. There is even talk of court-martial proceedings.

I just saw some of the investigators from Fort Rucker that have come to KAF to interview members of Apache Troop in regards to the Kenny Adams incident.

Special Note: PFC Kenny Adams was shot in the head accidentally by another soldier in his platoon while the soldier was cleaning and attempting to clear his M4 rifle. He was immediately evacuated to Germany and the U.S. and underwent many months of surgeries and rehabilitation. The bullet passed into his cheek and exited his temple, severing optical nerves and causing permanent blindness and brain damage.

So, I guess 2d Platoon is the only platoon not being investigated right now, and apart from dealing with the bullshit of day-to-day activities in KAF, things are OK here.

I'm told that in less than 60 days we will begin to load our containers and get our vehicles ready for shipment. That's the target. I'm shooting for that right now. Mid-April is templated for our home-bound plane ride. I'm still considering Fort Knox as an alternative to two more years at Fort Drum, but to be honest, I kind of like Fort Drum. I like that I can drive home on any weekend in time for dinner. I like the location in upstate New York, since there are so many new cities and places to explore. I actually like the prestige of being in the 10th Mountain Division. I don't like my current troop commander, however, but I am able to tolerate him. . . plus his time to go is only seven months away from the moment we get home. I'm excited to work in the 3-17 Squadron staff. I think there's a certain affinity you gain with your unit after a deployment, and I want to use my new veteran status in the unit to be that seasoned officer working on the staff, helping the new platoon leaders and butter bars as they start showing up. It sounds ridiculous but the only thing that really makes me want to leave is the Apache Troop bullshit and PT intensity. Working out used to be fun and enjoyable but with CPT B and the 1SG, it's only designed for pain endurance. It's become a real morale buster for someone like me who's never been in great cardio shape. I guess that means I just have a better reason to lose 10 pounds. Fort Knox, although I think I can offer Training Command a lot, I recognize that it's the easy way out.

There is another mission looming for us right now. The whole troop (less 1st platoon who just replaced us at firebase Qalat) will move to the west to about 60 miles away, near Gereshk in Helmand. They say it will be a 4-to-6-day mission, but we know by now to automatically triple or quadruple that estimate.

There is a small light at the end of this deployment tunnel but it's still too far away for any real excitement. I heard today that my good friend from Tulane—LT Chris Morrison—is heading to Kandahar Airfield soon to replace us as part of the 25th Infantry Division. It will be strange to see him here, if that actually happens. I also heard from some other Tulane friends, Pete Benninger, for one, that are on the front lines in Iraq with the 101st Airborne and the 2nd Armored Cavalry Regiment. Tulane's newly minted Army officers really moved into the force at the right time for some excitement. I think I've had enough of playing soldier 24/7 . . . and I'd like to go home.

CHAPTER 7

DETOUR TO HELMAND

13 February 2004. Firebase Gereshk, Helmand Province.

As planned, we moved to this Army Special Forces firebase, which is actually about 95 miles due west of Kandahar City and a few miles southwest of the village of Gereshk.[1] During our first week's rotation here much of the time was spent getting to know the rules of this new lifestyle, which was briefly interrupted with a 36-hour mission. This mission was supposed to be tied together with a larger 2-22 IN operation in the area, which is attempting to hunt down a key Taliban leader in our vicinity. But, the larger mission never happened. Despite this, 2nd Platoon went into the area of operation on our own. We pushed about 50 miles north of Gereshk, into the Sangin village region, along the Helmand River. Unlike driving around Kandahar City, not as many friendly faces and waving hands in Sangin. On 2 February, we returned back to the Gereshk firebase and conducted some routine presence patrols and village assessments in this immediate area.

We went back to KAF for three days, before returning back again to Gereshk on 8 February. This past week, I've been doing missions almost every other day out of the Gereshk firebase. Each mission is about 10 hours long and consists of presence patrols, village assessments and setting some traffic/vehicle checkpoints. When back in the firebase, we spend our time building up our living quarters. The Special Forces ODA team here had no room anywhere for

1 Firebase Gereshk was used primarily by U.S. Army Special Operations until 2006 when it was expanded and transformed into Main Operating Base Price, headquarters for the Danish Battle Group and British military forces until 2014.

us to billet, so we had to start building our quarters from scratch. I'm currently housed in a nice wooden hut. It was literally built by 2nd Platoon soldiers in their downtime. It's a little tight in here with all 20 of us together, but I secured a corner of the hut with enough space to be comfortable for as long as we're here . . . but there's no telling how long that will be before we receive orders to move back to KAF . . . to either refit for another rotation at Firebase Qalat, or resume new operations in the Kandahar City vicinity.

This firebase has lots of advantages, but some disadvantages. There's less living space and less of the typical KAF "luxuries" like access to the PX, a barber, and women to look at. But the advantages are less bullshit formations, no organized PT, and no lengthy pre-combat inspections. I can call the shots. The internet is also more accessible here and the phones are free. There are a couple of open computers for the guys to use to surf the web and email home. Unlike what we might see at the MWR tent in KAF, the screensavers are of a mostly naked Petra Nemcova. The SF team posted a warning that "screensavers on these computers must show some parts of the naked female anatomy…flowers, landscapes and family photos are strictly forbidden." The SF ODA team here runs a hot chow dining facility, and their cooks are local nationals. The food is pretty good. We're pulling our weight including rotating our soldiers (myself included) into the firebase guard tower for nightly shifts. The mission tempo has picked up significantly, which is making the time pass quicker. So, overall, I think 2nd platoon is enjoying this new change of scenery.

The 3rd platoon soldier (who accidentally shot Kenny Adams) has court-martial proceedings commencing this week. I'm told it will result in a conviction and possibly confinement for 30 days before he's discharged. LT Stenner is gone, but I don't know what the official result of that investigation was. I'm not sure if he's going to stay on KAF on staff, or just go back to Fort Drum. If possible, he might even leave the Army. No one knows right now. 45 days and counting until operations end and equipment gets containerized.

One year ago this weekend I was with all Tulane buds for a reunion in New Orleans. It was a great weekend. I need to be patient. Soon enough, this experience will also become a memory too, and it will become a story that I just retell—over and over again. I've been going at it now for 6 months and 8 days—mostly without a let up. We came in response. I must keep thinking on that. Home is going to feel like no other feeling in my life yet felt.

24 February 2004. KAF.

After spending almost 2 weeks at Firebase Gereshk (on our second rotation there) we returned to KAF on the night of 20 February. We were told to be ready to go back out for a new set of missions on 23 February—my 24th birthday. But unforeseen forces at hand prevented any future missions for the time being. We were told the Gereshk base was essentially shut down to 2-22 Forces, and consequently we left there in a hurry, presumably to begin operations around Kandahar City again. Sunday, 22 February was "Triple Deuce Day" in Kandahar. All Task Force Courage[2] forces consolidated on KAF for a battalion fun run, followed by presentation ceremonies of Combat Infantryman Badges and 10th Mountain Division Combat Patches for all soldiers to proudly wear. Afterwards, we received some good news, followed a few hours later by some not so good news.

The good news is that our deployment dates have been posted and A Troop will be one of the first elements returning home on/around 14 April. The other good news was that we were given a full week off from missions in order to complete much-needed maintenance on our vehicles, our weapons, and to properly inventory all of our sensitive items. The bad news was that the Army Inspector General was notified of another case of physical abuse against local nationals committed by Apache Troop while on missions.

Last month, SGT McElroy of 3rd Platoon butt-stroked a local when apparently, he claims, the local tried to grab his gun. But he was cleared of all charges. Now, a couple of guys from 2-22 are saying that they saw someone from 3rd Platoon kick a local national while he was on the ground during a village mission (back in December or January). Every Apache trooper had to write a sworn statement of our knowledge of the incidents, and all noncommissioned officers are being interviewed by the IG. This is not the kind of attention that we want, especially so soon to the end of our deployment.

The investigations are underway, and we were told that Apache Troop will not "leave the wire" until they are solved. We all know that 3rd Platoon's NCOs are hyper aggressive with the locals. In fact, this exact scenario was predicted by me and my soldiers, when 3rd Platoon left the wild lands of Gardez and consolidated here at KAF in November. No one is surprised either when you look at the leadership of 3rd Platoon, who have shown a pattern for this type of misconduct ever since I first encountered them earlier this year. There are

2 Task Force Courage was the official name of all joint forces assigned to 2-22 Infantry during the deployment.

the stories of 3rd Platoon's PSG and his rough behavior as a Drill Instructor previously at Fort Knox. Some of his former recruits are actually in Apache Troop now and remember seeing his abuse.

I will admit that I've allowed my men to do some things on missions that I now regret. During some of these static VCPs, we'd sit at these intersections for many hours and attract unwanted attention from the locals. For instance, we've had to throw rocks at large crowds that refused to move away from our vehicles. We even tied up and detained a young boy of probably 12 years old, that refused to comply with our orders to keep away from our vehicles. We did it to set an example, and to make them understand that we're not here to play and we needed to keep a certain degree of clearance from our trucks. If we need to shoot ACM, and we have large crowds in the area, we don't want to cause unnecessary collateral damage. The bottom line is that Alpha Troop does not have a very good reputation right now in the eyes of the Army. In the past five weeks, CPT Barnes has had three IG investigations, Kenny Adams shot in the head, LT Stenner removed from his position, and now all this.

In the middle of the drama was my 24th birthday. Yesterday, I turned 24 years old and I believe that I am an old man if hard work means making one old. The 23rd year of my life has been an eventful one for me, and after 21 months in the Army—seven of which in Afghanistan—I am beginning to feel like a veteran. If I look back at the young man of February 23, 2003, I'd see a fresh, young, second lieutenant, in my first month as a platoon leader. Now I've been in charge of this platoon for 13 months, and I've executed over 100 combat missions. I've traveled over 10,000 miles here since August. May God continue to grant success to my platoon, and good health in the 24th year to come.

13 March 2004. KAF.

Today is the first day on KAF to rest after conducting operations without a break for 14 straight days. On 29 February we left for our third and final rotation at Firebase Gereshk. It was supposed to be closed to conventional forces but things change here all the time. We executed missions out of Gereshk every day for about a week including conducting several village assessments in and around the provincial capital of Lashkar Gah. Locals working in opium fields down that way all the way to the horizon.

We made a return trip up the Helmand River valley towards Musa Qaleh in the Sangin District and had a bad feeling about it. Lots of pissed off looking locals, watching us along the way. When we got back to the firebase, the ODA commander told us "Hey, I don't think you guys should go back to Sangin. . . .

We're getting some intel reports of some bad dudes in there—they're planning something. Another ODA got ambushed along that route last year, so if you are going back that way, I'd beef up your security."[3] "No problem," I told him. "We've got orders to return to KAF and I don't think we'll be back there."

We did return to KAF . . . for all of 12 hours, only to leave on March 7th for a "deliberate operation" which included Apache 1st Platoon and a mortar truck section of 120mm Field Artillery guys. We conducted missions in the dunes northwest of Kandahar City for six straight days . . . mostly vehicle checkpoints and village reconnaissance. We returned to KAF yesterday at 0300, and we will now use the weekend to refit our equipment before we begin routine patrols around Kandahar City.

The pace has been fast for the past several weeks and I am tired, but I'm also confident in our success and eagerly anticipating homeward bound preparations. The weather has warmed considerably in the past couple of weeks. It's beginning of the spring season here and early summer and the temps are rising into the 80s and 90s.

CPT Barnes made a few of the NCOs quite discontented with his leadership lately. I define being a "squared away officer" as a direct correlation with the manner of respect and admiration you get from the soldiers around you. I am quite certain that my soldiers enjoy me as their leader. But CPT B is so frequently and severely slandered by the soldiers of A Troop, that its clear to me: He may know textbook tactics (or at least think he knows it) and he might be able to run a six-minute mile, but he does not understand how to feel the pulse of this men of his command. Therefore, his ignorance directly contributes to the lack of respect felt for him by the men.

Two more weeks of operations here, followed by two weeks of re-deployment preparation, and then, plane rides home.

3 He was referring to the coordinated ambush of ODA 774, part of 2nd Battalion, 7th Special Forces Group in Sangin, Helmand Province on 29 March 2003. Weapons Sergeant Orlando Morales and USAF close air controller, Staff Sgt. Jacob L. Frazier, were both killed in action.

CHAPTER 8

FINAL MISSIONS AND HOMEBOUND

20 March 2004. Saturday. KAF.

Nearing the end. This past week we conducted a local patrol around Kandahar City, where a villager led us to a landmine he had dug up near his home recently. It was destroyed by EOD the following day. A few days ago, 2nd Platoon was alerted to be ready to provide escort security for a team of U.S. State Department engineers, to take them along the highway from Kandahar all the way to Herat, which is 400 miles away near the border with Iran. We thought our big missions were behind us, but now this.

While preparing for the mission, there was some heavy contact between our A Company/2-22 and ACM near Tarin Kowt. On March 18th, two soldiers were killed and two wounded during the battle and we heard about 10 enemy fighters were killed. 18 March marked the first day that 2-22 IN men were killed in action during our deployment, and it comes with even more pain and shock when you look at the date on the calendar. This was the last leg of operations. Everyone's going home in a few weeks, and then these two guys get killed. Their names were Staff Sergeant Anthony Lagman and Sergeant Mike Esposito. I met SSG Lagman[1] briefly while at Gereshk firebase in late February. Poor guys so near the end. I attended the ceremony yesterday, and witnessed their caskets carried on the aircraft bound for the states.

1 SSG Anthony Lagman was killed in action while helping clear a village on March 18th, 2003, when he was 26 years old. 2-22 Infantry decided to name the firebase we built in Qalat after SSG Lagman. FOB Lagman served as a critical base for coalition forces for another ten years after we departed.

Back to this State Department mission. . . . After the ramp ceremony for the KIA, I took my platoon into Kandahar City's PRT building – which is right smack downtown in the busiest section of the city. Along with us was a large gaggle of U.S. State Department personnel, UN people, Civil Affairs, and senior military staffers who would assist with reconstruction projects in Herat. We staged at the PRT for the night and we planned to leave for Herat the next morning. Apparently, we found later in the night, our brigade HQ did not approve the mission and it was completely scrubbed. We also heard something about Ismail Khan, who's a big warlord in Herat, and how he did not approve our entry to Herat province—or something like that. So we returned to KAF this morning and now we're planning to leave for another Kandahar City patrol in the morning.

Three weeks from now I should be out of Afghanistan. I hope to never return. My theory of moving to the squadron staff and thereby missing any deployment to Iraq might be ill-conceived. There's talk of a huge change to the organization of the division and even the Army, happening in the next 6 to 12 months. It's hard to say where that might take me, but there is talk of building a new cavalry reconnaissance squadron in a newly established brigade, and that could be my new unit. We'll see. I've also been giving Military Intelligence more thought recently. Going to Fort Huachuca and being trained in MI may have its advantages for the civilian world later on. Although it would tack on another year of service at a new post, it still might be worth it.[2] Despite the lack of appeal of remaining in the Army, isn't Military Intelligence the whole reason why I joined? It is what I can see myself doing when I make the jump over to civilian life. Maybe one year in the Army somewhere as an MI captain might not be such a bad trade-off, if I need to spend one more year at Fort Drum somewhere?

24 March 2004.

I'm going out on my last mission tomorrow. It's a routine presence patrol in the villages Southwest of Kandahar. All very familiar ground and we're not expecting any surprises. At this point in our deployment, I'm very comfortable with the platoon and their ability to navigate the local terrain and make good decisions quickly. That said, however, as a student of military history, and on my ninth month here in Afghanistan, I know that I can make all the right decisions in the world but the enemy still gets a vote. Just like during our route recon to

2 Technically my branch detail in Armor ended in May 2005, so I figured I needed to find a job for a year at Fort Drum before I could make a move into Intel.

Oruzgan last October, "Murphy" still gets a vote. We've been going at this for nine straight months and the longer we do these missions the more I feel it's inevitable that something will go south on us. Our most recent patrol occurred during a dust storm and the visibility became zero during much of the route. Tomorrow we will travel down a wide dry creek bed strewn with old Soviet tanks. The Mujahidin must've used the high ground for ambush positions, and they targeted the Soviet convoy who were using the creek as a road.

It's nice to see moods lifting. There is a feeling of excitement in the air with only 15 days until we begin to leave this airfield. It's hard to imagine. I will fly through 15 days here like it's nothing. Missions and routines will pass the time away. 15 days from now I could very well be on an airplane bound for Fort Drum . . . only to be awaited by a welcome home ceremony, family, a car, a new apartment, beer, fast food. Freedom. America!

This has been a long "sophomore year," but an exciting one. With all this talk of a new division re-organization, and all of these professional career decisions to make in the coming months, things will continue to remain erratic. Maybe that's OK. If I were in some of my friends' shoes, with boring, cubicle, 9 to 5 jobs every day, I know I wouldn't be really content. But at the same time, I want some of my freedom back, after being held from it for almost nine months, it's had its due effect.

This weekend will begin final recovery for processing our equipment back to the states. CPT B leaves for Bagram soon to attend LT Stenner's Article 15 reading, with Brigadier General Lloyd Austin, who recently took over the 10th Mountain as the commanding general.

1 April 2004. KAF.

It feels really good to hit April—the official month of our homecoming. I can now honestly say that in just a few weeks I'll be back together with my family and friends once again able to enjoy life in the United States.

We completed our last mission on 25 March. Before we left the wire, I gathered all the men and NCOs of 2nd platoon for a group photo in front of our tents for one last time. I was blessed to have this NCO leadership team with me out here—SFC White, SSG Letunic, SSG Elsaesser, and SGT Stricker. Technically proficient in cavalry skills beyond reproach, and rough in their own ways for sure, but each one of them has a good heart and over the past nine months they've never wavered in their commitment to both prepare and care for our Joes. They've always been fair in how they've pushed the guys to meet our unit's high standards, while providing the genuine mentorship, sometimes even compassion. I've learned a lot from each of them—more than they probably realize.

If this deployment taught me anything it served as a reminder of how lucky I am to be living the life that I live in America. After passing through some of the most poverty-stricken villages in this third-world country over the past nine months, I'm absolutely floored by the life people continue to live here. It's almost hard to imagine that America—as I know it—actually coexists in the same space and time as how people live here in Afghanistan. Most parts of this country have truly been locked 1000 years in the past. It is difficult to fathom the prosperity and technological advances of countries like the United States, when seeing the depravity and burdens shared by the people here.

Nevertheless, I know that I did my duty and served my country to the best of my ability. I realize that although this deployment saw no real, active ground combat for my platoon, we still made an immense difference in the lives of people here, who know nothing about the liberties and freedoms that are so common to my men and me. I would have willingly given my life for this cause, and for my men, and for the sacrifices already made by so many throughout our country's military history. Not to say the thought of sacrificing my life didn't scare me—it did and still does. But I think I came to some sort of peace with the idea during this deployment. We came in response. I must keep remembering that.

We had a terrible sandstorm today that nearly shook our tents from the ground. The past few days have been productive. All of the troop's vehicles are now cleared through customs and they're en route to the States. The last of our equipment will be shipped off in a couple of days. Missions are over. Hard work is behind us and good thoughts of home, friends, and family, and new starts, await us at Fort Drum. By the time we get settled into Fort Drum, I will be moving into a new apartment in Sackets Harbor with my buddy John Torrealba, from 3rd Platoon. John was a couple rotations behind me at AOBC, and we easily found each other in a crowd there due to the distinctive 10th Mountain Patch on our shoulders.

I will begin a new job as the executive officer of Apache Troop, and I'll be turning over my platoon to a fresh second lieutenant—who I'm told has already arrived. And finally, we are all waiting to find out how the new 10th Mountain Division will be reorganized this summer. There is talk of breaking up Alpha Troop into three brigades, one platoon each, going separate ways. There's also talk of deactivating 3-17 Cavalry altogether.

By the time block leave ends in July, I'll be starting my "Junior Year" in the Army. There's no doubt it will be another year of change and excitement. Being

2nd Platoon, Apache Troop, 3-17 CAV, before leaving KAF on our last mission. 1LT Berkoff stands fourth from the right wearing his cavalry stetson. *George Elsaesser*

assigned to a new brigade will mean new training cycles, a deployment to the National Training Center or the Joint Readiness Training Center, to prepare for another combat deployment to Iraq? Will the Military Intelligence branch take me out of this division and send me to a new place, possibly preventing or delaying Iraq, or another deployment? Could it be possible for me to become a White House Fellow? I read about this yesterday and want to follow up with some research. For now, I have one more week left in Afghanistan. I can say that I've led my platoon over 12,000 miles, conducted over 200 missions, and everyone is coming home and everyone made it through without any serious issues. It's truly remarkable. I hope that my last entry here will be en route to the United States.

14 April 2004. Manas Air Force Base, Kyrgyzstan.

We flew out of KAF on the night of 8 April on C-130s. The troop, in various sections, conducted a glorious "Last March" through KAF, full battle-rattle with our rucksacks, then through the customs center, located along the airfield. After landing at Manas, we were corralled into a large airplane hangar and thus began the next phase of waiting.

A few days before we left KAF, the bulk of a new Army brigade combat team from Schofield Barracks, Hawaii (from the 25th Infantry Division) descended upon KAF. They were a sight for sore eyes, no doubt. Their brigade replaced our 1st BCT and their infantry battalions landed at KAF before fanning out to the firebases we had set up across RC South and RC East. One of my best friends from Tulane Army ROTC, Chris Morrison, sent me an email in advance of his arrival. So I sort of knew where to find him. I wandered along the airfield going from hangar to hangar, until there he was. He's a platoon leader with 2-27 Infantry and it sounds like he's headed to RC East where it's the real wild west. I came upon him sitting on a green Army cot in the hangar looking jet-lagged and petrified. Chris was a year ahead of me at Tulane, so he commissioned before me and completed Ranger School even before I was graduated. I've always been in awe of everything he accomplished as a cadet. He was our ROTC battalion commander, a scholar, and a PT stud. But, in this brief instant, *I ranked him.* I strolled up in my crumbled and weathered boonie cap, my discolored DCUs, compared to his that were still brilliant and creased. I mean, I did just finish nine punishing months out here and he's just getting started. So, I think he looked up to *me*, for a brief moment. Our exchange only lasted just a few minutes, unfortunately. I gave him a hug and wished him luck.

We've been here in Manas for almost a week now. Anxiety is high and patience is wearing thin, but I know we're happy for the change of scenery and not missing Afghanistan. This base is almost like a resort compared to Kandahar. My typical day here begins with waking up after 10 hours of solid sleep in the hangar. Springtime weather here in Kyrgyzstan is quite moderate and agreeable. Wearing only my PT shorts and tee-shirt, I'll take a brief bus ride to the main base and work out in their indoor gymnasium or run along paved pathways without a rifle slung over my shoulder. This will be followed by a hot shower in potable water. Next, a professional massage by some local women, and then a restful lunch in the dining facility while watching Armed Forces Network. I'm spending the afternoons either napping, playing video games, and wandering on the internet without a time limit. There are even some restaurants on the base, and they provide a delightful change to Army fare including french fries and pizza served by Kyrgyzstani waitresses, wearing tight jeans and skimpy tee-shirts. This week has certainly been an excellent relief after nine months of routine and austere living. If my family wasn't already waiting for me in Watertown right now, I don't think I'd mind if we were delayed in our return. We should be boarding a commercial airliner bound for the west at 0600 tomorrow morning. I still won't believe it until I am in the plane with the wheels up. I'm told we will layover at Incirlik Air Base in Turkey, but hopefully not for very long.

The boys in my platoon wasted no time in comforting their own desires in this new country. The past several nights they have catered to a large entourage of Kyrgyzstani prostitutes in a dark billiards room somewhere near post, and they've generally had a good time—so I understand. Leave it to GI Joe to take the initiative on that mission! It's the same initiative that has kept the oldest profession active for roaming armies going back hundreds of years.

So, this is the end. There's not much else to transpire. I wonder if my family will find me a changed man by this deployment. Although this tour was not witness to the amount of violence or tragedy so common in other war journals, I think it is a testament to a certain degree of endurance, leadership challenge, and relentless routine in dangerous lands. We came here as a direct response to what happened to our country, now 31 months ago. We were all just very lucky that most of that danger never really made its mark on Alpha Troop. Was it luck or just good professionalism?

A part of me is sad to see this go. This was Operation Enduring Freedom IV—according to the Defense Department—and it's a wrap. I'll never again be a platoon leader in a combat zone. Over the past few weeks, it was really an awesome sight to watch 2nd Platoon get ready for a mission and roll out the gate. Just watching them was enough. I stood back and watched veterans in action moving like pistons in an engine. I will miss that.

It will be an adjustment, albeit a welcome one, to move back into a normal life again. With access to civilian clothes, alcohol, women, privacy, and family. This job and my men will once again become a 6AM to 6PM occurrence. I'm sure the adjustment will be a smooth one for me. I hope it's a smooth one for my men—some of whom I've grown very close with, and I fear I will lose touch with many of them once we're back in the states. Right now, this lieutenant is coming home until the next time I'm needed to respond to my country's call to arms. With the current war in Iraq reaching new records for bloodshed that may be sooner than later. But that is talk for another chapter. Tomorrow, I'm going home sweet home.

Signed,
1LT Ross A. Berkoff
2nd Platoon Leader, Apache Troop, 3-17 Cavalry
10th Aviation Brigade, 10th Mountain Division

TOUR TWO:

COURAGE, RESILIENCE, AND HEARTBREAK

CHAPTER 9

FORMING THE TITANS

Apache Troop/3-17 CAV—as I knew it—was finished. In July 2004, the Department of the Army published this message to all units: "Our Nation remains at war. Our adversaries threaten the ideals and principles at the foundation of our society, the way of life those ideals enable, and the freedoms we enjoy. For the long term, the Nation must prepare itself to fight a protracted war of ideals against an irreconcilable and adaptive adversary. The Army is reshaping itself to conform to this new strategic reality. It will become an Army of campaign quality with joint and expeditionary capabilities—an Army capable of dominating the complex land environment and sustaining that dominance for as long as necessary."

For First Lieutenant Berkoff, that meant the dissolution of the 3-17 CAV's combined air and ground cavalry strength. 3-17 CAV would continue in the Army but as a pure *air cavalry* organization. The ground cavalry element (to which I belonged) would be pulled out completely. Enter the age of the RSTA Squadrons—Reconnaissance, Surveillance, & Target Acquisition. With the battlefield environments in Iraq and Afghanistan relying more and more on light maneuverability, the Army's Light Infantry Divisions, and their subordinate Brigade Combat Teams (BCT), needed new mobile, highly lethal, all-ground cavalry units. The RSTA Squadrons would fill that void and employ a deadly combination of mounted and dismounted reconnaissance and security.

RSTA Squadrons were composed of Alpha and Bravo Troops—each consisting of approximately 60 cavalry scouts (19 Delta MOS) with ability to fight in mounted and dismounted environments. Each was essentially modeled on the former Apache Troop organizational structure that I knew well, and each was equipped with the same heavy and light machine-guns, surveillance assets, and other weapons capabilities. RSTA Squadrons also included a Charlie Company: two Infantry reconnaissance platoons, designed to fight primarily dismounted, plus a mortar and sniper section. Alpha, Bravo, and Charlie "maneuver" units were supported by Delta Company—about 60 soldiers that specialized in forward-support logistics and sustainment services such as truck drivers, fuel technicians, welders, vehicle mechanics, cooks, and supply specialists. Delta Company would allow the squadron to operate somewhat self-sufficiently in more forward, remote locations. Each RSTA Squadron's Headquarters Troop would also provide administrative support, intelligence, command and control, and medical support to the squadron, and this was arrayed through four major staff sections: Personnel (S1), Intelligence (S2), Operations/Training (S3), Logistics/Supply (S4). During war-time deployment, a Civil Affairs Section (S5) would be activated.

In July 2004, I was informed that two RSTA Squadrons were standing up from scratch at Fort Drum—1-71 CAV which was going to be assigned to the 1st Brigade Combat Team, and 3-71 CAV, to be assigned to the 3rd Brigade Combat Team (3BCT). 3BCT did not exist at the time, so in addition to building 3-71 CAV from scratch, the entire brigade HQ and all units had to be formed and coalesced. One afternoon in July, 3-71 Cav's S3/Operations Chief, Maj. Rich Timmons, walked into my Apache Troop office and said "Hey Lieutenant Berkoff, I understand you just returned from an Afghanistan deployment. You were down in Kandahar, right? I take it you're the most senior LT here in Apache Troop, huh? I'd like you to come over to 3-71 CAV's temporary HQ and meet the 'SCO' (Squadron Commander), LTC Joe Fenty." Of course, I accepted.

When I sat down to be interviewed by LTC Fenty (for what sort of role, I had no idea), I immediately grasped that he was someone that could be an important mentor for me in my life and my career. We shared an instant connection founded upon mutual respect. He exuded confidence, emotional intelligence, authenticity, and compassion. He was extremely articulate. He spoke with enough pitch to be heard clearly, but not in such a way that he was determined to be heard by everyone in the room. But, when he spoke, people listened. As a Long Islander, I think he felt a kinship to my northern New Jersey and New York City roots, and I know he respected what I had just accomplished as a cavalry platoon leader in Afghanistan. He asked me lots of questions about my time in Afghanistan with 1st BCT. I told him that my recent tour was ostensibly the "ideal deployment scenario for a cavalry platoon." We were able to operate as a traditional cavalry force, implementing text-book maneuvers conducting reconnaissance, screening, and security operations, leveraging the wide-open deserts and mountainous landscapes—mostly to our advantage. Best of all, I continued, at least from my vantage point, the enemy watched us from a distance and was generally unwilling to engage us in direct contact.

Fenty confirmed that Apache Troop's recent deployment was the Army's first "test case" for employing light ground cavalry platoons on Afghanistan's battlefields. He told me that I was part of a very important mission and now the Army needed me to pass on what I had learned. In this first conversation, I got the sense that Lieutenant Colonel Fenty saw in me someone who could mentor and advise a new crop of lieutenants and captains—leaders who were going to be asked to do many of the things that I had just done. I had spent the better part of the last year trying to earn the respect of Captain Barnes, without much to show for it, but here in this office, in just a few minutes talking to these more senior officers (and strangers at that), I immediately felt that I belonged.

"Is 3-71 going to Afghanistan, sir? I just got back," I remember blurting out. "In time, I suspect, we will," was Fenty's reply. "But we have a lot of work do before we could even think about a deployment. I'd like you to be our first S1/Personnel Officer. You could help me bring some order to this chaos. You could also help me screen the Officer Record Briefs (ORBs; similar to a resume) of Armor officers looking to join us. I could use your advice on who you think might be a good fit for this type of organization." He continued, "we need people who could think like an independent operator but also be a strong team player."

I explained to him that I was branch-detailed Armor, and that my Armor Branch time (36 months) would be ending soon, in May 2005 to be exact. I told him that I was excited to transition into the Military Intelligence Branch, but I was not really sure if I intended to pursue an MI company command, a commitment which I knew would extend my active-duty service obligation by several years. He told me, when the time was right, he'd support me in my transition to Military Intelligence and perhaps, I might even continue to serve with 3-71 Cav as the next Squadron S2.

Fenty along with his XO, Maj. Paul Garcia, and the S3, Maj. Rich Timmons, were all professional infantry officers. They had each completed very successful infantry company commands and post-command assignments. They were all Army Ranger qualified. In the mid-1990s, Fenty served for two years as an exchange officer with the British Army as an instructor at Royal Military Academy Sandhurst, the United Kingdom's equivalent of the U.S. Military Academy at West Point. The Army only gives that assignment to the best of the best. The selection and assignment of these officers to lead this experimental unit, 3-71 Cav RSTA, was another signal of their superior status compared to their peers.

Still though, they were Infantrymen tasked with leading a maneuver unit primarily filled with Armor officers and 19 Delta Cavalry Scouts. Given this dynamic, I got the sense they needed *my* help to build and shape the organization, and I liked how that sounded. So, I happily accepted the role of S1, and I was the first officer assigned to 3-71 Cav from the Armor branch. As the S1, I would fill a senior staff position and serve as a chief advisor to the SCO—a role that is normally only given to captains. I am not sure I really had a choice in accepting this position, but when working with Joe Fenty, he always makes you feel like your voice counts.

By the summer of 2005, I completed the Army Military Intelligence Officer's Transition Course at Fort Huachuca, Arizona, and I rejoined the 3-71 Cav in time for its deployment to Fort Polk, Louisiana. Now as a member of 3-71's Squadron S2-Intelligence Section, the AS2 (assistant S2), I embarked with the rest of 3rd Brigade to "certify" our unit for our upcoming Afghanistan deployment. This meant completing two straight weeks of carefully scripted field exercises led by the Joint Readiness Training Center (JRTC) at Fort Polk.

Around this time, we were approved to begin secure communications with a task force operating in Afghanistan's Regional Command—East: the Area of Operations (AO) name given that covers the eastern provinces of Afghanistan. One unit in that AO was the 2nd Battalion of the 3rd Marine Regiment (2/3 Marines), and it was determined there was a very good chance 3-71 CAV would be taking over their Battalion AO, which encompassed parts of Konar and Nangarhar Provinces.

In late June 2005, just as we were finishing our mock village engagements and combat patrol exercises in the stifling humidity of central Louisiana, I received word from my S2 counterpart in 2/3 Marines of a major operation that had gone awry in Konar Province—called Operation Red Wings. On the evening of June 27, 2005, a four-man Navy SEAL reconnaissance and surveillance team, led by Lt. Michael Murphy, inserted into central Konar—near the Korangal and Narang Valleys.[1] They were on the hunt for a Taliban-aligned, Anti-Coalition Militia (ACM) cell leader who was suspected to be in a village on the valley floor. However, the next day, the team was compromised, and a fierce firefight ensued between the SEALs and the ACM fighters. Three of the four SEALs were killed during the gunfight, including Lieutenant Murphy, who was shot and killed

1 In 2007, Lt. Michael Murphy was the first service member to be awarded the Medal of Honor during the War in Afghanistan. Technical Sergeant John Chapman's 2002 acts of valor in Afghanistan preceded Murphy, but Chapman's posthumous Medal of Honor award date was not until 2018.

during a final act of selflessness and sacrifice for his team. While attempting to contact his Command Group and gain line-of-sight with his satellite phone to report the location of his forlorn team, Murphy deliberately stood exposed on top of an unprotected mountain peak attracting grueling enemy fire. The Army's 160th Special Operations Aviation Regiment (the Nightstalkers) launched as a quick reaction force, but just as they neared the SEALs' position, their CH-47 Chinook was shot down by an RPG and everyone on board was killed in the crash: all eight Army Nightstalker crewmen, and eight Navy SEALs onboard who were hoping to rescue the compromised team. June 2005 had just become the deadliest month for Americans during the Afghanistan War to date.

Following Operation Red Wings, I continued to receive intelligence reports from 2/3 Marines suggesting the ACM were becoming faster, deadlier, and applying new levels of ingenuity and resolve. I thought to myself—this coming deployment is going to be *very* different from my previous. Later in the summer, over a secure military IT network, the Intel Section from 2/3 Marines sent me a Taliban propaganda video to analyze. It showed graphic scenes of Taliban fighters pilfering through the belongings of the dead Navy SEALs they had just killed on June 27th, on that mountaintop. The video also showed the Taliban trying to exploit the data on their captured "Toughbook"—a small hard-shelled laptop carried by the SEALs to collect and share intelligence. I started to receive more and more reports suggesting the insurgency was growing stronger, becoming more organized. After several years of observing, learning, and adjusting their tactics against us, combined with the extreme terrain, I knew we were going to be facing an enemy force in RC-East that would pose a significant challenge. I realized then that I needed to learn everything I could about their patterns, their motives, their strengths and weaknesses, their tribal history and loyalties.

By the late summer of 2005, I was promoted to Captain and officially assigned as the S2 or Chief Intelligence Officer of 3-71 Cav. 3BCT and all its subordinate units, including 3-71, now had firm deployment orders. Starting in January 2006, the 10th Mountain Division HQ, along with 3BCT, would begin deployment to RC-East to replace the 82nd Airborne Division that had overall operating authority in RC-East. Our Brigade's RC-East AO would stretch across six of Afghanistan's eastern border provinces, from Paktika, Paktia, and Khowst (in the southern section), to Nangarhar, Konar, and Nuristan (in the northern section). The entire AO covered over 500 miles of border country, and comprised over 40,000 total square miles, roughly the size of Pennsylvania.

In the late Fall, LTC Fenty and a few other leaders across the brigade deployed to the AO for a brief, one week, pre-deployment site survey to conduct terrain familiarization. When he returned, he briefed everyone in 3-71 Cav on what he had learned: We would be assigned to FOB Salerno in Khowst Province, and as the brigade's only cavalry force, we needed to be ready to deploy to any and all parts of the brigade's AO. Built in late 2002 by elements of the 82nd Airborne, FOB Salerno was named to recognize the Italian beachhead that was secured by the 82nd's 505th Parachute Infantry Regiment in 1943.

We would start by conducting reconnaissance and security operations along Khowst's border with Pakistan. All of my coordination efforts with 2/3 Marines—who held the more northern AO section of Nangarhar and Konar—were not for nothing, Fenty told me. The brigade, he said, is already planning a major operation in central Konar to finally destroy the Taliban cells that remained following Operation Red Wings. "We need to be ready to flex up there, to move quickly, wherever the commander needs us," Fenty said. To me, it sounded like we were going to be picking up just where Special Operations and the Marines had left off.

Joe Fenty, remember, was a professional Infantry Officer. The avid historian in me, and the consummate cavalry admirer, I was constantly pestering him to accept and embrace some of the cavalry traditions that came along with our new unit. He allowed me to communicate with the Society of the 71st Cavalry Regiment, and I shared the news with some of those World War II tank destroyer-veterans that the old 71st Cavalry had been reactivated. I told the veterans our new cavalry squadron looks very different today than it did back in their day, but that might not have been entirely accurate. In the Army's haste to reorganize, the 10th Mountain Division simply did not have the space to house this influx of new soldiers. 3-71 Cav's Squadron HQ and Troop HQ offices were situated on Fort Drum's "Old Post." This meant we had to occupy 1940s-era barracks-style buildings to conduct our daily business, and these buildings had seen much better days. Still though, I encouraged Fenty to require all officers and NCOs to purchase their Cavalry Stetsons, with proper cord braiding and insignia. He and Command Sergeant Major, Del Byers, another stern and steadfast Infantryman, eventually caved and even donned Stetsons for themselves.

Before we deployed, I tried to get LTC Fenty to approve a Squadron level Spur Ride. Similar to the Infantrymen's arduous trial of attaining the coveted Expert Infantryman Badge (EIB), the Spur Ride was designed to test the mental, technical, and physical fortitude of Cavalry Troopers, by demonstrating the employment of Cavalry skills while under contrived duress. Afterwards, those that complete the training are afforded the right and privilege of wearing silver spurs on their boots and dress shoes. I completed my Spur Ride in 2003, with Apache Troop, just before I first deployed to Afghanistan. It was a grueling 18-hour day of land navigation. I remember after reaching each checkpoint, I was confronted with a new technical task to overcome, while undergoing physical and mental pain: "LT Berkoff, go assemble and disassemble that .50 Caliber Machine gun." "Which one?" I responded. "That one over there, lying in that muddy swamp. And do it in the prone position. And when you're done, do flutter kicks in the mud until I say stop." Then, on to the next station which was a few kilometers away through the woods. All the while, Troopers showing off their own proudly earned boot-strapped spurs would throw eggs at us or engage us in close range combat with super soaker water guns. Despite all my prodding, LTC Fenty never did prioritize our pre-deployment training enough for it to include a Spur Ride. Instead, as it turned out, we all went off and would earn our gold spurs. The golden colored variety were exclusively worn by Cavalry Troopers that had been tested in combat.

3rd BCT was the Spartan Brigade. While I was his S1, Fenty asked me to form an advisory group of staff officers and troop commanders that would vote on 3-71 Cavalry's call-sign. He asked me to bring him some proposals that aligned with our brigade's Hellenistic theme. "Wait, we get to vote?" was the response I received from my fellow officers as I scheduled our first meeting. That was a signature Joe Fenty leadership tactic: empower your officers through "leadership-by-consensus." Not all decisions would be made in this manner, but this was an easy win for him to quickly build esprit de corps and camaraderie amongst the unit's officers. We settled on the "Titan Squadron." We didn't know much about Greek mythology, but the name "Titans" suggested an entity of power and strength; plus it sounded short and snappy over the radio. As the S2 my call-sign would be Titan 2.

"With Your Shields or On It" was our Spartan Brigade motto, which harkened back to Ancient Greece, when the Spartan mothers apparently told their warrior sons to return home "With your shield, or on it." I remember explaining to LTC Fenty that our brigade's motto reminded me of the story that a young George Armstrong Custer would tell of his experience killing his first man in combat during the early years of the American Civil War. Custer recounted that he hunted down and killed a Confederate officer and took his sword. On the sword's inscription, it said "Draw me not without provocation. Sheath me not, without honor." "That's interesting, Ross, I appreciate that," Fenty responded. "But I hope you are not going to next try and draw a parallel to Custer's battle at the Little Big Horn, and our fight coming up in Afghanistan." "No, Sir," I said. "I am NOT going to go there."

Of course, it turned out, approximately a year after this conversation, Joe Fenty was gone from this world, and his replacement had in fact ordered 3-71 Cav to establish and defend a cavalry outpost in an utterly remote valley floor.

We would be surrounded on all sides by steep, mountainous cliffs, and by a tribal foe with overwhelming numbers, that not unlike the Sioux and the Cheyenne were also determined to band together to oust a foreign invader by any means necessary. This outpost, later be called Combat Outpost (COP) Keating, would become indefensible.

As the Task Force Titan S2, I helped lead the operations and planning team that first built and established COP Keating, more recently popularized by Jake Tapper's best-selling book and Rod Lurie's Netflix movie, both named *The Outpost.* Over a three-year period that began on my watch, COP Keating would cost the Army tens of millions of dollars to man and sustain, and over a dozen soldiers would lose their lives in its defense, before the Army ultimately declared it unnecessary, obsolete even. In 2009, COP Keating was overrun by the enemy, and then intentionally obliterated by the U.S. Army. As we were building the Outpost in 2006, I requested specialized imagery of the area from our intelligence analysts at brigade HQ. The analyst sent the images over secure email, and I recall that he used a new subject line: "Imagery for Camp Custer." I remember at the time thinking: "I wish Joe Fenty was still here with us right now. He wouldn't allow this."

CHAPTER 10

THE CALL TO ARMS, AGAIN

12 February 2006. Wheeler Sack Airfield, Fort Drum, NY.

I am writing this aboard a commercial airliner bound for central Asia, which will be closely followed by a military aircraft ride into the volatile country of Afghanistan. Exactly 22 months after my departure from there, I am scheduled to return . . . to bring the fight back to my country's enemies: the Taliban (TB) and Al Qaeda (AQ), and other associated militias that are attempting to slow the process of a democratic and free Afghanistan (AFG).

My role will be dramatically different during OEF VII, compared to OEF IV. I am no longer a green, shaved-tail lieutenant for starters. I was promoted to captain last August. Having made the jump over to Military Intelligence, I am no longer a combat arms officer, technically. I am, however, still in the Cavalry, but this time as the chief intelligence officer, (or S2) of the 3rd Squadron, 71st Cavalry (3-71 CAV), and the squadron commander's advisor on all things Intelligence. I'm leading an Intelligence Section composed of 1LT Clay Huffman, MSG Carlos Debose (S2 NCOIC), SSG Clint Gaston (our senior analyst) and six enlisted analysts. Task organized to my S2 section for the deployment are attachment personnel from our Military Intelligence company that specialize in Signals Intelligence, Human Intelligence, and Counterintelligence. My team of analysts and collectors will array across the battlefield, providing their firsthand accounts, their assessments and analysis, and reporting back to my station at the Task Force Titan TOC in Khowst Province, Forward Operating Base Salerno. I presume most of my time will be spent outside the wire, visiting my intelligence teams and moving with the commander LTC Joseph Fenty, as he circulates across the battlefield. My call sign will be Titan 2. LTC Fenty's is Titan 6.

I have mixed feelings about this deployment. Not about the cause but just more personal consternation. As I described in my previous journal, I was counting down my four years of active duty associating each year with collegiate grades, freshman and sophomore, etc. I'm currently supposed to be "graduating" in about two months, and my four-year term of service will be complete in May 2006. But one never knows how or why events transpire, and I will now recall on some of the events that occurred over the past 22 months since I returned from Afghanistan to help explain why it is that I'm becoming a "5th Year Senior." It's been over four years since 9/11. And, just like my last tour, I need to keep focused on why we're here. We're here in response.

As expected, the old Apache Troop, 3-17 CAV deactivated, and each platoon was dispersed into new RSTA (Reconnaissance Surveillance Target Acquisition) Cavalry Squadrons across the 10th Mountain Division. Most of my 2nd platoon soldiers and NCOs from Apache Troop went over to 1-71 CAV in 1st Brigade and they're now bound for Iraq. In August 2004 I was assigned to a new cavalry unit in a new brigade—the 3rd Brigade Combat Team, commanded by COL John "Mick" Nicholson. I helped stand up 3-71 CAV from scratch as their first Personnel Officer, or S1. I served in this capacity for about nine months before I left for Fort Huachuca, Arizona to complete a one-month crash-course on how to become an S2 Intel officer for a battalion or squadron sized element. When I returned to Fort Drum in May 2005 I began working as the Assistant S2 in 3-71 CAV. In June, I completed a deployment with the squadron to the Joint Readiness Training Center (JRTC) at Fort Polk, Louisiana, and then I took over as the primary S2 in August 2005. Since then, I've been living and breathing the Afghanistan enemy situation, and threats to Coalition Forces, day in and day out with intense research and training. I completed several specialized intelligence officers courses tailored to the Afghanistan theater of operations, including a week at the National Ground Intelligence Center (NGIC) in Virginia, and three weeks working with the U.S. CENTCOM J2 at McDill AFB, Tampa, Florida.

I'm more ready today for this deployment—both physically and mentally—than I ever was in 2003. There was a time in 2004, only a month after I began building up 3-71 CAV, that I could've been transferred out of the unit, and possibly have been able to separate from active duty as scheduled. But there were too many what-if scenarios involved with reassignment, so I volunteered to stay the course, and go back to Afghanistan to see the unit that I had helped create from scratch go to war and hopefully see everyone return home safely.

We are now four hours from Germany. I hope and pray this coming year brings peace to Afghanistan, and a safe deployment to the men of 3-71 CAV.

16 February 2006. FOB Salerno.

After about 18 months of pre-deployment training, 3-71 CAV is finally in Afghanistan, and it's been exactly 22 months—to the day—that I returned home from my first tour here. I'm back.

We arrived in Manas Air Force Base in Kyrgyzstan without any issues. 14 hours of flying followed by a three-hour layover in Germany. We moved into transient barracks on the Air Force Base, not a hanger like last time. This was the first sign that we might actually be here for more than just a few hours. Although we had ample access to phones and Internet, we were jammed into tents with barely enough room for our gear. I was thrown into a small tent with about 20 other guys, and we had to assemble a stack of old green Army cots which were waiting for us, nicely stacked up. This rite of frustration is known all too well to me, as I've been assembling Army cots since my ROTC field exercise days at Camp Shelby, MS, so I should be a master at this. Lining up the cot's crossbars requires more brute force than finesse, and when you're sure you've got it, the bar slams into your knuckles, pinching skin off the bone. Still better than the cold ground. On top of that lovely experience, there was a biting wind chill, the latrine shower facilities, crowded, and confusion, rampant.

After two nights at Manas, we flew on a C-130 onto the airfield at FOB Salerno directly, in Khowst Province, AFG. This FOB has a fully operational airfield and is more built up than I was expecting. I first moved into a really nice wooden building and spent a couple of nights on an actual bed with a mattress, and with more space than I could've ever imagined for a living quarters. But now, I'm being told to get ready to squeeze 10 or 12 more guys into this room which I guess would give each man about as minimal space possible to be moderately comfortable.

Operationally speaking we are building our TOC and preparing to receive equipment and conduct orientation rides of the area. Everything about 3-71 CAV requires us to build it from scratch. Everything back at Fort Drum, from moving into vacant 1940's era barracks as our headquarters, to collecting enough men and equipment to finally fill the ranks of a platoon. We're literally building a wooden TOC right now and wiring up the entire place on our own. We've been forecasted to arrive here for months. Wasn't the Army expecting us? Frustrating.

Yesterday I rode in a Blackhawk helicopter along the border of Pakistan and Khowst Province. I flew all over the AFG border security posts that I've read so much about these past many months. Enemy activity never ceases in the meantime. Yesterday during my Blackhawk flight, someone tossed a grenade at a U.S. convoy just outside our FOB. South of here, in Deh Rah Wod district, four U.S. Special Operators were killed when their truck struck an IED. Today, an ANA patrol was ambushed near Asadabad, along the same route that we're now being told we will be taking to move operations north, towards Naray District in northern Konar Province.

I will try to pick the brain of my 82nd Airborne S2 counterparts as much as I can before they leave next week.

16 February 2006. Letter Home from FOB Salerno.

> Arrived to Afghanistan safely. KBR has done a lot to this country since I left 2 years ago. No more tents for me, instead I moved into this first-rate brick structure with a few other staff officers and we are getting along fine. Our big task now is to build our operational center, literally from scratch. The food isn't bad, and the amenities here are actually better than Kandahar's in 2003.
>
> Today, I went on an aerial reconnaissance (Blackhawk helo) of the Pakistan border with Afg. I got to see a close up view of the area that I've been studying so deliberately these past many months, including the ground of previous large scale border attacks conducted by Al Qaeda and Taliban forces in recent months/years. Luckily, they were not out playing today to take a shot at us. I think I'll remain in this FOB for about another month, until I relocate for a while. I'll stay in touch either way. Send mail to:
>
> CPT Ross Berkoff
> 3-71 CAV, TF SPARTAN
> FOB SALERNO
> APO AE 09314

23 February 2006. FOB Salerno, Khowst.

Another birthday passed in the Army. This is now my second birthday in Afghanistan. That's 2 out of 26 . . . doesn't that equate to about 8 percent or something? This past week has been very active and passed very quickly.

I joined a ground patrol into Khowst City with some of the high-ranking officers of the unit we're replacing here (2nd BN-504th Parachute Infantry

Regiment, 82nd Airborne Division). We went to FOB Chapman[1] which is a headquarters for all local U.S. Special Forces, and "Other Government Agencies" (OGA)—a catch-all term that we're being asked to use to categorize a number of federal law enforcement and intelligence community agencies operating in this area. We had a synchronization meeting with them to confirm our intelligence assessments on the enemy situation in Khowst and the neighboring districts. Afterwards, our patrol moved west towards the infamous "Khowst Ambush Alley," a narrow canyon that leads directly into Gardez. I remember hearing stories about this pass during my last deployment. We made no enemy contact, but we stopped at a small village on the other side of the pass and talked with some local elders. The intent was to introduce new American soldiers (10th Mountain) to the prominent mullahs and elders around here.

This past week has seen intense periods of staff mission planning. We're planning two major operations right now not to mention just trying to get our own bearings straight on this base, while also building our TOC, while also receiving our combat power and equipment that's been rolling off the containers—so much of it broken. One of the operations we are planning includes about 75 percent of the squadron—250 men and 50 trucks—to a small U.S. Special Forces operating base in northern Konar called FOB Naray (after the name of the local government district center). Naray is about 300 miles north of here. This type of move would be difficult even for grizzled veterans but considering it would be our first operation here it's going to prove extremely complicated.

I will be moving up to FOB Naray as well, part of LTC Fenty's TAC. Actually, I'll be riding in his personal Humvee. I don't know how long I'll be gone—maybe a month? The base at FOB Naray will be an exciting place for a tactical intelligence officer. There have never been U.S. Army conventional forces in that area before, and according to the SF ODA at Naray, it's a "target rich environment" for those that are looking in the right places for the bad guys. It's also literally the northernmost frontier of our Coalition Forces' footprint along Afghanistan's border with Pakistan. This area is a known sanctuary for large networks of Al Qaeda and Hezb-e Islami Gulbuddin (HIG) militants, or terrorists. The bad guys in this region exploit the relative lack of U.S. Forces there, and it's very easy for them to move in and out of Pakistan, over the porous border. I hope we can make a difference up there because it clearly is the forgotten frontier, and the loyal Afghan civilians deserve to have some peace of mind.

1 FOB Chapman received global attention on December 30th, 2009, after a suicide attack by Al Qaeda-linked Jordanian targeted CIA personnel stationed at the base. Seven American CIA officers and contractors were killed and six Americans were wounded.

Captain Berkoff engaging with Afghan children in Khowst Province just a few days after arriving in Afghanistan, February 2006. *Author Collection*

I heard today that I might be scheduled for my mid tour leave/R&R sometime in August, but I know that's a far away off.

27 February 2006. FOB Salerno.

15 days now into the deployment. It's not a bright idea to count days or even weeks but at least I can say the past two weeks have gone by relatively fast. Although at the same time, it feels like ages ago when I spent my last weekend in Sackets Harbor, NY. These past few days on the base have found 3-71 CAV plagued with

problems that we shouldn't have to be dealing with, especially considering our mission tasks that lay ahead of us. Two different soldiers accidentally discharged their weapons—coming very close to killing those around them. Another officer, the bravo Troop XO, said some immature and insulting comments to a female lieutenant and has since been removed from his leadership position and placed on the squadron staff. All this in the midst of preparing for a significant operation into Konar province. Are they such maladroits that they can't carry a weapon without discharging it adventitiously? It's a clear case of poor discipline, and such mistakes could easily become fatal in this country, especially considering we have 12 months of combat operations coming up.

2 March 2006. Letter Home. FOB Salerno.

Hey all,

Operations are picking up and I am working 16 hour days in the TOC. To make matters worse, guys in my unit are having problems with discharging their weapons adventitiously. In the past week, we've had 2 weapons discharged negligently, and one happened to be an AT-4 (anti-armor rocket launcher). Never a good thing. Luckily, no one was hurt.

We are running at 1000mph. I think everyone is stressed out and forgetting to breathe. Things will work themselves out once our routine is set. I finally moved into a larger building and I have a pretty decent set up. The local Afghans are hired to do just about everything. Every shitty job on the base, and they flock to the opportunity for 5 dollars per day. Cleaning out porta potties, jumping into our dumpsters, doing our laundry. I walked into the laundry tent and saw 20 singing Afghan men in an assembly line. They pump out 400 clean bags of folded laundry every week. Not bad.

Enemy activity is consistent, and we had our first "run for the bunker" event last week, when about 20 Taliban tried to set up a rocket launcher near the base. Our artillery response time was pretty good and took care of them. I should be here for about two more weeks until I relocate temporarily. Miss everyone.

Ross

CHAPTER 11

BETWEEN THE OUTPOSTS

13 March 2006. Firebase Gardez, Paktia Province, Afghanistan.

Officially one month down. The past two weeks since my last entry have been exceptionally busy with almost no time for maintaining this journal and certainly very little energy for it. But I'll give it a go. I write tonight from FOB Gardez having left FOB Salerno early this morning. I'll get back to that later.

Deployment work schedules as a primary staff officer require long days of mission planning; especially grueling when your days are interlaced with going out on real missions with the SCO. Since we arrived last month, 3-71 CAV conducted two large, named operations: Operation Southern Watch-1 and Op Southern Watch-2. Both were focused on reconnaissance and surveillance of Khowst's southern border with Pakistan. A third "Southern Watch" operation will soon be underway.

I moved with LTC Fenty's vehicle during Southern Watch-1, which was a three-day mission in Khowst's Tanai District, right along the border of Pakistan. While conducting an area reconnaissance out there, we received reports of Troops in Contact, and heard some booms in the distance. We thought we may have stumbled upon some real AQAM activity when actually it turned out to be a case of Green-on-Green clashes in our area. Green on Green is a term for when Afghan Security Forces or Afghan Military Forces fight each other. This one might have had the added complexity of an ongoing tribal rivalry, and one local man was shot dead. We drove around the valley for three days and it turned up very little in the way of actionable intelligence. That mission was from March 3–6.

On March 6, I returned to FOB Salerno and I helped plan the next two operations, while also planning and preparing for the GAC operation to FOB Naray. After months of planning, briefings and tedious application of the Military Decision-Making Process, we finally left FOB Salerno this morning bound for Naray. We will be staggering our GACs to Naray and I left in the SCO's truck as part of a 12-vehicle convoy.

We left this morning on the heels of what was probably the most bloody day—most "enemy active" day in many months—certainly the bloodiest day for U.S. forces in a long time. On 12 March there were significant enemy attacks all across RC East: suicide attacks occurred in Khowst, Ghazni, and in Kabul. There was a coordinated IED strike against a U.S. Marine convoy that killed four Marines near Asadabad, which is very close to our upcoming convoy route as we head to Naray later this week. I think it temporally jolted our leaders and soldiers who are part of this GAC, and it really impacted me. There's no discrimination with these IEDs. I don't recall the IED activity being such a significant threat when I was here last time. Whether I am riding in LTC Fenty's truck or not, I'm just as vulnerable as anyone else as these remote-control operated or pressure-plated mines are buried 12 inches under the road soil. It did scare me and I'm thinking about it more and more now than I did two years ago here. This country and especially this particular area has gotten more dangerous since 2004. Sometimes I feel like I'm just in a big hunk of tin moving down the valley road with a sign saying "IED Me." We are seriously that easy of a target. OK enough on that for now.

We have taken every measure available to us to protect our soldiers from these threats, including all Humvees are all up-armored now (no more sandbags). We also ensure our convoys are tightly integrated with overhead aerial assets for reconnaissance and for aerial-based electronic jamming of enemy frequencies. We have devices on our trucks that monitor and jam enemy frequencies as well. We integrate route clearing teams/engineers in front of our vehicles, with robots and tractors, used to clear the route. We also try to use old-fashioned common sense.

I'm told I'll be living at FOB Naray in northern Konar for the next eight to ten weeks. The Naray firebase has never seen conventional U.S. forces before. For the past couple years, it's been used exclusively by U.S. Special Forces and OGA, quite literally as a frontier outpost on the extreme northern border of our U.S. influence along the Pakistani line. Recently, KBR contractors were tasked to build up the base to accommodate our arrival, almost 250 soldiers.

The area surrounding FOB Naray is a known sanctuary for bad guys. The SF ODA team up there has already told us they have more actionable targets than they have the forces to prosecute them. But apparently the local bad guys don't like to mess around with U.S. SOF, because they don't want to spoil their sanctuary and bring unnecessary attention. No more of that now, as 3-71 is coming up to go knocking down some doors. I'm confident we will succeed.

I was not thrilled with the idea of going up to Naray. First of all, it's one hell of a long ride, and then we have to drive all the way back to FOB Salerno again?! Imagine driving a road equal in distance from New York City to Richmond, Virginia, but instead of a nice highway, you switchback over mountain tops the size of central Colorado the entire time. Oh yeah, not to mention there are no barriers on the sides of the road here. The lines of communication in this region are typically along river valley floors which means the enemy lies in wait, always in control of the higher ground. We are constantly just a big target for a well-placed ambush.

I have no idea how austere the living accommodations will be at Naray, but you can bet that I won't be able to call home or use hot showers with the same frequency. I probably won't be able to do any physical training or have any privacy in my living quarters. So the bottom line is that I'm going to be roughing it for a while. It's not like I'll be the first soldier in history to do that right?

So, our GAC left FOB Salerno early this morning and we moved north and west about 100 km today. Tonight we're staying at the Gardez firebase (where elements of Apache 3-17 CAV stayed during my last deployment). Tomorrow we will drive towards Kabul and then onto Jalalabad or "JBAD." We're going to spend a couple of days in JBAD with our sister unit, 1-32 Infantry, before moving to Naray. May God please watch over our column as we continue to traverse this dangerous country.

19 March 2006. FOB Asadabad, Konar Province.

I'm writing tonight from another new outpost that I can cross off my list. Firebase Asadabad. Lots of OGA and Special Forces here. Continuing my scenic tour of this country. Just in time too. Apparently the last base that I was staying in was only about 2 miles away from where that human bird flu strain popped up.

After leaving Firebase Gardez on 14 March, we traveled about 120 km to an ISAF base in Kabul City, not too far from the international airport. Here, we conducted a short refuel and resupply, but then pushed on. We had another 150 km ahead of us to reach Jalalabad Airfield (JAF). Somewhere near the Surobi Dam, our lead vehicle reported that the road ahead was out. This was very troubling because it was almost dusk, and we'd been traveling for about 12 straight hours. Vehicles required maintenance, and our drivers and gunners (who would rotate those duties every other hour) were beyond exhausted. We were able to find an alternate route, completely off-roading it for a while, but then again, the "roads" here would not qualify as roads to any 1st world country population.

We finally reached JAF during the early morning hours of March 15th, after completing a very long and dangerous movement that lasted about 18 hours. JAF will be the HQ for 1-32 Infantry, one of our sister maneuver units in 3rd BCT. 1-32 is commanded by LTC Chris Cavoli. We arrived both mentally and physically exhausted and our trucks needed some rapid maintenance. LTC Cavoli was very gracious to us, opening sleeping tents, the motor pool, and working space in his battalion TOC so that we could continue mission planning and coordination for a few days, before we continued our push onward to Naray. LTC Cavoli and LTC Fenty are good friends. As our squadron commander, the majority of my interactions with LTC Fenty are cases where he's the most senior guy in the room. So, he talks like a commander would. I also get the sense that Joe Fenty is a social introvert at heart. Around his staff, he's almost always all business. So, it was calming for me, even refreshing, to watch him converse more casually with an old friend, a peer commander, like LTC Cavoli, who also happens to be high energy and a humorous extrovert.

Before reaching Asadabad today, we passed by a few famous passes in history . . . the Khyber and Nawa mountain passes. Both were used extensively by armies throughout this country's history. Alexander the Great, Genghis Khan, and Tamerlane, to name a few. For the first time in all my experiences here (last tour too) I found myself using the word "beautiful" to describe the scenery around me. I am staying in a small camp in a deep valley near the Nawa Pass right now. It's very green and lush, with raging rivers, and tall mountains that surround us. It also a huge sanctuary for Taliban fighters, so go figure. Tomorrow should be the final push to our destination. I have a Cuban cigar waiting to be smoked when we get there, and another one waiting for later.

21 March 2006. Letter Home. FOB Naray.

One week and 300 something miles later, we finally made it to Naray, in Konar Province. I am at a small camp along the Pakistan border called Firebase Naray. No conventional forces have ever been here before. It's really the wild frontier. The base is not at all prepared for a surge of conventional forces. Hopefully it's just temporary (a few weeks?) but so far there is no running water, no showers, and no hot food. There are PVC tubes stuck in the ground and holes dug with a wooden plank on top to do our business in. The Afghan militia

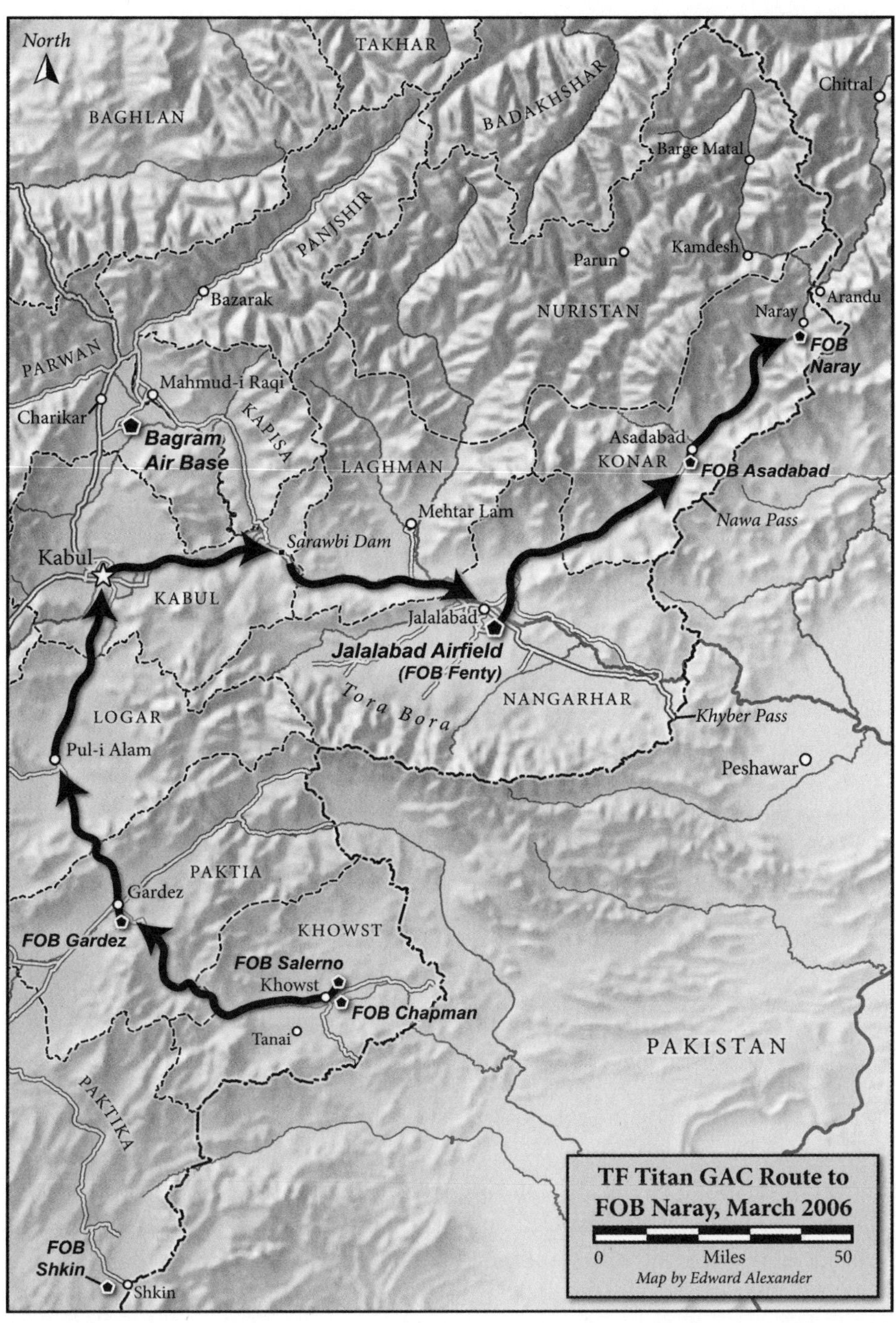
North
TAKHAR
BAGHLAN
BADAKHSHAR
Chitral
Barge Matal
PANJSHIR
Parun
Kamdesh
Bazarak
NURISTAN
Arandu
Naray
FOB Naray
PARWAN
Mahmud-i Raqi
Charikar
Bagram Air Base
KAPISA
Asadabad
KONAR
FOB Asadabad
LAGHMAN
Mehtar Lam
Nawa Pass
Sarawbi Dam
Kabul
KABUL
Jalalabad
Jalalabad Airfield (FOB Fenty)
Tora Bora
NANGARHAR
Khyber Pass
LOGAR
Pul-i Alam
Peshawar
PAKTIA
Gardez
FOB Gardez
KHOWST
FOB Salerno
Khowst
FOB Chapman
Tanai
PAKISTAN
PAKTIKA
FOB Shkin
Shkin
TF Titan GAC Route to FOB Naray, March 2006
0 Miles 50
Map by Edward Alexander

moved out of their "barracks" and we moved in . . . Now, it smelled pretty bad after 40 Afghans moved out, imagine it's not going to get any better after all our smelly bodies settle in. Plans are in the works to improve this place, but it might take some time.

I have been very busy building intelligence frameworks around here. Today, I sat in on a meeting with local militia commanders. They brought in some bad guys that wanted to reconcile/pardon. A very interesting discourse followed. They expect us to believe them that they will never attack U.S. soldiers again, and want to walk away with an ID card saying they are "reconciled" so that we can't bother them anymore. We're not that dumb. I was told by the ODA intelligence guy here that I should try to keep some anonymity during these engagements. He gave me a Harley Davidson black leather jacket to wear over my brown tee-shirt. "Don't let them see your name-tape," he keeps telling me.

Well, it doesn't get much worse than this place as far as accommodations go. No hot chow yet. No running water. We piss into PVC tubes that have been partially buried into a sand and gravel mixture. So, whatever you would like to send my way would be much appreciated. I don't how long it will take to get to me, but the idea that something is en route is gratifying enough. The scenery around us is still awe-inspiring, (lord of the rings-esque) and the raging Konar River runs past our camp. I'm feeling fine. There are phones and net to use, so I can stay in touch.

Love, Ross

1 April 2006. FOB Naray.

I have been working quickly to gain the trust and respect of the local Special Forces team, ODA 773. They are beginning to share their lessons-learned with me and we are starting to develop intelligence leads together. With their help, I've started to map out the surrounding settlements and valleys and marking some as NAIs for future targeting. I'm also analyzing the illicit lines of communications used by both timber smugglers and ACM to cross into Afghanistan from Pakistan, and vice versa. There is only one legal international crossing point and that's at Bari-Kowt (on the Afghan side), about 10 km north of here.

The sudden increase in U.S. troop presence here at Naray was quickly noticed by the enemy who conducted small arms attacks and rocket attacks against the base almost every night from 26 March to 29 March. None of these attacks were particularly effective and no one was wounded. Some intelligence reports tied the recent attacks to the Ayoub brothers and their band of not-somerry men in the nearby Kotya valley. I'm not exactly sure we can pinpoint their allegiance to the HIG or if they're just trigger-happy jihadists, but we wanted to find out more.

On 29 March we conducted a very successful operation in the Kotya valley, which is about 10 miles north of our firebase. A large convoy consisting mostly of Charlie Troop moved up to the mouth of the valley and then dismounted and faced west. LTC Fenty and CSM Byers personally led the dismounted ground movement through the rugged and graduated ascent up the valley floor. During mission planning, it appeared to be only a 3–4 km movement to reach the village itself, but we continue to blunder in our underestimation of the "suck" that's involved in navigating this terrain. Those 3–4 km, with full-battle rattle, were filled with punishing, climbing switchbacks and it kicked our ass.

After LTC Fenty conducted a village engagement with elders and announced our return to base, he quietly ordered our sniper team to find cover and concealment and then watch and wait. Lo and behold, once our main effort finished their retrograde out of the valley, our snipers radioed back to the TOC and reported enemy activity: military-aged males popping out of the brush carrying weapons. From the TOC at Naray, I picked up the net and listened to lead sniper SSG John Hawes's report sighting a man holding a long antenna radio and an AK-47. He said this guy looked to be monitoring our troops, and sending a message to others, as we walked out of the valley. I told him: "Sounds like you have a Positive Identifiable Threat. Engage when ready." Hawes sent three rounds to the chest of Daoud Ayoub, the leader of the Ayoub clan (we confirmed his identity a bit later). We estimate he was trying to organize his fighters to rally against us. The killing of the lead Ayoub shook the valley and caused most of the fighters to flee for fear of more U.S. attacks with such precision. Although I did pass out suspected photos of the Ayoub brothers to the sniper team before they left, we honestly just got really lucky.

It was not until a few days after the operation did word spread amongst the locals and back to FOB Naray: the American snipers killed Daoud Ayoub, the leader of the Ayoub clan. Suddenly our firebase was flooded with local elders that wanted to talk about PTS and reconstruction projects. PTS is also known as Program Takhm-e Sohl ("Strengthening the Peace" or Peace Through Strength), and it's essentially the Afghan government's reconciliation program. We tried to encourage local elders to support PTS and bring in the young ACM to help build up their country instead of tearing it down. We had a few local insurgents come down from the mountains to swear allegiance to the Government of Afghanistan. The elders said they would not allow ACM back into their valley. So, I would call the Kotya operation a blazing success.

As part of the intel debrief following the operation in Kotya, I sat down with Hawes and looked through his photographs of Ayoub's compound and his body, stained crimson red through his white man-jammies. He said just moments after he took the shot, he watched as members of Ayoub's family, women and children mostly, casually collected his weapon and radio and other personal belongings and stashed it all away in a mud hut. When Hawes reached the target area, he found and secured Ayoub's Kalashnikov cached in the home where the women had left it.

It was a strange feeling to hold that weapon in my hands. I closely examined it. The previous owner scratched carvings into the wooden stock, which I couldn't make out. He also festooned it with bright colored strings, similar to how the locals dress up their gypsy-like jingle trucks. This rifle could have been in his family for 20+ years. It bore scars of rust and neglect and was probably used to fight the Soviets as they passed through this part of Nuristan. Now, it was mine, or at least in possession of the U.S. Army. I may not have marched down the Kotya valley and I certainly didn't take the shot but holding that weapon and viewing the sensitive site exploitation photographs reminded me why I decided to pursue military intelligence to begin with. It's my job to inform the commander on *where* to bring the fight to the enemy. This time, it paid off. During my first deployment here as a platoon leader, I went on 200 combat missions and most were dry holes. Maybe because the enemy is better organized now, or maybe because of where we are along the Pakistan border, but for our very first deliberate operation since arriving to Naray last week to have produced actual ACM KIA results? I'll take it. I tried to ship the rifle through our military customs and back to Fort Drum's museum, thinking it would make a nice exhibit one day. We'll see how that goes. I'm betting someone claims it as a nice souvenir first.

2 April 2006. Letter Home. FOB Naray.

> Things are slowly being built to improve the quality of life at Firebase Naray. Showers and laundry facilities are starting to go up. The shower water is pumped in from the nearby Konar River and say good night if you accidentally swallow some. Flush toilets go in next. Thanks to our Delta company cooks, we are now eating a hot lunch each day on wooden picnic tables that we built. Breakfast and dinner are MREs, but once in a while, we will see a hot breakfast. USAF jets are dropping in resupply bundles, lowering slowly from the sky on a parachute. Every once in a while the bundle will accidentally land in the Konar River, but before we could even react, local farmers are quick to dive

FOB Naray and the Konar River, facing east, with part of Naray village visible in the background. *Author Collection*

in, retrieve it, and deliver it to base, knowing they will be paid. Mail packages came in today for the first time, and we're told it will continue about once per week. In a nutshell, I am doing fine. I feel healthy, but tired. No beer and no pizza for the past 2 months is causing the old belt to slip a few notches. I think I lost about 10 pounds so far.

Love, Ross

10 April 2006. Letter Home. JBAD Airfield.

Hey everyone,

I keep moving around here. At this rate, I don't think I will ever have one place to call "home" during this entire deployment. So far, I've left 2 bases with the expectation (and instruction) that I would be returning soon. In reality, I will not be returning to any of those places and my already meager supply of equipment is slowly dwindling. Right now, I'm staying on the airfield and U.S. Marine base in Jalalabad.

This city is sort of the summer vacation spot for Afghans. The downtown is lined with palm trees, and lush gardens, the surrounding mountains are ice-capped and the Konar River runs past the city sustaining the agrarian Pashtu tribespeople. I heard that Bin Laden once had a villa here in Jalalabad. I got a quick view of this scene, but most of my days are in an operations center along the busy airfield, reading intelligence reports and pouring over maps. I've had some unique experiences so far here. I gave an intel assessment brief to Major General Ben Freakley, the commander of the Combined Joint Task Force 76 and the commander of the 10th Mountain Division—which is basically all the forces in this theater. I've also been able to tap into some of the national intelligence agencies that have representation out here. It's good to see the agency sharing with the military. Isn't that how things are supposed to work?

Facilities on this base are pretty despicable—considering there are over 1,000 soldiers here. This base has been occupied by Marines for the past couple years, and their tours only last about 4–6 months. So basically, the contractors haven't done much to improve life here because the Marines just suck it up for 4–6 months. Now that the Army has moved in, and for a yearlong deployment, we all hope things start changing. There are 50-inch plasma TVs on Bagram airfield in the TOC and in the chow halls, but here on JBAD, there aren't even working public phones to use, so that the soldiers can call back to the U.S. Oh and TVs? Forget it. Please direct mail to the following new address. I think I'll be here for a month or longer. Either way, this address will be permanent for mail.

Ross Berkoff
3-71 CAV TF SPARTAN
APO AE 09354

18 percent of the deployment down, and about 100 days until mid tour leave, but who's counting?

25 April 2006. Letter Home. JBAD Airfield.

If you have been keeping track of the news out here, you would know that we have been conducting very successful operations in Konar so far. Operation Mountain Lion is in full swing. Lots of bad guys have been killed and captured and lots of weapons caches discovered but unfortunately we had our first major setback this morning. My unit—like many Army battalions here—have ANA companies attached to us. We've trained them on everything we do as an Army—in all the different specialties. I even had members of the budding Afghan Military Intelligence Corps in my office, getting classes on how to organize information and how to collect it. Today, one of our ANA units was ambushed alongside our own Troopers, and four Afghan soldiers were killed, many others wounded. It's a double- edged sword. Of course, we're happy that our guys are OK, but remorseful for our local comrades and feeling frustrated with the guerrilla war.

We've had some close calls of our own out here that maybe we can chock up to miracles. A 10th Mountain soldier had an RPG slice through and lodge in his abdomen. He remained alive and the doctors would not operate at first until Explosives Teams were sure the RPG would not go off in front of them. He's back in Maryland now, and will make a full recovery. Last night a Marine sergeant was shot in the chest, but the round deflected off his body armor and scraped his arm, breaking some ribs.

To make things more interesting we just received a new batch of "replacement soldiers" from Fort Drum. Skinny privates right out of basic training all of them saying "born in 1987, sir." Amazing. Their first duty here on Jalalabad was guarding the building with ANA caskets in it, until the local government can arrange for proper transport. That should bring a speedy reality to their new-chosen profession.

It's sort of like Groundhog Day here since this operation began, and although each day brings in new reports, it is the same basic routine. I'm in the TOC by 7 AM and I leave by midnight. I'll have some short meals in between. I did get a chance to get out of the wire last week, but only for a day. I attended a meeting with a Pakistani Army unit along the border. The Pakistanis were surprisingly well educated, articulate, and very proud. They were happy to hear that Operation Mountain Lion was going well, and they said they wanted to help from their side of the border. They spoke with partial British accents, and they took a lot of pride in their British heritage. Of course, when we asked them about the hard questions, about the bad guys in their own country they would deny that Pakistan provides sanctuary for terrorists or "miscreants" as they liked to call them. If so, they would say they would be "the first people to know about it." It's the same hubris that's probably kept Bin Laden hiding in Pakistan for as long as he has.

I also got a chance to fly out to our 3-71 CAV rented operating base. Right along the Konar River main road, south of Asadabad, in the Chowkay District. We literally bought or are renting a local farmers house, which is a mud compound structure a bit smaller than a football field, and in the shape of a rectangle, walled in firmly on all sides by 6 foot high mud walls. We established a little Forward Logistics Element (FLE), which we're calling "The Flea" as those little buggers are everywhere we sleep and eat. The local economy loves that we set up here. Every day, we get people at the front door wanting to work the labor force of the camp, or vendors springing up outside the walls to sell soda or chips. They all want U.S. dollars.

Our 3-71 Cav soldiers there are dirty, smelly, and tired. Two straight weeks of operations without a rest, and without a night of uninterrupted sleep, and without a shower or hot meal, or change of clothes. Certainly, puts things in perspective even for me. Hell, I am deployed out here too but every day I see how hard some other soldiers have it . . . harder than me. But at the same time everyone has their own specialty and expertise. The last time I was here my expertise was ground reconnaissance, so I was just as dirty and tired as they are. Now I'm typing and reading all day—so it's a very different kind of tired.

It's getting warm here, mid to upper 90s. I'm not looking forward to seeing how bad the actual summer temps will be. Thanks for all the packages and well wishes. I'm getting along fine here in general. In my spare time, I'm working on my résumé. I work closely with civilian contractors, supporting the intelligence work out here, and their companies represent some of the better-known Fortune 500 Defense contractors. They tell me I shouldn't worry too much about my résumé—two tours in Afghanistan should say enough about me.

Love, Ross

1 May 2006. Jalalabad Airfield, Nangarhar Province.

It's been a long time since I've had a chance to really sit down and transcribe in the journal. I've logged a couple entries and I sent out some quick emails mostly for the past month. Part of that is due to the sheer exhaustion at the end of the day. The other part of that is because I've been separated from many of my personal belongings, including this journal. How do I begin to summarize the past six weeks of activity? I hope this journal will one day include all of my letters that I've been sending home to friends and family because that will also give a good assessment.

Well, I'll try to begin. In mid-March, we continued our movement to JBAD, by the way of Kabul City. My first time there. 14 March was a long, hard day of traveling through the country. Many route detours and other obstacles turned the ride from Kabul to JBAD into an 18-hour long journey. I spent about a week in JBAD with other staff to conduct mission planning for Operation Mountain Lion, which was the next big operation to take place in Konar province. Then we continued our move north to Firebase Naray. The road north from Jalalabad to Naray was very scenic. The raging Konar River gave life and vegetation to the area, green and lush, with jagged mountains, still snowcapped.

We spent the night of 19 March in Firebase Asadabad. I'm carrying my college copy of Arrian's Alexander the Great with me, and I was reading about his passage through this part of Afghanistan, and in particular the Nawa Pass which leads into modern-day Pakistan—visible to the eastern mountains. Nawa Pass is still a "Named Area of Interest" today. I linked up with the CIA and Special Forces teams at Asadabad to get a better idea as to the enemy threats in this part of Konar. I approached the CIA so that I could gain access to their sources in the Afghan NDS—the Afghan version of the CIA. Apparently there are NDS agents near Naray, so I wanted to begin the intel sharing process.

On 20 March I finally reached Naray. The base was more isolated than I had imagined. The facilities at Naray were under construction when we arrived so that meant no running water, no hot meals, no flush toilets. I joined about 40 other smelly men crammed into tight concrete barracks, which still reeked of the local Afghan militia, who were the previous occupants.

Right after the Kotya valley operation, on 3 April, I was told to move back to JBAD by helicopter (thankfully) to conduct rehearsals and planning for Operation Mountain Lion, with other leaders in the brigade. I left with only enough personal supplies to sustain me for 3 to 5 days—the amount of time I was told that I'd be gone. I didn't take much with me. I left my journal behind, which I had flown in with some of my other stuff in late April. It's been almost a month now and I have not returned to Naray, and I'm not sure when or if I settle back there with any permanence.

Preparation and rehearsals lasted a grueling week in early April before Op Mountain Lion finally begun on 12 April. So far, it's been a very successful operation. We killed between 25 and 50 enemy fighters with many more wounded and captured. We found many IEDs and weapons caches, and we've been destroying them in place. 3-71 CAV has made a significant contribution to the cumulative battle damage assessment. The best of all: we've not had a single wounded or killed soldier yet. We are seeing lots of broken bones, ankle sprains, tired limbs—but nothing serious.

The worst day for casualties came on 25 April during a joint mounted patrol with ANA. The ANA—as per their MO—were riding all crammed into a Ford Ranger when it struck an IED, set off by a trigger-man watching from above. Four ANA soldiers were killed and 3 wounded. They were moving in a convoy that had 3-71 CAV soldiers, so it could've easily been one of our own.

Our soldiers have been out there in the mountains for almost 20 straight days and there's no real clear end in sight. Our biggest fight occurred on 29 April in the rugged forested mountain-top village of Chalas. The battle raged here for many hours between our ground troops and about 30 to 40 fighters who held some high ground and they were armed with heavy machine guns and mortars. The next day our patrol found nothing left of them, but large pools of blood and body parts.

I'm not really sure what's next for me. We're being told JBAD will be our permanent home for the deployment but we don't have a HQ or structure here to work from. So things are up in the air. We do believe that Alpha Troop will be deployed to RC-South in late May, to Kandahar or Helmand (my old stomping ground) for a 60-day operation along with our brigade's 2-87 Infantry, and some British/ISAF troops. The rest of us will continue operations in Konar with the focus along the border as well as Nuristan Province. No forces have ever conducted sustained operations in Nuristan province, and it remains the last untouched sanctuary of Al Qaeda and other extremist groups. Some analysts report that even Osama Bin Laden is hiding up there.[1]

It's finally May now and with another month down it brings me over closer to a homeward-bound ride, or at least mid-tour leave to look forward to in August. I never experienced a mid-tour leave during my first tour here. It seems it would be such a strange feeling to be whisked out of this atmosphere and into the company of friends and family. Then, all of a sudden, to be whisked out once again and placed back in the shit.

There will be a day in the not so far ahead future that I will miss all this. Although right now I just seem so cut off—so unimportant—similar to my last deployment. I'm sure this experience will have great meaning to me in the years to come. I have 9 months left out here, What's nine months in the grand scheme of things? It's an academic school year. I have nine months to serve my country proudly and honorably in a combat zone. Then I can come home and begin a new kind of life somewhere. I'll recall my days as a young captain serving in Afghanistan with pride.

1 Bin Laden was eventually found and killed by U.S. Navy Seals in 2011 in Abbottabad—about 400 KM away from Nuristan.

CHAPTER 12

THE REAL ENEMY WILL BE THE TERRAIN

5 May 2006. Jalalabad Airfield.

A terrible day, maybe the worst day of my life, next to the death of my father in 1987. I don't have the strength to even write about it. LTC Fenty, along with three other Alpha Troop/3-71 CAV Troopers, and five aircraft crewmen, are all feared dead. Their Chinook CH-47 helicopter had a malfunction while extracting our soldiers off a side of a mountain tonight. It somehow lost control and tumbled down the cliff. There is very little left of the helo, and it's burning still as I writing this, six hours after the accident.

I will write again when there is some sort of resolution and confirmation of the dead. I lost a good friend today, a mentor, a father-figure even. My boss. My Commander. I don't have the stomach to write much more.

6 May 2006.

Still holding onto a bit of hope that our commander and possibly another soldier somehow managed to survive the crash. Two soldiers have not been positively identified. It's been a hard day and I would trade almost anything not to have to relive the past 18 hours. Yesterday at about 1540 Zulu, 810pm local time, 1140am on the East Coast, LTC Fenty and six aircraft crewman touched-down (rear two wheels only) onto the side of a mountain near the Chowkay valley to extract 2nd Platoon/Alpha Troop from their observation posts.

At this time, we believe a combination of high winds and maybe a rotary blade striking a tree caused the helicopter to lose control during boarding. The men from 2nd Platoon were PV2 Brian Moquin, PFC David Timmons, and Specialist Justin O'Donohoe. They all boarded the helicopter before the helicopter started to tumble down into a ravine and explode. So far, our recovery efforts found the remains of eight men, but unfortunately only six of the eight could be identified. The six were aircraft crew so their bodies were partially protected from the fire, due to their nomex fire-resistant flight suits. Their suits allowed for an easier assessment of the remains. Of the other four men—two were burned beyond any recognition, and the other two are still missing. LTC Fenty is one of the missing. It brings me to chills just to write the words.

Joe Fenty had an amazing career having just reached 20 years in the Army this month. He was getting ready to retire and start his family with his new baby Lauren—who was just born four weeks ago. His first and only child and he never got a chance to meet her.

The loss of our commander and three other soldiers from Alpha Troop is just too hard to fathom. Never did we think that such an incident could happen to us—not to my unit. I met Joe Fenty for the first time in August 2004 when he was screening me for the role of the S1—the senior personnel officer of 3-71 CAV. In the past 21 months since, we've become very close. I served as his advisor on personnel and human resources topics for the first nine months. I helped him build the squadron from scratch. As the S1, every morning I came to work at Fort Drum's Old Post, in a WWII-era barracks, and I sat outside his office at my desk. I thought he was going to be one of those lifelong mentors that you're always happy to have on your side, because of his genuine kindness and his sincere interest in me as a person. He really wanted to set me up for success in my life. In fact, one of the last things he said to me—only a few hours before the crash—"Hey Ross, did you ever see that Rabbi that came through here for Passover?" With all that must be going on in his head—both operationally and personally—he always had a vested interest in my well-being to the very end.

Where do we even go from here? The chances of any survivors amongst the two missing men has already been ruled out by all of the leadership here. So, it's only a matter of finding and identifying them, so that we can begin the notification and grieving process. But how do we even grieve? We have 9 more months of combat operations here.

The military historian in me tries to seek some solace and wisdom in the lessons learned by previous Army units that were also beget by tragedy. Easy Company LT Winters lost his Commanding Officer on D-Day. They were Civil War companies and regiments that routinely lost their leadership during combat. We have to pick up our heads right now, and remember they died for something larger than themselves.

But LTC Fenty did not even *have* to be on that helicopter. In fact, he wasn't even supposed to. Three hours before he lifted off the airfield, we were briefing Brigadier General Terry (the 10th Mountain Division's deputy commander), and he was asking us questions about the extraction. BG Terry's concern was that there was not enough Command and Control in the air during the extraction for the number of 3-71 CAV soldiers coming off their observation posts. So, always leading from the front, Joe Fenty strapped himself into the cockpit, in the jump seat of the first Chinook that left the airfield. There was plenty of mention of the danger involved in the night-time extraction . . . actually I stood next to LTC Fenty in the TOC, when he was asked by BG Terry, "What are your concerns?" Fenty's exact words to Terry were: "Sir, I think the real enemy out there will be the terrain."

On Friday night, that terrible night, there was a scene that played out in front of me, and that I was party to, which I probably will never forget. CPT Frank Brooks, our B Troop Commander, was the most senior officer on the ground near the crash site. I was in the TOC at JAF, with MAJ Timmons and CSM Byers. Reports of the crash had just come in. They were trying to get Brooks to give a BDA of the crash. At first, they used lots of military jargon and acronyms over the radio to inquire, but then CSM Byers just blurted it out on the radio, showing raw emotion which for him was very rare. He also broke radio protocol by not using Brooks's call-sign, Barbarian 6, which he never did. He said forcefully: "Captain Brooks, do you or do you not believe there are any survivors?!" Brooks responded with "No way, Sergeant Major. There is no way anyone could have survived that." The whole TOC heard that—about 40 guys all went completely silent. That was hard for us all to hear.

I took a deep breath and then walked towards the TOC exit and bumped into the Brigade Chaplain standing there. We locked eyes, and he saw the look on my face, and he opened his arms as if to provide comfort, but I wasn't ready for it. I walked past him, then ran outside and found a dark corner of the building. I dropped to my knees, cursed god, and then just wept. LTC Chris Cavoli (Commander, 1-32 Infantry) came outside and found me like that.[1] He tried to offer me some comfort, and coming from him, I was eager to accept it. He and Joe Fenty were best friends.

I might be flying to BAF to attend the memorial service. There will be an informal ceremony here on Jalalabad airfield when we send the remains out by C-130. It's hard to know how to feel. Why wasn't I on that helicopter with him?

1 Chris Cavoli went on to be promoted to a four-star general and is currently the Supreme Allied Commander, Europe since 2022.

My job is to go wherever he goes . . . to circulate with him and provide on-the-spot intelligence assessments. I've flown in helicopters with him all over this country over the past couple months. A few months before we deployed, my parents visited our 3-71 CAV HQ on Old Post, and I introduced them to LTC Fenty. He told my mother "Not to worry. I'll take good care of him. He'll be attached to my hip—so to speak." That gave my mom some comfort.

This really hits home hard—just how dangerous the things that we're doing every day really are. We don't think about the danger—and we try to block it out. It could've been anyone of us on that helicopter with them. I'd be lying if I told myself that didn't scare the hell out of me. All the more, it makes me want to serve with honor out here, but to return home safely and live out my years in peace and start to lay some family roots. Life is so precious, and we often neglect to realize how precious it is until someone is taken away from us so tragically. I just have to keep remembering the bigger picture: we came here in response. Our backdoor was kicked in hard, and we're doing our best to bring the fight back to their doorstep.

The intelligence analyst in me thinks back to "what if" this or "what if" that. After all if it had not been for all of my prodding and phone calls and emails, pushing LTC Fenty to move our operations into the Chalas Ghar mountains . . . maybe this would not have happened? There are countless variables to ponder. But nothing worth our time to consider viable. In the end, we're just doing what we can to continue business as usual. In fact, it's almost sickening to me to watch people go on about their routines. In particular, our S3 Operations Officer, who seemed to butt heads frequently with Fenty over the past year, does not seem the least bit affected. Part of me wants to pull him aside and say "does any of this actually fucking bother you?" But I guess he's doing what maybe we all should be doing . . . and that's moving on, mentally, to the next mission. We're in a war zone here and things don't just stop, even if it's for the death of your Squadron Commander.

7 May 2006. Letter Home. JAF.

> Tragedy has struck my Squadron. Many of you have probably read the news reports about a Chinook helicopter carrying 10 soldiers from the 10th Mountain has crashed in the mountains near Asadabad. Six of them were helicopter crewmen and three were Soldiers in my unit, all from Alpha Troop, and the last man was my boss, my mentor and my friend LTC Joe Fenty. We're still in a state of shock that our commander is gone. I worked with LTC Fenty closer than anyone else since we activated this unit two years ago. I served as

(Top) LTC Joe Fenty, CPT Matt Gooding, and CPT Frank Brooks (L-R) taken in the Chowkay Valley, just days before the tragic May 5, 2006, helicopter crash. (Bottom) A CH-47 attempts a rear-wheel landing to resupply 3-71 CAV during Operation Mountain Lion in the Chowkay Valley in early May 2006. *Matt Gooding*

his S1 and his S2. The worst of it is, his wife just gave birth to a baby girl named Lauren only four weeks ago. He never got to meet her. The three other soldiers were all so very young and they had so much potential. I knew one of them well, Justin. He had a college degree, which is rare for an enlisted man, and he always asked me about how he could get into OCS and becoming an officer after we returned home.

My job here has been to circulate the battlefield with LTC Fenty, and provide on the spot assessments of the enemy strength, their motives, their disposition. Up to this point I've gone almost everywhere he went. Why was I not on that aircraft with him is a question that I will have to ask myself for the rest of my life. I gave him the intelligence brief two hours before he took off, and we agreed that terrain would be the biggest threat. He wanted to be in the Chinook to make sure all of his soldiers got extracted from their mountaintop positions safely. It was decided that there was no reason I needed to go along with him. At high elevation, and during the night, his Chinook hovered over the platoon, and put only its two rear wheels down. After three soldiers boarded, high winds pushed the aircraft's rotor blades into the side of a mountain and cut the aircraft into pieces, and then it dropped off a cliff and exploded. The rest of the platoon had to watch the awful scene, play out in front of them, and bear the difficult task of securing their comrades from the wreckage. All of this after four straight weeks of continuous operations in these mountains. I can't imagine their fatigue and now their state of mind.

It's hard to know where to go from here. The officers and men loved and respected LTC Fenty and we're trying to go about our business with the understanding that they wouldn't have wanted us to stop pushing a fight to the enemy.

Our XO, Major Rich Timmons is taking over 3-71 command. Memorial services and chaplains and combat stress teams have been ongoing to keep the soldiers mentally fit. I think when the commander is killed, everyone starts reimagining how vulnerable they are out here. This certainly exposed an open wound in me that will take some time to heal. LTC Fenty was a father figure for me always looking out for my best.

It looks like I'll be leaving Jalalabad in a couple of weeks to go back to FOB Naray, which we hope will be renamed FOB Fenty. I will most likely stay there for a while, at least until the Fall. All this moving around has been getting to me and the rest of us. It would be nice to have one place we can call Home, in which we could operate from. I guess combat deployments are not supposed to be convenient, yet there are so many out here that have it better and easier than us.

> In better news, Gary Sinise came out here to visit at JAF. I had a five-minute conversation with him while he stopped by on a USO tour. We took a photo together and I'll send it out when I can. He said to me, "I have nothing but respect for you Marines, my nephew is a Marine." I just smiled back. He made a great Lieutenant Dan, but too bad he cannot tell the difference between an Army uniform, and a Marine's. It's printed on our chest.

8 May 2006.

LTC Fenty's remains, along with all the other nine men, were identified and all found, officially on Sunday morning on 7 May at 440z. They have all been brought back to Bagram for a ramp ceremony. I am departing for Bagram right now to see my commander go home.

8 May 2006. Letter Home.

> Family,
>
> I'm in Bagram right now. I flew here this morning from JBAD (in a Chinook of all things) to attend the ramp ceremony in the C-17. I helped carry LTC Fenty's casket onto the aircraft, among 9 other flag draped coffins. In the C-17, MG Freakley made some comments, choking back tears. Our Chaplain led us in a nice prayer. Then, I kneeled alongside each of the caskets and said goodbye. We took the 4 flags over our guys and will hoist them over our FOB at Naray, and bring them back to the states next year. MAJ Timmons and CSM Byers were just distraught. Other BN Commanders in the brigade were present, some were best friends with LTC Fenty since their lieutenant days. There were a lot of grown men openly weeping in that C-17, myself included and general officers. It's just unreal. I'm returning to JBAD in the morning and prepping for my move.
>
> Love, Ross

19 May 2006. FOB Naray.

It's been exactly two weeks since the CH-47 crashed, carrying LTC Fenty and three other 3-71 CAV soldiers. I left to take part in the ramp ceremony at Bagram, which was a very moving tribute. We conducted several memorial ceremonies in the following week both at JAF and here at Naray.

On 13 May, I arrived at Naray for a ceremony and now I believe I'm here to stay. The majority of our squadron has consolidated on this base. Operation

Mountain Lion is officially over. Alpha Troop, still reeling from such a devasting loss in 2nd Platoon, had no time to think about it. They were deployed down south in Kandahar/Helmand region to help the Brits keep the pressure on.

The space at FOB Naray has become increasingly scarce over the past few days with so many soldiers coming here. I'm happy that we've re-grouped here. The unit needs to be together right now. LTC Mike Howard is en route from Fort Drum to take over 3-71 CAV as our next commander. I don't know much about him other than he commanded 1-87 Infantry while I was deployed here in 2003 to 2004. I was chatting with some of the guys that said Howard had a reputation as a ball-buster.

I'm approaching my 100th day in this deployment. It's a good feeling. Another 70 days or so before I go home for my mid-tour leave and see family and friends.

17 May 2006. Letter Home.

> Just want to give a quick update. I left Jalalabad last week for Naray. Hopefully, I will be staying here at least until I come home in August for mid tour leave. The camp's quality of life has improved a little bit since I left 7 weeks ago. We have a sit down dining facility now, with 3 meals a day . . . some new weight lifting equipment, showers, laundry facilities. Air conditioners are scarce and don't work well. . . its a good thing I'm so far north and in the mountains, the average day time temp here is about 90. Much nicer than 113 degrees in the Jalalabad dustbowl everyday.
>
> I drove into Arandu, Pakistan yesterday and had a very interesting meeting with a group of Pakistan army officers. I had to walk through the downtown bazaar to get to their army headquarters . . . not a very pleasant walk. Lots of evil stares from shop owners. The town is out of an old west movie. . . one dirt strip road jam packed with cattle and pack animals . . . with two story shops and hotels on either sides, wooden plank sidewalks, everyone walks around with guns . . . just amazing. We are the first conventional American forces to step foot, so the reaction was not surprising. Once the meeting began, we talked about everything from where Osama was hiding, to world politics, to local lore. Always the student of history, they entertained my questions regarding Alexander the Great and the impression his armies left on this area over 2,000 years later. There is a small tribe, called Kalash, that live near here who are the direct descendants of Alexander's Greek army. Or, so, that's the local lore. The Kalash people seem to share some of the genetic traits, lighter skin tone and hair color, more common to the modern-day Greek or Balkan than Afghan.

North
Chitral
Kalasha Valley
Ayun
Barge Matal
BANDAKHSHAN
PROVINCE
Landay-Sin River
Paprok
Pitigal
Mandigal
Parun
NURISTAN
PROVINCE
Kamdesh
Pashki
Arandu
Kotya
Naray
Waygal Valley
Nishagam
Aranas
Wanat
Asmar
Bar Kanday
Pech River
Korengal Valley
Asadabad
KONAR
PROVINCE
Chalas
PAKISTAN
Konar River
Bajaur River
Nawa Pass
Chowkay
TF Titan Area of Operation
Konar & Nuristan Provinces
0
Miles
20
Contour Interval - 1,000 feet
Map by Edward Alexander

LTC Chris Cavoli, commander of 1-32 Infantry, and best friend of the late Joe Fenty, prays at a memorial service for the four fallen men of 3-71 Cav, JAF, May 2006. *Jeb Ridgeway*

They still practice animism and other pagan-like rituals, much like the ancient Macedonians. The Pakistani officers told me to get a visa, and they would take me on a tour of their ancient battlefields . . . an enticing offer but I think I've had my fill of third worlds after this deployment.

So many of you responded to my last email with words of comfort and wisdom. Every email helped. So, I thank you for that. We've had many memorial services here (since our squadron is spread so thin) and I attended every one. I even went to Bagram Airfield to act as a pallbearer and attend the ramp ceremony inside the aircraft holding all 10 of the flag-draped caskets bound for Dover AF base. It was a moving tribute, causing even general officers to openly weep. So, we are getting through this . . . our new commander, LTC Howard, is on his way to Afghanistan as I write. We've got a lot of work to do in this part of the world and can't stop to mourn. But we will never forget and continue to honor them. FYI, LTC Fenty will be buried at Arlington on 23 MAY.

Take care, Thanks again for the flood of email support.

CHAPTER 13

NOT A PASSING MOMENT OF COURAGE

27 May 2006. FOB Naray.

LTC Mike Howard, the former commander of 1-87 IN, and the former rear detachment commander for the 10th Mountain, just assumed command of 3-71 Cavalry. I've certainly seen this unit change, grow. I've seen its formation and inception, its ups and downs in garrison and in-country, the battlefield death of its first commander, to the gaining of new one. LTC Howard has made a good first impression so far. He has openly acknowledged that he has a lot to learn, and he's showing his desire to do so.

Our operations have significantly slackened lately, although there have been several opportunities presenting themselves, but for a good number of reasons we are just not pursuing them. I think most of this is due to the new command, the changeover, and generally still reeling from May 5th, and getting acclimated to LTC Howard.

Last week I traveled into Pakistan with a small ground patrol. We drove about 20 km north of here to the border village called Arandu. Then, we walked over the foot bridge into another country. It was exciting to walk through this border town almost resembling an Old West movie set. We had a mission to meet with the Afghan Border Police on their side, and the Pakistan military on the other side. The Pakistanis invited us to tea and cookies in their headquarters and we talked about everything from religion to politics to the history of this region.

Embedded media journalists are not an uncommon thing out here. But today, I was told by our XO that I should brief up the author Jon Krakauer on the security situation in this part of Konar. Apparently, Jon signed up to embed with 3-71 CAV for a couple of weeks and he recently showed up. Jon told me he's in Afghanistan primarily to conduct research for his future book on Pat Tillman—a former NFL player turned Army Ranger who was killed by friendly fire in 2004. Tillman's unit was conducting operations a bit further south of Konar, closer to Khowst I believe. I think Jon has plans to go down there too. Anyway, Jon seems like a really interesting fellow and of course I'm familiar with his Mount Everest story and book.

I talked about this with some of the guys here: we all think that it takes some serious guts and dedication, as a journalist, to come out to a FOB like this one, and spend real time here. Jon is supposed to be here for three weeks. According to the XO, Krakauer was hand-picked by LTC Fenty back in March (off a list of journalists) to embed with us. LTC Fenty was a fan of Jon's books and his outdoor adventures. Having Jon out here, it makes us all feel that America has not completely forgotten about us, in this far flung and remote corner of the world. Jon is billeted in one of the soldier barracks and when I found him, he was piled in between about 20 smelly, loud soldiers, while quietly reading his book. I checked in on him and made sure he's ready for joining a patrol that was going out the next morning—to climb up to the observation post overwatching FOB Naray. When I introduced Jon to the patrol leader, a SGT who had no idea that Jon scaled Everest and is a pretty hardcore outdoorsmen, the SGT expressed some concern to me that "this journalist" better keep up with his squad. Hah. SSG Monti did recognize Jon's name and his COLT (Combat Observation Laser Team) appears to be joining them on the patrol.

Future operations are a big topic of discussion right now. We've been tasked by higher headquarters to build a new combat outpost about 40 miles north of here in Kamdesh. To our knowledge, no U.S. forces have ever had a permanent presence in that valley. It's going to be a significant challenge and the next 60 days before I go home on leave will be intense.

29 May 2006. Memorial Day.

My brother used to work as a legislative correspondent in the U.S. House of Representatives and still has some connections with friends working for various congressmen, and the President. He shared LTC Fenty's story of sacrifice with his former colleague, Chris Michel, who now works as President Bush's Special Assistant for Speechwriting. A few weeks ago, my brother mentioned to me that the White House is waiting for more information from press reports on the crash and were very moved by LTC Fenty's story and his sacrifice. Today, during the President's annual Memorial Day speech at Arlington National Cemetery,

3-71 CAV squadron staff at FOB Naray in June 2006 (CPT Berkoff, seated). *Author Collection*

LTC Fenty was mentioned. I first heard about it from our public affairs officer that sent around an email. President Bush said:

> Last week, the family of Lieutenant Colonel Joseph Fenty Jr. gathered here at Arlington to pay their last respects to the husband, son, and father they loved. Colonel Fenty was killed with nine of his fellow soldiers in a helicopter crash in Afghanistan earlier this month. Hours before that crash, he had spoken to his wife Kristen about their newborn daughter he was waiting to meet. Some day she will learn about her dad from the men with whom she served—he served. And one of them said this about her father: "We all wanted to be more like Joe Fenty. We were all in awe of him." I am in awe of the men and women who sacrifice for the freedom of the United States of America.

30 May 2006. FOB Naray.

Another thought on the President's speech yesterday. I met Chris Michel in 2005 when he was kind enough to treat my brother and I to breakfast at the White House mess, and give us a tour of the White House, along with his pretty amazing office and balcony views from the Old Executive Office Building. I just wrote Chris a letter to express my appreciation—from the entire 10th Mountain Division—for recognizing our fallen commander. My letter to him:

> Chris, I am writing to you to thank you and to thank the President for recognizing our fallen commander. I hope you can pass this message of appreciation to him. We knew that LTC Fenty was awe inspiring, well before May 5th. But, to hear the President say it really lifted our spirits and made us feel that we truly are in the thoughts of our Commander in Chief. So, on behalf of the new Squadron Commander, LTC Michael Howard, and the men of 3-71 CAV, thank you for including LTC Fenty into this year's Memorial Day speech. It made the holiday really mean something to all of us out here in the mountains, where the joys of American holidays and American comforts are so out of touch.

Chris was very quick to reply:

> Ross,
>
> Thanks for sharing your experience with LTC Fenty. Having heard from you and read some of the news accounts, I am blown away by what a special man and unique leader he was. I was glad that your brother mentioned the story to me a couple of weeks ago, and it was the least I could do to suggest it for the speech. I know the President was honored to tell it. It's a touching and important reminder of the sacrifices all of you are making in Afghanistan, along with your comrades in Iraq and beyond. Hope all is well, and thanks again for the idea of mentioning LTC Fenty's story—like I said, it's the very least we can do to honor someone like him.
>
> Regards,
>
> Chris Michel

22 June 2006. FOB Naray.

The past few days we have seen the worst this war has to offer, at least since the crash on May 5. We now can report that 3-71 CAV has sustained KIA as a result of enemy contact. And once again, I don't have the heart to write about it. I have been sending emails home frequently enough to allow for the month to have elapsed without an entry. I'm just so exhausted mentally and physically that any free time I have been getting is devoted exclusively to just relaxing my brain, reading books and watching movies. But I have to maintain this journal properly, so I need to describe the events of 20–21 June 2006, and how those events affected our small squadron.

The past few weeks we have been conducting relatively low impact, brief operations in the general vicinity of FOB Naray. All of this has been gearing up for a main event of pushing to Kamdesh, Nuristan Province, and a large 4-5-week operation that would end after we have "cleared out" insurgent groups operating in all of the villages along the main line of communications—the main road leading to Kamdesh, such as Gowardesh, Baz Gal, and Mirdish. LTC Howard is calling it "village hopping." Clearing these villages would finally allow us to lay groundwork for what would become a new Kamdesh Provincial Reconstruction Team compound in the village of Kamdesh, the district capital.

The operation took weeks to plan, to rehearse, and to brief, and from a staff officer perspective, I think we were as ready as we could be. But on the evening of 20 June during a routine patrol to the Dugalam village, about 30 minutes north of here, the "enemy had a vote," as LTC Howard would say. Local bad guys detonated an IED against one of our mounted patrols, which we determined was a pressure cooker filled with about 20 pounds of Semtex explosives. The IED went off under the Humvee of Staff Sergeant Flores from Charlie Company. Fortunately, it blew up too early to destroy the entire vehicle, but it did take out the front engine block. SSG Flores and his driver, PFC Frank, sustained leg wounds. Frank was able to return to duty, but SSG Flores's wounds were more serious, and he had to go back home. That attack was followed by some small arms fire, so it was a coordinated multi-prong attack: the first of which we have seen here.

This is also our first case of WIA as a result of enemy fire, since we arrived in country, and it honestly could not have happened to a more depleted and fatigued company as Charlie Company. Charlie Company has already sent 15 men home in the past three months due to mission-related injuries, broken bones, broken backs, etc. Back in April, one of their platoon sergeants, SFC Brock, jumped into the Konar River to save a drowning soldier, and SFC Brock later fell ill to pneumonia or something . . . probably the result of accidentally drinking the river water. He lost 30 pounds and was apparently close to death. But he beat it, and he returned to FOB Naray a few weeks ago. Tough SOB.

It's clear the enemy does not want us moving any further north into Nuristan. On 9 June Charlie Company was ambushed on a route reconnaissance mission to Kamdesh. Although no one was hurt, it was the first real eye-opener to what sort of fighting was waiting for us in that area.

The IED from 20 June forced LTC Howard to delay a bigger operation that was already underway in Gowardesh. Just a day or so prior to the IED attack, we had inserted a 17-man recon element of snipers and forward observers, led by sniper SSG Chris Cunningham, and lead FO and COLT (Combat Observation Laser Team) leader, SSG Jared Monti, to overwatch enemy positions in Gowardesh—covertly. The plan was to get this team high in the hills, with good cover and concealment, and get eyes and intelligence on the objective—the village of Gowardesh—prior to launching a larger ground patrol into the village directly.

They had a strong overwatch position on Hilltop 2610. They were in place and doing okay. But after the IED attack, LTC Howard decided to delay the main effort (moving directly into Gowardesh) by two days. This meant our recon team on Hilltop 2610 needed a resupply—they were already just about out of water—which we could only do by Blackhawk/aerial drop. So, on 21 June, and only an hour or so after the aerial resupply, our recon team was attacked.

The positions of the recon team, of Cunningham and Monti, were obviously compromised by the helicopter activity. During the night of 21 June, they were attacked by a regular hornet's nest of enemy fighters, and they gave us one hell of a fight. They attacked our observation post positions from multiple approaches and with significant numbers.

Before the operation began, I told Monti that he needs to monitor certain enemy frequencies, but I did not realize that they inserted into positions without an interpreter. At 1400 Zulu 21 June, I called them on the net from FOB Naray and I spoke to SSG Monti. Monti and I were one of the few guys in 3-71 CAV that deployed with 1st Brigade, 10th Mountain during OEF IV. He was a popular NCO in 3-71, a veteran of 1-87 Infantry, our COLT Leader and one of the best NCOs in the unit. They were attacked close range by over 30 fighters with RPG and PKMs. They were hit by multiple RPGs. Almost immediately, we received a report of a KIA. It was SSG Patrick Lybert, an infantryman and squad leader from Charlie Company. I later learned that he was shot in the face and instantly fell dead.

From what I can tell happened next, PFC James and SPC Bradbury occupied one of the fighting positions about 20 meters from SSG Monti. After the shooting started, an RPG tore off Bradbury's arm and gunshot wounds riddled his other arm. His foxhole buddy PFC James also took shrapnel to one arm, and a bullet passed through the side of his back. SSG Monti made several attempts to reach their position, but the enemy fire was too intense. Monti came back on the net after we were constantly requesting a situation report. I heard him say clearly, that he's under heavy fire, and if he were to lift up his head from his covered position, he'd be shot down. That was the last thing we heard from him. Later on, I learned that Monti made several attempts to rescue James and Bradbury. During his last attempt, Monti rushed to their position with hope for administering first aid when multiple RPG rounds tore him apart.[1]

The fighting lasted for another two or three hours. We dropped five B1 bombs and dozens of 105 mm and 120 mm howitzers and mortars on the enemy from our gun pits at Naray. What was left of the assault force melted away.

But now came time for the extraction. The recon team was perched on a narrow ridgeline, heavily forested. There were no good places for a Blackhawk helicopter to land and pick up the dead and wounded. So a special team of flight medics arrived and pushed out a cable and a basket for the wounded Bradbury and James to hoist themselves on. James was first to be lifted out without any incidents. I saw him get off the helicopter at Naray and watched as he was carried into our aid station on a litter. He was our third WIA to enter that aid station in only the last 24 hours. James will recover. The bullet somehow missed all his internal organs and just lacerated his muscle tissue.

We stood out in front of the aid station, hoping that Bradbury would be next to make it back without any problems. I walked back to the TOC, and I heard SSG Cunningham's voice coming over the net: "Fuck, the cable broke. "Bradbury fell." "The medic fell." "I'm gonna go get them. Out." Only God knows why, but somehow the cable snapped that was lifting out Bradbury and the medic attending to him.[2] They both dropped 40 feet to the earth and died. So we now have four dead men on that damn hill. There is not going to be another risky nighttime extraction to attempt to pull anyone else out. Cunningham and his guys did their best to find the bodies to cover them up and to wait out the night.

The following afternoon extraction teams by Blackhawk did have success pulling out the four dead men. We lined up on the landing strip at Naray, and we presented arms to our fallen comrades as their bodies were pulled off of the birds and placed into body bags. Their limbs were chewed up and blackened. It was grotesque, and I wish I could erase that scene from my memory. The recon team now has 13 men who are currently walking down the mountain top to link up with a mounted patrol, which will return them to Naray.

We have some really hard brave man in this unit and we're already too small of an outfit to take these types of casualties. So far in the last 50 days we've had

1 Jared Monti received the Medal of Honor, posthumously, for his actions near Gowardesh, Afghanistan. I attended the White House ceremony and watched President Barack Obama place the medal around Jared's father, Paul, on September 17, 2009.

2 The combat medic was Staff Sergeant Heathe N. Craig, who grew up in Mechanicsville, Virginia, and served with the 159th Air Medical Company.

seven KIA, three WIA, and numerous others sent home due to broken bodies and bones, from the mountain climbing. It's having its due effect on our unit morale. I think we are all, for the first time now, doubting if we will be able to achieve our mission here with the time that we've been given.

This deployment has already proved to be more volatile and bloodier than my first tour. I know it sounds crazy but sometimes I wish that I could be slightly wounded so I can go home. But then I wake up and smell the coffee . . . I want to see this damn deployment through. Although I've given more than my fair share to the service of my country—4 years and 37 days and counting . . . I realize that civilian life is waiting for me on the other end. So I need to buck up and face the cruelty out here for another seven months, so I can go home to my country to my family as a veteran and ready to start anew. I'm nearing halfway through this deployment, and I've lost some good friends. I'm weary and I'm homesick. I've done all this for my country. I love my country, but if this deployment ever ends and brings me home safely to my loved ones, I'll be damned if I ever love another.

28 June 2006. FOB Naray.

No time to mourn our friends here. On 23 June, the bulk of 3-71 CAV moved by air and by ground into the villages of Baz Gal and Gowardesh. These are the two largest villages and closest to the fight from 21 June. We believe most of the enemy fighters came from these villages. On 25 June, Charlie Company observed a large group of enemy fighters moving into a compound. We dropped everything in our arsenal on top of them: 120 mm mortars, 105 mm Howitzers, A10 warthogs, 2000-pound bombs. I'm confident we killed those responsible for attacking our recon team. They should be wrapping up operations in the next couple of days and returning to Naray, after which we will have a memorial ceremony for SFC Monti, SSG Lybert, SPC Brian Bradbury, and the flight medic who tried to extract Bradbury.

On 26 June, one of the ANA trucks flipped over and killed the driver. I hear the ANA company that has been serving with us is beginning to quit.

I got my first case of the Afghan Bug on the night of 26 June. I was nauseous all night long with chills and spins. I woke up to use the bathroom and vomited. Medics gave me an IV and some medicine for my nausea and then I slept a lot. I'm feeling better now.

Nearing July now and I might very well be leaving Naray for Newark International Airport in about 34 days.

CHAPTER 14

SURVEILLING KAMDESH

4 July 2006. FOB Naray.

The Glorious Fourth has come again, although you might have to remind our unit that it's our nation's birthday because today was a day just like any other.

This will be my fifth July 4th in the Army. My first was in 2002 while training to become a platoon leader at Fort Knox, Kentucky. I spent that holiday weekend on leave with my friends in Nashville and Memphis. My second was passed on leave traveling to Florida and Houston with friends just before my first deployment to Afghanistan in 2003. Last year at this time I was in the company of great friends enjoying fireworks overlooking Sackets Harbor in New York. And today, this holiday finds me in my fifth month of a yearlong deployment to northeastern Afghanistan. There will be a pig-roast barbecue meal for the soldiers today. That's the only stamp of occasion but considering we're surrounded by Muslims observing halal we'll take it as an opportunity to celebrate.

I'm actually gearing up as I write this, about to go up in an aerial reconnaissance of Kamdesh district with our Brigade Commander, Colonel Nicholson. We will be launching another big operation in the coming week and all intelligence reports suggest serious enemy threats waiting for us there.

Hopefully this air reconnaissance will shed some light on what we're about to encounter. I am being asked by LTC Howard to find a suitable location for a future PRT in Kamdesh district. We thought Naray was the Wild West. The Kamdesh hive is a whole new level of wretchedness, scum and villainy, to quote Obi Wan. We have started to send some patrols up that way to scout out possible locations for the PRT. A few weeks ago, some of the Charlie Company guys traveled the 20+ miles up the river valley using mostly ATVs and were ambushed along the way. No one was seriously wounded. They took lots of photos and I'm starting to analyze our options. None of them look any good.

5 July 2006. FOB Naray.

The enemy provided us with all with a bit of fireworks show last night. For the first time in about two months and certainly the first type of attack with this much determination, the enemy launched a series of rockets down on FOB Naray. We think about five rockets were fired—passing overhead or landing short. We responded well into the morning hours with our own mortars, howitzers, and heavy machine guns. During a lull in the fighting, some of our soldiers took advantage by launching some real July 4th fireworks that were purchased over in the haji-mart.[1] Overall was an impressive display. We heard a five-year-old was accidentally wounded by shrapnel up in the mountains over the FOB and is being cared for at our aid station right now.

I took a ride in a Blackhawk yesterday that I mentioned. It was an exciting ride with open doors at elevations in excess of 15,000 feet. We landed safely and then we gave a briefing to Colonel Nicholson who joined me on the helo ride. We provided him our current assessment of the enemy and tribes. Colonel John Nicholson is someone I've gotten to know well over the past two years in this brigade, and I very much respect his leadership style.[2] His father, John Nicholson, is on President Bush's cabinet—I believe as a secretary of the VA. After the briefing, COL Nicholson, who is my senior rater, asked to see me in private for a counseling session. He asked me about my intentions to remain on active duty after this deployment, and generally my professional career goals.

This next operation will be delayed a few days. It's now templated to begin on 8 July and will last for about a week. We're also planning another squadron level operation in late July right before I begin my mid-tour leave.

I'm supposed to get a new Assistant S2 soon. My current AS2 is 1LT Clay Huffman. He's been in this role for almost 2 years. He's highly competent, very intelligent, and he gets shit done quickly without any supervision. I'll be sorry to see him go, but I know he needs to move on to continue to grow professionally.

1 Haji-marts were soldiers' crass vernacular to describe an Afghan market or bazaar.

2 Colonel Nicholson went on to become a four-star general and was the second to last commander of NATO-led Resolute Support Mission and United States Forces-Afghanistan from 2016–2018. He is currently the chief executive of Lockheed Martin operations in the Middle East.

In a rare selection for a Military Intelligence junior officer, Clay was selected to become the next Charlie Company XO—a position that is reserved for the most senior Infantry or Armor lieutenants in the squadron. It says a lot about the competence of Clay, and perhaps the paucity of really strong LTs left in the squadron after several months of combat-mission-related mishaps. My new AS2 will be 2LT Ward Yoder. He's been working in the brigade S2 Shop for the past many months. I met him briefly before we deployed and I'm confident he'll fit in well here.

30 July 2006. FOB Naray.

I am about to board a UH-60 Blackhawk for Bagram Airfield, to finally begin my mid-tour leave.

We were rocketed this morning from the southwest. Six or seven rockets whizzed over the base. I stumbled out of my hooch to take a look and no more than a few seconds later I heard the sound of a hummingbird flying over my head. Kind of sounded like a lifeguard whistle. We could see the rockets exploding far off in the distance on the other side of the river.

The past three or four weeks have been relatively uneventful, though, the new "Kamdesh PRT" was formally set up. We did not face too much enemy resistance while setting it up, although we think the honeymoon period is ending. They've been watching us closely, and we are expecting a big gunfight any day now. There is a quiet concern amongst our staff officers of the feasibility and sustainability of keeping our troopers at the Kamdesh PRT for the long haul. We were told that due to the lack of helicopters in country, we'd need to resupply ourselves, and that by ground. So that ruled out placing the PRT on top of the mountain, which is actually closer to Kamdesh village proper and many of the key village elders. The PRT will need direct access to the main supply line connecting back to FOB Naray. That left only one possible site and that's on the valley floor, alongside the river road, and surrounded on all sides by steep cliffs and blind spots—perfect terrain for lobbing rockets in. We are constructing an observation post, about halfway up the mountain, to help cover those blind spots. But that just means we need to keep it manned 24/7, and we're already strung out pretty good. I sent imagery requests for the Kamdesh PRT site to the brigade S2 shop, and they came back calling it "Camp Custer." Not very funny.

There is a new talk of pushing even further north into Barge Matal district. The CIA here are beginning to take a greater interest in our operations. They are thinking that Bin Laden is hiding somewhere up there or near Barge Matal. OGA established a footprint on FOB Naray, and their numbers, and the size of their compound, has grown considerably. Their ranks include several "Ground Branch" officers, who are responsible for training the "Afghan Mohawks," a local conglomerate of Afghan special operations fighters. I've gotten pretty friendly with some of the CIA guys, but we never use their agency name out here. Only OGA or Other Government Agency. I'm most friendly with a fella named Mike, who reminds me of my scoutmaster when I was in Boy Scouting. Soft spoken, wise, highly competent and eager to mentor. He actually retired from CIA Clandestine Operations, but he's back here in some kind of consulting fashion, as he explained it to me.

The month of July went by fast despite my calendar-day counting until I was finally scheduled to leave Naray. I expect I'll spend about a week in Bagram, most likely spending money on crap in the PX and being bored. I hope to fly out of BAF on 6 August and arrive in New Jersey on 8 Aug. I can hardly wait for some of the luxuries that I've been so deprived of these past six months. I will pick up this journal again after my return in late August.

31 August 2006. FOB Naray.

I'm back to work again at Naray. My leave went from 7–23 August with a few relaxing days laying around Bagram Airfield on both ends.

20 September 2006. FOB Naray.

I regret that I've lost some desire in keeping this journal updated lately. Between my mid-tour leave and the last eight weeks of combat operations, I don't even know where to begin.

On the battlefront—the Kamdesh outpost continues to gain in personnel size and strength. Its establishment in July was followed by the building of another outpost that we set up on top of the mountain near Gowardesh in early September. This outpost we named Camp Lybert after SSG Patrick Lybert who was killed that fateful day in June, nearby there. Charlie Company has taken ownership of Camp Lybert, and from that perch, they have a pretty good vantage point of some of the ingress routes and mountain passes leading into Konar from Pakistan. Bravo Troop is finishing their rotation at Kamdesh, and Alpha Troop—coming right from the battlefields in Helmand Province—are set to replace them there. These two outposts will keep 3-71 CAV occupied for the long haul.

Enemy attacks and ambushes started in early August against Kamdesh, just as I was leaving country. They continue almost every day with regularity, mostly attacking us along the valley road (only one road leads to Kamdesh), targeting our slow-moving convoys. On 11 September (intentional?), enemy fighters conducted a large, coordinated ambush along the valley road (from both sides of the river), wounding four troopers from Alpha Troop. My friend SFC Milt Yagel (who essentially took over as PSG for my old 2nd Platoon/3-17 CAV back in 2004) received shrapnel wounds. His mortarman who was riding with him, SGT Kline, lost his hand to an RPG round.

We continue to fight across our area of operations with a small glimmer of light at the end of the tunnel. The 1st Infantry battalion of the 508 PIR (1-508) from the 82nd Airborne, we're told, is slotted to take our place here at FOB Naray. I have been corresponding with their S2—a guy named CPT Dave Hammerschmidt, who actually went through the MI Transition course with me back in April 2005.

I'm not really sure what's ahead of us, operationally speaking. I plan to make my way up to the Kamdesh outpost in about two weeks. 1LT Huffman has been the S2 up there and I want him to return to get ready for his mid-tour leave before he officially moves over to Charlie Company as their XO. I might spend the month of October in Kamdesh. Then we've got 60 days of operations in November and December and by early January we should be sending the advanced party of 3-71 CAV back to Fort Drum. 1-508 will arrive here in late January and then that's it. That's a year of deployment. It's been a hard year. I've now been deployed for 220 days.

This weekend is Rosh Hashanah, and I was going to BAF to attend a Jewish service with a rabbi or chaplain that I heard is coming there.

CHAPTER 15

SURVIVING KAMDESH

9 October 2006. Letter Home from Kamdesh.

Hey all,

I moved up north into Nuristan, to one of our new outposts. It's about as rough as living can get in today's so called modern Army. We have had soldiers living here for almost three months now, and there is still no running water, no flush toilets, no hot food, and electricity is scarce. We occupied what used to be an Afghan militia compound. We live in their mud huts, which have been fortified with thousands of sandbags. The sand brings the fleas, unfortunately, so it's a toss-up . . . seek protection from the rockets and get the fleas.

The road leading up to the base is littered with the shells of Soviet-era tanks, now battlefield trophies to the local Nuristanis who are very proud of their part in the ousting of the Russians from Afghanistan.

Everyday local elders and mullahs come to the base eager to contract reconstruction projects in their villages. We've hired local masons and carpenters to build our new homes. For the first time ever, these people are seeing the breadth of the USA . . . the local economy is picking up, schools are being built, mosques are being rebuilt, and the bad guys are starting to get desperate with their tactics. They will lob rockets into our camp, but remain completely exposed along the edge of the cliffs, like mountain goats. Then, our mortars will do their work and blast 'em to bits. In the meantime, it's hard living for our guys.

I'll be here a few weeks, maybe a month. Drop me a line, the internet connection is our only lifeline to the outside world, and I can usually check it everyday.

18 October 2006. Letter Home from Kamdesh.

Hi Family,

I did see our PA here and took some Motrin and Benadryl, combined with a couple nights of solid sleep and I feel better.

Yesterday was a rather action-packed day here. Occasionally, I jump along with one of the Humvee patrols and I guess I might have accompanied the patrol on the wrong day. It was seriously the ambush scene from the movie Clear and Present Danger. I was in the middle of a long convoy of trucks that were snaking along a one lane dirt road in a narrow river canyon . . . the enemy ambushed our lead trucks, leaving one Humvee completely burnt out and destroyed (luckily, they all jumped out in time). In our rear, we had a convoy of local pickup trucks and cargo trucks (we hire the locals to do this because their trucks are not as wide as ours) . . . this convoy was attacked, and every truck was set ablaze by the enemy. And there I was stuck in the middle, with no way good way to go.

Air support eventually picked them off, but we had to wait for the burning trucks to extinguish as they were causing a serious roadblock. It wasn't until early the next morning when we were able to completely put out the flames and push them into the river—which cleared the way for our return back to base. Thankfully no one was seriously hurt . . . but those trucks were carrying all the hot food that we had been waiting so patiently for. As I cleared through the rubbish, I could smell what was supposed to be that night's dinner. Now just charred black steaks and chickens mixed in with the pile of burning aluminum.

It's frustrating . . . such a primitive enemy and yet on some days, like today, they beat us good. And this was the first time we've ever lost one of our own Humvees to the enemy. I hope to have better news to report in the future.

Love, Ross

30 October 2006. Back at FOB Naray.

I spent the last 24 days at the Kamdesh Outpost. I could not fit my journal into my rucksack for the trip, so I will do my best to describe the last month of operations at Kamdesh.

Ambush Alley: The road between Kamdesh and Kamu. Smoke in the distance after U.S. close-air support destroyed enemy machine gun nests. *Jeb Ridgeway*

Although I think the intent of this location is for us to call it Kamdesh "PRT." LTC Howard gets angry with us when we call it a "Combat Outpost" when he has orders from higher to use the site as a PRT. It's all an optics game. He has to report progress and establish security in this region, but we all know that this is a Combat Outpost right now and there's not much time or space for reconstruction efforts until we can first establish some damn order.

There was a definable decrease in enemy activity starting in late September. I think we went a full two weeks without being shot at. But that all changed once October started and Ramadan began. I think the Ramadan holiday corresponds with increase in local Jihad seekers wishing to martyr themselves. The local bad guys use it as an excuse to conduct attacks and they believe if martyred during Ramadan, then Allah and paradise are even more magnificent. Attacks did tick up during the first and second week of October, mostly directed against Kamdesh Outpost. On October 6th, I boarded a CH-47 bound for Kamdesh Outpost to assist with intelligence and operations' planning from Alpha Troop's TOC there. I was somewhat relieved that I did not have to make that trek by convoy over the ground.

At COP Kamdesh over the past few weeks, I continued to discharge my duties as the S2. But I also played a role as an operations officer in the TOC for Alpha Troop. During my 24 days there, we were rocketed six different times from small teams of HIG fighters looking to shoot down our helicopters.

The dynamics of the tribal populations continue to amaze me. The Nuristani people have known only one way of life for thousands of years, and they are really hesitant to accept our construction or reconstruction efforts, despite the incredible rates at which their people die from curable diseases and fixable problems. I sat down with Tamim Nuristani, during a shura, who's a local politician here. He spoke good English. He said before 9/11, he managed a fried chicken restaurant in Brooklyn, NY, and owned a home in Fort Lee, NJ. Small world, quite literally.

The security along the river road between Naray and Kamdesh has worsened. Just about every patrol that goes down that road gets ambushed. There's only one road to Kamdesh and it's along a deep river valley floor that locals have been using to ambush foreign invaders for centuries. The roadside is littered with the shells of broken Soviet personnel carriers. Our guys have been eating RPGs and heavy machine gunfire almost every time we travel down that damn road to send fresh supplies and troops to Kamdesh, to and from FOB Naray. Not only does the enemy own the high ground along that route, but they have an effective early warning system in place that alerts local cells of fighters (on both sides of the river) to our presence, and they're consequently able to organize rather effective ambushes against us. This is to say nothing of the fact that the road in many places is barely wide enough for a Humvee, with no road barriers to protect our trucks from the formidable drop off to the river in some sections.

On 17 October, I joined an Alpha Troop platoon on their mounted patrol along the river valley, along Ambush Alley. We rode to a key village along the main road towards Naray, the village of Kamu. It has a strong, defensible compound that sits on top of a commanding hill overlooking the road and river. This compound is believed to belong to the local police. We met with the Kamu village elders and talked about construction projects.

During one of these patrols, we were responding to an ambush that had destroyed several large jingle trucks that were in-bound from Naray to Kamdesh to deliver food and supplies to us. "Jingle trucks" is our term for these large supply vans driven by the locals, loaded down with wind chimes and gypsy-like ornaments. Not very tactical. When I arrived on the scene, the local truck drivers had fled or were killed and their trucks were on fire, tipped over, or had actually dropped (or were pushed) off the cliff and landed in the river. Our long-anticipated resupply of food and other stuff, gone or going up flames.

Life at the Kamdesh Outpost was hard living—the most austere of any continuous living conditions that I have yet been exposed. Showers were funneled into a hose, in a small tent, directly from the mountain stream, so the water was really cold. On sunny days we would hang bags filled with river water out in the sun and then wait until the evening to shower under them when it became lukewarm. The river is close but technically outside the wire so just securing enough water to carry back to the base, for god's sakes, manifests into a squad-level combat patrol. I managed to take one shower during the 4 weeks.

Task organized from our Delta Troop (Combat Support for logistics, maintenance, fuel, etc.) were Army cooks that served us T-Rations, called "tee-rats" for breakfast, which were some mix of potato hash and sausage, which left an old, sour, mellow taste in your mouth. A few nights (when our food resupply convoy was not getting blown up) the cooks had real meat—probably local goat or lamb—that we barbecued. I also paid a local translator to bring some potatoes, rice, and flatbread into the camp from a half-way house in the nearby village. During the Eid party,[1] we were served up a fine selection of goat and lamb by our ANA brothers here on the camp.

The land around Kamdesh is breathtakingly beautiful. The mountain range extends up 14,000 feet. The nights were crisp and clear and never have I seen so many stars. I often took my pipe out to a stone quarry in the evenings, and I sat on a rock and smoked and played my harmonica softly. It was pleasant to be out of the "line of fire" of all the field grade officers back at Naray. I was able to run my own show out here. I got my work done and I didn't have to stress over dozens of "Hey, I need you to do this" tasks, that I would normally get at Naray. Sure, I had to dodge the occasional 107mm rocket and a wear a flea collar on my belt, but aside from that, it was a "break" from the Naray routine.

On the day that I was scheduled to return to Naray, 29 October, a convoy from Naray was en route to Kamdesh to pick up equipment and people (and to take me back). However, on their way to Kamdesh they were attacked in two separate points along the road. Both were coordinated ambushes, and when they finally fought their way through the ambush, they arrived at Kamdesh shaken, then in shock when they got a look at where the camp is situated.

Six soldiers were wounded during the ambush and they went to our local aid station. Most of them will return to duty with minor shrapnel wounds. My new assistant S2, LT Ward Yoder, was among the men in this convoy, intent on replacing me at Kamdesh as the "S2 Forward." Ward stepped out of his bullet-ridden Humvee as white as a ghost. I think he was in a state of temporary

1 It's a tradition among Muslims to celebrate the end of Ramadan, or Eid, with feasting.

shock. Just about every truck in the convoy had wounded men in it (mostly our gunners), but Ward, a rear seat passenger, somehow escaped unscathed. During the lovely ride through the valley that day, Ward's gunner, SPC Cuong Vo, took a round directly to his Kevlar helmet. Ward said Vo let out a holler and slumped over into his lap inside the truck. He laid there limp until he finally came to. The round lodged in his Kevlar Helmut but didn't penetrate it. Just unreal.

Later in the day I was to join a patrol of six trucks that was returning to Naray. The patrol leader decided (or was ordered) to launch out at 0100—ensuring we'd be driving while local bad guys were either sleeping or ill-equipped to attack us during night-time, poor visibility. It was a smart decision. Wearing our night vision goggles, we rode through all the infamous ambush MGRS grids that I had spent the last few months plotting as "kill points." We sailed right through without making any enemy contact. I arrived at Naray in time for a hot breakfast.

In any case I am now back in Naray, and I've quickly noticed all the luxuries that this place offers when compared to Kamdesh. Everything must be viewed in relative terms. As a unit here we can expect another 70 or 80 days of steady state operations before being relieved by 1-508 IN and finally getting the relief-in-place procedures.

I have now been deployed for 262 days and even when you subtract the time that I was home on leave, I've been in Afghanistan longer than my first tour.

23 November 2006. Thanksgiving Day. FOB Naray.

Another Thanksgiving has passed in the Army, and this will be my second in Afghanistan. Uncle Sam has made a good effort to bring us turkey fare for the holiday. It didn't look like the weather would ever clear enough to allow the helicopters to drop in the turkey feasts, but alas, it's a beautiful sunny day today at Naray. We had a good meal. The Commanding General, Major General Freakley, arrived here to inspect the troops, and enjoy his turkey dinner with all of us. Just before dinner, the general gathered all soldiers around him for a motivational speech, and then he asked our Squadron Chaplain, CPT Doug Weaver, to bless the meal and pray for our country during these perilous times.

The past four weeks since I returned to Naray from Kamdesh have been exciting. Enemy attacks in this area significantly increased. On 8 November rockets came flying into camp and one exploded near my quarters and shook all the dust off our walls. Our artillery howitzers responded with overwhelming fire along the entire mountain side. It was nighttime so the exploding shells lit up in the countryside. I went to inspect the impact crater with CPT Brooks (Bravo Troop Commander) when we both saw the hills flashing, thinking rockets

(Top) 3-71 CAV trooper looks down at Combat Outpost Kamdesh, Fall 2006. (Bottom) 3-71 CAV Humvee destroyed after an October 2006 ambush (near Kamu), along the road to Kamdesh. *Jeb Ridgeway*

Troopers from 3-71 CAV pause for a smoke while on patrol near Kamdesh, Fall 2006.

Jeb Ridgeway

were bound for Naray again. Frank pushed me down and yelled "Incoming!" We laid down in silence for a few seconds. It seems one of our shells had detonated an enemy rocket or ammunition cache in the mountains, causing an unexpected, delayed flash.

We recently read the findings from the Army's Accident Investigation Division of the U.S. Army Combat Readiness Center, after the past many months' investigation into the 5 May crash that took the lives of LTC Fenty and nine other men. It was also published in an Associated Press article that I printed off here and shared with my family over email. The report said that the crash was caused by a "series of mishaps." We knew all this already, but the report went on to say that a nighttime landing on a small mountaintop landing zone was part of the cause. The complicated landing maneuver combined with the small LZ was not compatible with the pilots' technical knowledge of the terrain. Not in the report, but I did hear the pilots that night came from an aviation unit that was relatively new to operating in our AO. The aviators that had previously supported us in these mountains were apparently conducting a safety stand-down day on May 5th, so Division HQ assigned a less-experienced CH-47 crew to extract our guys. What in the fuck, over. Also, the report blames a large, foot-wide tree that was too close to the LZ. Our Alpha Troopers tried to hack the tree down as quickly as they could using hammers and pocketknives. All they had to work with.

I learned that the Chinook made one successful landing, but when they returned the pilots saw "glowing spots" nearby and thought they were taking enemy fire. So, the pilots took off again, but the crew soon realized the glowing spots were actually hot embers from a trash pit used by the soldiers, which were tossed up into the air. When the CH-47 came in on its third attempt, and from an angle that was ill-advised by our guys on the ground waving them in, the rear rotor hit that damned tree. The Chinook then crashed and rolled down the cliff and burst into flames. Not much in this report was real news to anyone here, but it is the first time we've seen anything published on the topic, aside from the initial report of the crash back in May. Not in the public report, but some of the guys on brigade staff told me that LTC Fenty's body/skeleton was found still strapped into his jump-seat near the cockpit. I could have gone without learning that grisly detail.

The pass of Thanksgiving is another mark on the calendar to check off as we grow closer to the end of this tour. I left Wheeler Sack Army Airfield 285 days ago. 11 weeks from now I will finally be home again ready to don a civilian suit and leave my time in the Army behind me.

CHAPTER 16

AN AWFUL TRAGEDY

26 November 2006. FOB Naray.

Another one of my good friends in the Army is gone. They go now with almost peculiar regularity and a sense of normalcy, and it makes my stomach knot up inside. 1LT Benjamin Keating, a fellow officer that I've come to know and respect since our first meeting almost two years ago, is gone. Ben started in 3-71 CAV as a Scout Platoon Leader. An Armor Officer (and, like me, branched detailed with Military Intelligence) he came to the squadron during its formative months, and he quickly earned the respect of all he served with. He's quiet, professional, intelligent, deliberate, and extremely competent. He moved to Alpha Troop as the XO a few months before we deployed, and he has since been the glue holding together that small, tired company of men. They've all seen so much senseless bloodshed these past 10 months.

Things were going great in the unit. We just finished a very successful operation in Baz Gal. Thanksgiving came and lit everyone's spirits and then tragedy strikes when you least expect it. About 1830, Ben was leading a convoy of trucks back to Naray when the road gave way under his LMTV truck.

Special Note: I later learned that Ben volunteered to not only lead the LMTV back to FOB Naray, but he decided he would personally drive the vehicle back to base, knowing full well the deteriorating conditions of the road due to recent washouts, and the dangers of driving at night. Officers are prohibited from driving military vehicles during combat missions so they can better command and control operations from the front passenger seat. His bravery and selflessness, however brash or impulsive, epitomized Ben Keating, a leader who always talked about "not assigning a soldier a task that he would not do himself." He died by this creed.

The vehicle rolled 300 feet down a cliff into the river. A precious two hours passed before Ben and SFC Tiller, who sat shotgun, could be extracted safely. Alpha Troopers had to hoist them out by rope. Ben stopped breathing somewhere between the rope and the aid station at Kamdesh.

I went to see him when he was brought here to Naray into the medical tent. I wanted to pay my respects, but really just say goodbye to a good man. I walked into the tent and there was a small line of other officers. We found Ben lying on a gurney, covered in a green wool Army blanket which was tucked up to his chin. We walked by him slowly, touching his arm under the blanket. While I stood there, the surgeon asked me if I wanted to know what happened to him. I said yes of course. He told me that he died of a massive internal bleeding caused from a broken pelvis. SFC Tiller was badly hurt, but he will live.

Everyone here is just in shock. We will muster up the strength to grieve and then continue operations. Ben was a popular officer, a good person, and a loyal friend to everyone around him. It was just about a week ago when Ben was here at Naray, and I saw him in the chow hall. I sat down and we chatted over lunch about his future in the Army. Like me, he was branch-detailed Armor and set to go MI. There was even talk of Ben joining my S2 shop. Ben told me he wanted to stay in the Armor branch, and he wanted to join a tank unit in Korea. I told him I would help him get out of the intelligence detail if I could. And now Ben Keating, 24 or 25 years old, is gone. He is the eighth man in my small unit to go since the crash on 5 May. I pray there will be no more.

LTC Howard told me this evening that I've been ordered to serve as the Summary Court Martial Officer for Ben's personal effects—which apparently are spread across Kamdesh, Naray, and Bagram. I don't want this job.

May God give us all the strength and will to see this deployment through with no more fallen comrades to grieve.

28 November 2006. Letter Home. FOB Naray.

Hey everyone,

I wish I could write under better circumstances, but I wanted to let you all know that I am ok in case you heard something in the news about a death in our unit. Another tragic accident has struck 3-71 CAV. Ben Keating was one of our Troop executive officers, a highly intelligent, well-liked and respected guy. Back home, he was one of my beer drinking buddies, during this deployment we

LT Ben Keating with Able Troop as they moved north to Naray in March 2006. *Author Collection*

grew even closer, as deployments do, but Ben was soon supposed to transfer to military intelligence just like I did last year.

Ben was leading a convoy along the same roads we travel every day, but he was doing it at night, and he was doing it from the widest load vehicle in our squadron, a LMTV. Why on earth he was trying to drive this truck down

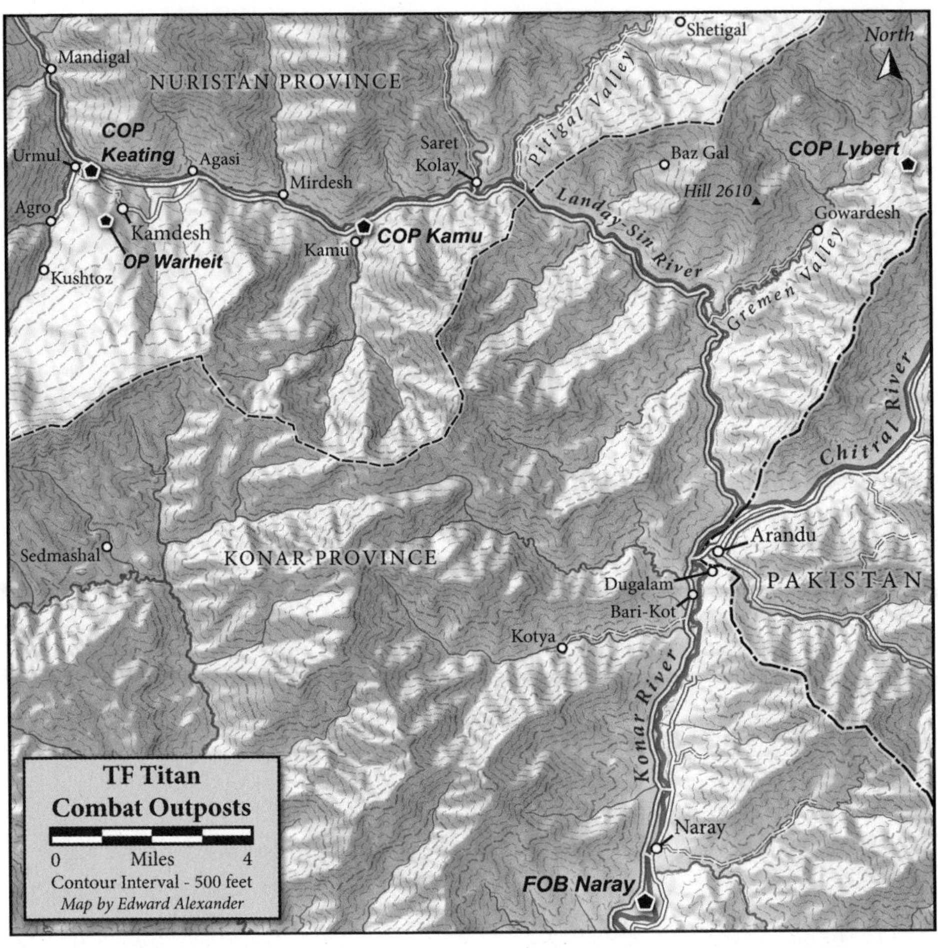

a narrow muddy road, at night, and as the driver, I'm not really sure (officers do not typically drive trucks, we sit the "shotgun seat" so we can Command and Control the convoy movements). The road gave way underneath his truck, and it rolled 300 feet down a steep cliff and into the river. The driver sustained serious injuries, but he will live. The canyon was too steep to drop a rescue hoist, so we had to pull him up using a rappelling rope from the road. By that time, his internal bleeding was irreparable, and he stopped breathing.

Conducting night-time convoys is a gamble that our commander recently decided to take . . . do we face the dangers of night driving on terrible roads or face a barrage of RPGs while driving during the day? For a while, the latter was taking its toll of wounded men, so we switched tactics hoping that events like yesterday would never happen.

It was such a senseless death of a kid with such unlimited potential . . . and so near the end of this tour it just makes everyone angry. Because I was close to Ben, I was appointed to serve as the officer in charge of inventorying all of his belongings and making sure everything is packaged correctly and shipped to his family in Maine without incident. This inventory will take me to 2 or 3 bases over the next couple of days, dealing with lawyers and mortuary affairs teams trying to make sure everything he owned is safeguarded. I am writing now from Kamdesh at the beginning of this inventory process.

On a lighter note, we had a nice Thanksgiving holiday here, it was of course before the incident. The weather finally cleared, and helos dropped in prime rib, real turkey, ham, sweet potatoes, shrimp, stuffing and cranberries. President Bush called our base and was connected to one of our soldiers to commend him for his work. This, of course, was well scripted and rehearsed. He called 9 other servicemen across the globe that day. After dinner, I even conducted my traditional post-turkey-dinner food coma nap, which is a rare treat for me.

We have now lost 8 men since May, two were from enemy fire and the rest were just terrible accidents. Overall, God has really blessed our unit because there have been so many close calls to speak of. Continue to pray for us . . . God willing we will all be home in 10 weeks. Please don't send mail after Jan 1st, since I might not get it in time before I leave.

Thanks so much, I miss everyone.

Please stay in touch, Ross

Special Note: As the Summary Court Martial Officer, I oversaw collecting Ben's personal items. To accomplish this, I needed to follow the trail of 3-71 CAV's footprints across eastern Afghanistan. Like me, Ben spent time and left personal gear at Bagram, JBAD, Naray, and Kamdesh. In mid-December, I processed the shipment and signed the forms with Mortuary Affairs at Bagram. I then felt compelled to send a personal letter to the parents of Ben Keating. I wanted to share with them my love and respect for their son, and to ensure they knew I tried my best to care for and package up all of his things. I sent the following letter to Ben's parents, and I also received a reply from them. During the summer of 2007, following my redeployment home, I made the trip to pay my final respects to Ben at the Riverside Cemetery in Springvale, Maine. Here is that correspondence:

17 December 2006

Mr. and Mrs. Keating,

Hello. My name is CPT Ross Berkoff and I am the Intelligence Officer for 3-71 CAV at FB Naray. I am writing to you both today with a very heavy heart. Ben was a good friend of mine in this unit and so loved and respected by his soldiers, peers, and superiors.

He had this great reputation among everyone in 3-71 CAV. . . When people thought of Ben Keating they thought of someone that is not only extremely intelligent and reliable, but with a certain charisma that motivated everyone around him to pick their heads up and keep on pushing on. I've known Ben since he first arrived at Fort Drum in 2004–05. At that time, I was the Personnel Officer and tried to help ease the transition of in-coming officers to the Post and to our organization. Ben was the immediate favorite of LTC Joe Fenty, our first commander. He was the epitome of the quiet professional. Just give him a task, and it gets done.

As an aside here, I would like to share with you a story from the Fenty family that they shared with me a few days after Ben's death. You may have already heard this. During the night of 26 Nov, Kristen Fenty (the wife of LTC Fenty) was going through some of her husband's personal things at home. While sorting through documents, a piece of paper slipped to the floor with LTC Fenty's writing on it. It was Ben's performance evaluation, Joe Fenty had written them out before putting them to the actual form—as you can imagine, all glowing remarks. Kristen read the comments and thought how much Joe Fenty respected Ben Keating as an officer and person. She believes that was Joe's way of telling her that Joe has found Ben in heaven and is watching out for him. I thought it was a nice sentiment and I shared it w/some of the officers here.

I would like you both to know that I was assigned to inventory and package Ben's personal belongings and prepare them for shipment to the U.S. The items left Afghanistan last week and are en-route to Aberdeen Proving Ground, Maryland. Issued military gear such as his helmet and rucksack will be separated from his personal belongings, the latter will be sent to your home address. They will contact you and make sure they have the right address before they send it. It should arrive sometime between 5–15 January. If you have any questions about his stuff, please don't hesitate to email me. I tried to do my best to sort through and organize what I could into like items.

I hope we meet one day. I know 3-71 CAV is very eager to meet the Keating family. I am sorry it has taken me so long to write this letter. To be honest, I didn't know where to begin. I also wanted to make sure his belongings were on the way to the U.S.

Ben was like a brother to many of us and will be sorely missed. I know there are no words of mine that could possibly attempt to assuage your bereavement at a time like this, but please know that Ben was a true American patriot, incredibly brave, modest and professional, a true gentleman, and an inspiration to all those he served with. I wish you and your entire family my heart-felt sympathies, and I hope you are all blessed with inspirational Christmas season.

My Warmest Regards, Ross Berkoff

12-17-2006

Dear Captain Berkoff,

I just want you to know how much we appreciate your kind words and the attention you have paid to gathering up Ben's personal belongings. On more than one occasion in the last couple of years, I told Ben that I would consider it *an awful tragedy* if he didn't survive this deployment. I was convinced that with his unique blend of intelligence, strength and courage he could make a more valuable contribution to this society in pursuit of his lofty ambitions in the civilian world. He agreed but felt that military service was a necessary prerequisite for things to come.

In truth, we saw an amazing transformation in him, starting with his R.O.T.C. experience at the University of New Hampshire and continuing with 3-71 Cav. We were consistently impressed by the quality of the young men we met when we attended Ben's graduation from AOBC at Ft. Knox in November of 2004 and during his final weekend at Fort Drum, last January.

Ben was just one among the brightest and best who currently serve in harm's way and who have the potential to become America's next Greatest Generation. When Ben was home for R&R in October, he was lean, strong and seemed larger than life. The many tributes to Ben's memory given in the last three weeks by Army colleagues deployed in Afghanistan, Iraq, South Korea and stationed at posts around the continental U.S. have helped us to understand that his life counted a great deal, despite its brevity.

Your message was written by a man whose parents must be very proud, and it is a source of genuine comfort to know that Ben was valued by such men.

Sincerely,

Ken Keating

13 December 2006. Letter Home. FOB Naray.

Hi everyone,

I just wanted to send out a quick update and let you all know that I am ok and nearing the end out here. We had a very nice memorial ceremony for Ben, and I understand his family has been remarkably strong through all of this. His parents are both Methodist pastors with an unshakable faith.

Our rear-detachment at Fort Drum had a large presence at Ben's funeral held in Maine last week. We renamed our outpost in Kamdesh to Camp Keating in his honor. He did so much to make that place what it is today. I spent last week at the Bagram Air Base near Kabul sorting through Ben's things and making sure it was prepared to be sent home. It was not a fun task, but I was nevertheless happy to get off Naray for a while to decompress.

Take a look at the attachment. I thought you may be interested in seeing some photos taken by a Spanish photographer last month during his embed time with 3-71 Cav. Some of the photos are really beautiful. I especially like the ones of the Catholic Chaplain offering the Eucharist to some of our soldiers at Camp Lybert—one of our mountain top outposts in Nuristan. That particular chaplain had to be inserted by helicopter for the day. No Rabbis in-bound on the calendar yet:) Even I made it into his photo collage, see page 12. It's a really eerie looking photo taken during a meeting with the Naray District police chief and governor. It almost looks like two different photos cropped together, modern day on the left and historic on the right. Sitting next to me is the Squadron S3 operations officer.

We are now in constant communication with our 82nd Airborne replacements and it seems like 80 percent of our daily duties consist of re-deployment tasks. Operations are slowing down immensely, mostly due to the annual winter lull in enemy activity. We are less than 8 weeks from starting our move home. Thanks so much for all of your prayers and emails following Ben's death. It meant a lot to me. Happy Holidays to everyone and stay in touch.

Love, Ross

22 December 2006. Letter Home. FOB Naray.

The Sergeant Major of the Army is arriving at FOB Naray today. He is the highest-ranking NCO in the Army. He wanted to experience Christmas with the Soldiers at one of the border bases in Afghanistan. The Army is trying make Dec 25 special for the Soldiers and right now our staff officers are busy coordinating a helicopter-inserted Holiday dinner to be dropped into Camp Lybert and Camp Keating. Quite literally dropped in, by a sling, since the terrain does not permit unnecessary landings. Whether Christmas or Hanukkah, it does not matter here. All normal feelings of American holidays in December tends to get drowned out by the local Mullah's daily prayer calls over the loudspeaker here, five times per day. All good though. I'm almost done. In six weeks, I will begin my journey home. I am looking forward to seeing everyone then.

Love, Ross

CHAPTER 17

HOME STRETCH

31 December 2006. FOB Naray.

Well, the old year is finally drawing to a close. When I look back on all the places I've been and things I've done over the past year, my mind rains reminiscences of the good men and friends that have been lost while fulfilling the duties of their nation's service. I'm going to try and sum up the past 12 months.

I rang in the new year of 2006 while standing with best friends on the 700-year-old Charles Bridge in the center of Prague in the Czech Republic. I returned to Sackets Harbor, New York in early Jan. and resumed my duties at Fort Drum, in final preparation for this deployment, and enjoying my last couple of weeks of freedom.

On 12 February, I left the United States with 3-71 Cav and the rest of 3rd BCT, the Spartan Brigade, aka Task Force Spartan, of the 10th Mountain Division. I spent the first month in Afghanistan in a large airfield base named FOB Salerno outside Khowst City. Here the squadron conducted a few minor operations along the Pakistan border, while preparing for a major operation to come—Mountain Lion—which took place in April and May in central Konar province.

On 13 March, I left Salerno with LTC Fenty, and a large 3-71 CAV convoy bound for what would become our squadron's official home—FOB Naray. With the local ODA 773, we conducted operations in late March around Naray, including engaging and killing enemy fighters for the first time, dismantling the Ayoub brothers hold over the valley. It would be the first of hundreds of enemy kills for Taskforce (TF) Titan, the 3-71 Cavalry's combined combat and combat support elements.

From 3 April 3 to 13 May, I remained at JBAD conducting intelligence analysis, and staff planning while the bulk of 3-71 CAV fought Op Mountain Lion. Less than a year before Mountain Lion, and in the same hills, Mike Murphy and his team of Navy Seals were killed during Operation Red Wings. Although we never found the cell leader responsible for that attack, Mountain Lion was still an extremely effective operation. Not one U.S. soldier was killed or wounded from enemy fire, and we inflicted heavy casualties on the enemy side, mostly during the battle of Chalas, 28 April through 3 May. But it was here, in the process of exfiltrating our men from Chalas, that our unit suffered a terrible tragedy: the loss of our beloved commander, LTC Fenty, and three other A Troopers: O'Donohue, Timmons, and Moquin. They died during a helicopter extraction that went wrong. The rest of May was spent consolidating the entire squadron at FOB Naray and recovering from 30 straight days of continuous combat operations.

In June, under a new commander, LTC Howard, we conducted our first reconnaissance patrols into the unchartered lands near Kamdesh in Nuristan province. No U.S. forces had ever entered this area, and there had not been an ANA presence here either. During one of these recon missions, we lost our first soldiers to enemy fire. On 21 June, SSG Jared Monti led a small 15-man team up a mountain top near Gowardesh village, but they were compromised and attacked by a much larger force. SSG Monti, SSG Lybert, and SPC Bradbury were killed in action, along with the medic, SSG Heathe Craig, who fell to his death, trying to rescue the wounded during a helicopter extraction.

In late July, we laid the first stones of our new outpost in Kamdesh, now officially called Camp Keating. The base was the target of enemy forces for the next few months. We built another base in early September near the same spot where the action of 21 June occurred. That base was named Camp Lybert, in honor of another of our fallen comrades. Throughout the Fall, we conducted continuous operations between our three bases, and many more good men were wounded in action, but thankfully no one killed.

I spent the month of August on leave with family and friends. On 6 October I left for COP Kamdesh to assist in the intelligence collection and analysis there. I stayed there for about four weeks. Another tragedy struck not long after I returned—on 26 November Ben Keating died of wounds received during a truck rollover. He was instrumental in the building of the camp in Kamdesh, and he died leading a convoy out of the base and back to Naray. Ben was posthumously promoted to the rank of captain and he was buried in Maine near his family's home. We recently held a ceremony at the Kamdesh outpost, on a very snowy cold day, renaming it Camp Keating.

The accident that took Ben's life caused us to take a serious look at the dangers of this road, and the road was officially closed to U.S. forces for an entire month. We are now just starting to get back on the road and conduct operations again. Not sure it's any safer today than it was a month ago, but what do I know? The LMTV that Ben was trying to take back to Naray should never have been at Kamdesh to begin with. LTC Howard wanted to prove to someone in at Brigade or Division command that he's making progress widening the road between the outposts, and he wouldn't listen to the advice of his commanders and staff officers who all said that road was not trafficable for a LMTV. Ben thought he could avoid another complex day-time ambush by launching in the middle of the night. Now that damned truck is sitting at the bottom of the Landay-Sin River. I still can't believe that Ben Keating is gone.

With our time ebbing to a close here, there's not much more we could do. Our 82nd Airborne replacements will begin arriving in country in about 10 days. I hope the story of this hard year and deployment ends with that. It has to. Right? In two weeks, our Advanced Party will begin its journey back to Fort Drum and I will follow about three weeks after that.

So, the question remains, what's next for me? I wish I knew for sure. A few days ago, I was offered a possible slot to begin a master's degree program at Columbia University, paid for by the Army. Following school, I would begin duty at West Point as a tactical instructor. Grad School + West Point . . . that's like five years of more active duty time. The Army is quick to just map out your life in 3- or 5-year chunks. I'm not sure I am ready to continue committing myself to all that time. I'll spend the next couple of weeks researching that program to see if it's viable for me.

May God bless our labors in the year about to open and grant some sense of peace to our Nation in these troublesome times. 2006, your time has finally come up and your departure is not regretted. So, goodbye 2006. I welcome the coming year with open arms, for it leads us ever closer to our homeward-bound journey.

15 January 2007. FOB Naray.

I've spent the better half of the last two weeks preparing for my replacement officer to arrive, the battalion S2 from the 82nd Airborne Regiment, and also supporting our final combat operation here.

From 11 January through 14 January we conducted our last squadron level deliberate operation to disrupt enemy sanctuaries in Kamdesh district. We were very successful when everyone returned safely.

(Top) 3-71 Cavalry Troopers at COP Lybert during the winter of 2007. COP Lybert was established along the border with Pakistan to conduct surveillance along illicit smuggling routes. (Bottom) Kamdesh village in the winter of 2006, overlooking the Landay-Sin River Valley. *Jeb Ridgeway*

On 11 January, CPT Dave Hammerschmidt from the 82nd Airborne arrived at Naray with a small S2 section, beginning the relief in place process between 3-71 and 1-508 PIR. For all major intents and purposes, my job is really done here. One week from now the rest of 1-508 will begin to flow in and hopefully I will move down to JBAD to begin staging there for our final push to Manas Air Base in Kyrgyzstan. Tentative dates to return to New York are 11–14 February—truly making this a one-year deployment.

I decided that after we redeploy and refit this spring, I will not remain on active duty, despite some of the very enticing offers including grad school. Instead, I will pursue a career in the Defense Intelligence Community as a civilian contractor. I do plan to continue to serve my country in the Army National Guard. With combat operations continuing to pick up in Iraq right now, I'm told not to risk it by joining the Individual Ready Reserve. By joining the National Guard, however, I will shorten my remaining service obligation. At least, that's the deal they're offering right now. Upon accepting the ROTC scholarship and getting commissioned, I contracted for a total of an 8-year service obligation which would come up in 2010—but I'm told by choosing to complete my service time in the Guard, I can officially "check out" and separate from the Army all together in 2009. I'll make that deal. Also, I think the Virginia or DC Guard units that I am looking at will probably not receive orders to Iraq or Afghanistan any time soon. At least, I like to tell myself that.

I have about 20 days left in Naray, after which I'll start heading home. I'm hoping next entry will be my last one in this journal.

16 January 2007. Letter Home. FOB Naray.

Hey everyone,

Sorry it's been so long since I sent out an update but as you can imagine we've all been incredibly busy trying to wrap up operations and conduct the change-out with the 82nd Airborne. We passed the holidays here as nicely as can be expected. On Christmas, my friends and I popped in Ralphie and *The Christmas Story* . . . we tried our best to keep it going for 24 straight hours, but there is just no one day here where we can blow off our job.

On New Years Eve, our howitzers lit up the mountainside surrounding Naray . . . we had reports that the enemy would attempt to rocket us that night (in deference to the Haj Pilgrimage in Mecca, if that makes any sense) . . . they didn't, but we did get to see a pretty stunning fireworks display on the taxpayers' bill. So, thanks. Last week, I returned from our last major operation, and it was a great success.

My replacement arrived here a few days ago and the bulk of the 82nd Airborne will fall in behind him. I've already started passing off my daily duties to the new S2. It feels pretty good, but I'm still 3 weeks away from leaving this base forever and it's going to crawl by.

I attached some photos taken during our Golden Spur ceremony today. It's a long tradition in the U.S. Cavalry to issue brass or golden-like spurs to Cavalry Troopers after proving themselves in combat. I earned mine while I was here back in 2003 but I guess now I'll have a second pair. We brought in some horses for the ceremony and then tried to kick off our own game of Buzkashi, which is a traditional sport among the horse cultures in northern Afghanistan and other parts of Central Asia. Just think horse polo, but replace the ball with the carcass of a goat. You may have seen it in Rambo 3. It's actually a pretty fun game.

I've been seriously contemplating "what's next" for me during these past few weeks. I voiced my complaint with the Army that the primary reason for getting out of active duty is the operational tempo that I've been running with the past few years. So, in an attempt to keep me in their ranks, Army HR proposed some very tempting offers to include admission to Columbia University's graduate school beginning this summer, among other institutions. The catch is that once I finally graduated, I'd be indebted to the Army until I was at least 33 years old. As much I want an Ivy League MS, I also want a life.

So I decided to finish my service in the Army National Guard instead. The Guard will guarantee me "stabilization" from ever deploying again until I can officially resign my officer's commission, two years from now. It's an opportunity for me to finally start a normal civilian life, while continuing to finish my service with honor, and not have to worry about ever being recalled. I knew there was a loophole out there somewhere. I'll keep you posted on which state I eventually land in. I'll be wrapping up Active Duty at Ft Drum this May, and I hope to take the summer off before I begin work as an intelligence contractor for the DoD or analyst for one of the Intelligence Community agencies.

So, that's my plan. For now, I'm just trying to get home. We don't know exactly when we will land in the U.S., but it will be sometime around Feb 12th . . . exactly 365 days after we left. Oh, I also attached a photo of me and my intelligence analysts . . . they broke the cigars out when they heard that the first group of the 82nd Airborne hit the ground here to replace us. I'll write one last time, a few weeks from now, when I know my exact arrival date. Thanks to all who kept our

CPT Berkoff on horseback at FOB Naray in January 2007, after receiving his second pair of golden spurs and preparing for a game of Buzkashi. *Author Collection*

spirits high with the packages and letters. I can't tell you how it makes us all feel, to know that we are so well supported from everyone back home . . . from best friends to complete strangers. Thank you!

Love, Ross

CHAPTER 18

EXTRA INNINGS

25 January 2007. Letter Home. FOB Naray.

Hi Family,

No words can describe how I felt when I was shaken out of a cold sleep, only to be told that we've been extended another four months. I should have realized something was up when we just received a new shipment of uniforms that were long overdue. I'm sure the Defense Sec Gates, who's been in his office for all of 2 weeks and came out here to visit, listened to some NATO general say that we needed more troops in Afghanistan—and that's it. The entire 3rd Brigade, and the 10th Mountain HQ all ordered to remain. We are now calling back hundreds of soldiers that already went home to return to their posts out here. All our equipment that we sent away, its coming back, or so we hope. It's just unreal. God help the man that made this decision when we lose another soldier. I've now been getting shot at for 12 months, lost good friends, jeopardized relationships, and even sprouted a few silver locks, and I've done all this for my country. I love my country, but if this deployment ever ends, I'll be damned if I love another. I'm trying to laugh at this, but I doubt I'll be able to sleep tonight.

I love you all and I'll be home whenever, Ross

26 January 2007. Letter Home. FOB Naray.

Hey Family,

It hasn't really set in yet that our homebound plans have been postponed for as long as 4 months. I would characterize the overall morale of our soldiers right now at an all-time low. Everyone is moping around, feeling bad for themselves, canceling hotel and plane reservations, including myself. I think it's healthy to be upset. It's not too dissimilar to losing comrades in a strange way. Everyone out here thought they would 100% be going home, but now, each of us can continue to ponder our own mortality a little bit longer. We need to show our grief but then get over it. We cannot allow our unit to implode from disappointment but just trying to overcome this and still get the job done.

I'm in no way hiding my disgust with the Army right now. Politicians in Washington and Generals so out of touch with the ground truth of soldier life on this frontier, are asking their soldiers to do things that they themselves could not do. The Allied Forces invaded Europe, defeated the 3rd Reich, and went back home to Baby Boom, in less time than 3-71 CAV will serve in this forgotten corner of the world. It's just unreal. I'm told we're going to be getting an extra compensation of $1000 for each month we're extended. My response has been that I'll pay the U.S. Government $2000 per month just to let me go home. We all feel as if we've earned the right to rejoin society. I paid my debt of gratitude to my father's father, for serving in their own times, and then some. But we're still here and we will attempt to start the projects and resume the operations that we thought we would be passing off to the 82nd Airborne.

I can tell you that Army Human Resources will be losing almost every single officer in this unit—largely due to the extension. Some of our best and brightest officers and soldiers, many of whom had 20-year careers in their futures, are now completely disenfranchised with the military. Many soldiers are dealing with marriages that were holding on by a thread, and now have to figure out, how to keep that thread from completely splintering.

Tell all of that to our policy makers who think they know what's best. Thanks again for your love and support.

Love, Ross

13 February 2007. Letter Home. FOB Naray.

Hey Everyone,

Well, I just passed my 365th day in country so in the spirit of that hallmark accomplishment I thought it was time for another update. First, I want to thank you all for the flood of emails I received offering the morale support. Getting through another four months out here is going to be a serious test on my mental constitution. It helps to know that you all have my back. Our

Soldiers that were en-route home, were recalled and found their way back to their homes here at FB Naray. I've been very busy these past few weeks trying to plan our Spring Campaign operations . . . every year in this country the Taliban and Al Q try to gain some momentum during the spring by launching new attacks. So, as long as we're still here, we might as well give it to em' hard and fast before we leave. We are now starting our 13th month in country, and the Squadron that I see before me is a mere skeleton of the unit that deployed last Feb. Sick, broken, weary from so much discipline has led to the undisciplined, on top of those missing from our ranks from wounds and death . . . so many men are no longer present for duty. To remedy this, we're getting a battery of artillerymen to help increase our fighting force. We even pushed some staff captains back down to the companies to fill platoon leader positions.

I attached some photos that I took during a recent trip into Pakistan. In an attempt to improve the relations with the Pakistani military, I often meet with Pakistani intel officers and commanders that occupy the border outposts on the other side. This particular unit is an elite group known as the Chitral Scouts (named after the district they cover). They repeatedly mentioned their pride regarding their ancestral ties to Alexander the Great, and their role in the War on Terror as the most critical since many believe Bin Laden has been hiding in Chitral (they were quick to aver, however, that the Bin Laden claims are nothing but rumors, and that the Chitralis are all peace-loving moderates). Their officers are all college educated, English-speaking, and carry themselves with a smidgeon of British aristocracy that must have carried over. Their "orderlies" laid out a fine spread of fried potatoes, chicken and vegetables, and steamed milk served with a pasty cocoa substance (I haven't hit the can yet, but I'm not looking forward to it). Interestingly enough, their soldiers have the same concerns that we have . . . the international border is inherently porous and there is no way to fully protect insurgents from crossing over at will—all we can do is make it harder for them. We discussed the pros and cons to using landmines (which are a hard sell for the civilians and goat herders that live along the border), and then the famous Border Fence we keep hearing about. The enemies we are fighting are too intelligent and resilient to be stopped by a fence. It's just a completely absurd idea. Say nothing of the monumental task it would be to build a fence at altitudes of 12–16,000 feet. Anyways, overall it was a good meeting . . . I didn't get shot at, I ate off of real dishes, and they even presented me with a Chitrali Scout "Pakol" hat, festooned with a mountain lion—their unit crest—a very appropriate token considering my own division.

So, the Army chiefs got what they wanted—two combat brigades fighting side by side in the volatile northeast. It just comes at the expense of 3,500 Ft Drum Soldiers who have not had a rest in a long time. Some of my soldiers were the first to go on their block leaves, last April, so we are now trying to send them on a four-day pass to Qatar—an R & R spot for soldiers where beer and entertainment is plentiful. Four days of heaven for another four months of hell, we're saying.

I won't be making it to Qatar, but maybe I'll get another trip to Pakistan! I think I've hit rock bottom if I'm getting excited over that. Please keep sending your emails and packages . . . they are so very much appreciated by everyone here. I miss you all and can't wait to get home for good.

Be in touch, Ross

14 February 2007. FOB Naray. Still Here.

During the early morning hours of 25 January, well before sunrise, I was woken up and told to report to LTC Howard's quarters. This was unusual. As I walked over, I thought either someone important was just killed, or some major attack had taken place in country that changed the ballgame. I walked into his room and saw somber faces of my fellow officers, as the word had already gotten out: we're being extended another four months. I've written about this extensively in my letters home over the past two weeks.

I suppose worse things could happen to units deployed. For instance, we are fortunate to have only sustained relatively light casualties compared to other units in country. 1-508th PIR was slotted to take our place and they have now been shifted south to Kandahar. By 25 January, I was only days away from going home. In fact, our advanced party did actually make it all the way home to Fort Drum and they were setting up a reception area for us (to process our weapons and sensitive items, etc.). We were so confident we were leaving that I gave away most of my personal belongings that I didn't want to lug home—books, DVDs, magazines, pillows, blankets and mattresses we bought at the Hajimart, even my damned bunk.

Secretary Gates was here, meeting with brass, and the decision was made. We need more troops in country to accomplish our mission. So, the 3rd BCT in its entirety has been extended until June. Our Division HQ, however, went home to Fort Drum and they have been replaced by a new Joint Task Force from the 82nd Airborne Division HQ. So now I begin OEF VIII? I guess this is technically my third OEF rotation.

(Top) CPT Berkoff wearing a traditional pakol (hat) with members of Pakistan's Chitrali Scouts during one of his several trips across the border to share intelligence. (Bottom) CPT Berkoff (far left) with MAJ Drew Ornelas, 3-71 CAV Operations S3, during an engagement with Naray's district governor and district police chief (far right). *Author Collection*

I went on another patrol into Arandu, Pakistan, yesterday to meet with their military. It was a good meeting, and they laid out a fine spread of local foods served on real dishes. The staff has been busy the last few days planning future operations. The countdown has been reset and we are now roughly 90 days until we begin the next RIP. This will be with elements of the 173rd Airborne Brigade Combat Team, I am told, stationed in Europe.

28 February 2007. Letter Home. FOB Naray.

Hey Family,

Not much new on my end. We built another operating base along the Pak border, south of here, calling it Camp Monti. Missions and routines continue. I passed another birthday in this country, which was my third in the past four years, but even worse another Mardi Gras missed. We are soon to be starting our 14th month in country. I find that whatever curiosity that was had by our men, with respect to this country, has been fully satisfied . . . and all we can do is think about home.

Last week, we lost another soldier . . . SGT Buddy Hughie, who was actually in the Oklahoma National Guard, but assigned to our unit for the deployment. He fell from enemy fire while trying to save wounded Afghan soldiers during an ambush near our Kamu outpost (east of Kamdesh). I didn't know him well, but it hurts every time.

The packages have been coming in and are so appreciated. The Washington Redskins cheerleaders are touring several nearby bases in this corner of Afghanistan but decided to skip out on Naray. Big surprise. So, friends have sent pics of their dance performances, but somehow it's not the same.

I received an email from my future replacement a few days ago which was a good feeling. He is with the 173rd Airborne in Europe and claims he's coming here to take my place in May. I think this guy is like the third officer who has written to me in the last 6 months, saying that he will replace me at Naray . . . so I'll believe it when I see it.

Missing you all, Ross

CHAPTER 19

ANOTHER SPRING OFFENSIVE

25 March 2007. Letter Home. FOB Naray.

Hey everyone,

I realized that it's been a while since I sent out a mass update so here we go. March has been rolling by pretty fast and we are now about 8 weeks away from turning over our area of responsibility to our replacements from the 173rd Airborne. Right now we are planning on an arrival date at Fort Drum during the first week of June, which would officially make this deployment 16 months. Its just hard to believe sometimes. The packages have been coming in by friends and strangers alike, and after picking through my favorite junkfood vices, I usually pass them off to our out-lying bases on the mountain tops. They are all so very much appreciated.

I attached some pics (via PowerPoint) that show just how difficult a process it is to mail here sometimes. In many cases, the boxes you are sending go through three or four different air bases, before being loaded up into our own convoys, who then begin the 150 mile (8 hours on Afghan roads) trip to Firebase Naray. With a second combat brigade now in country, the mail delivery system has been considerably stressed, not to mention the phone connectivity . . . it's been harder and harder to reach the Army switchboard operators to call home lately, but I'm persistent.

Operationally speaking, we have all been very busy as usual. We built two more outposts in the last 2 months. One of those posts is being manned by our Bravo Troop and is called Camp Monti—named after SFC Jared Monti,

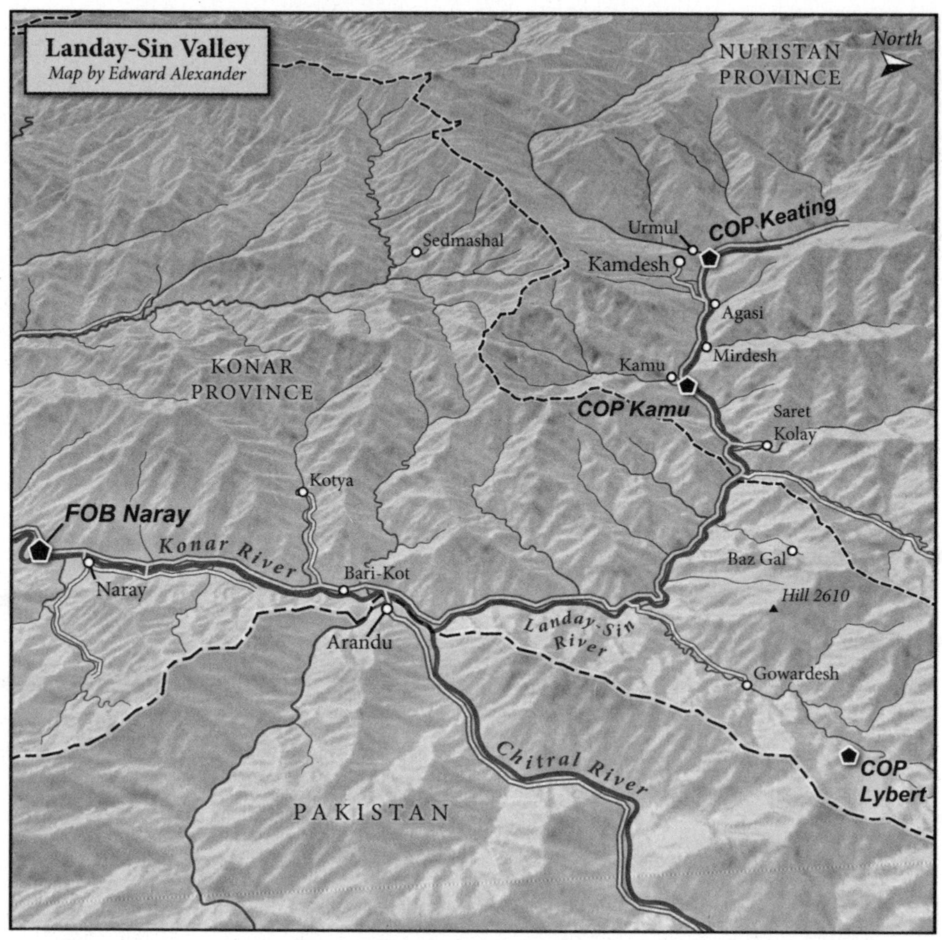

undoubtedly our finest non-com, who was killed last summer in a firefight (he was submitted for a posthumous Medal of Honor, which we are waiting to hear back from).

I also went along for a large operation into the northern frontier of our boundary, in the Barge Matal district. In the mountains of the Hindu Kush, we air assaulted into one of the most remote and lawless corners along the Pakistani border. U.S. forces have not yet settled this area, and the people were very frightened to see us to say the least. We calmed them down over tea and explained our intentions and they became very receptive. It's an area where foreign fighters are thought to be training, so if we can gain the support of the populace, than maybe they will start pushing out the bad guys—a standard counter-insurgency tactic. On my second day in the village, a huge snowball fight erupted between the local kids and our platoons, followed by snowman building lessons—all in good fun but also integral tasks in defeating the insurgency here in Afghanistan.

I'm sure those kids will have some good stories to tell their kids and grandkids, when the Americans landed in our village and pelted us with snowballs and showed us how to build snowmen. I included a couple shots of the snow filled village and mountains, just before I landed there.

Love, Ross

13 April 2007. Letter Home. FOB Naray.

Things have been really hectic here lately with our "spring offensive" operations. We've been trying to pre-empt the Taliban's plans by conducting our own deliberate operations in certain areas and in many cases we stirred up the hornets' nest. We've actually found ourselves back in some of the same mountains and valleys where we were fighting last April this time—during Operation Mountain Lion.

You may recall that operation because it was the area where the Chinook crashed, and LTC Fenty died along with 9 others. It's frustrating, because by going back there it almost feels like we didn't get anywhere in the last 12 months of fighting. But that's not really the case. Some of you may have seen the Diane Sawyer interview with MG Rodriguez and her coverage in my corner of Afghanistan. She met with the overall U.S. commander, MG Rodriguez, who in my opinion did a very poor job of articulating our accomplishments here. I suppose Diane's stature can be intimidating to even our most seasoned U.S. generals. She mentions that the general's helicopter was shot at by RPGs a few days before the interview took place. Well, it was on Easter Sunday, the General came out here to Naray to pin awards and eat turkey and ham with the troops. . . . Once he arrived at Naray I gave him an intelligence update, and then he flew around our battlefield to see our outposts. Well, we can thank the local bad guys that I track so closely for making that day memorable—luckily they were bad shots and I'm glad to report that those particular miscreants are no longer with us.

I had a chance to experience my own holiday service here. A lay-leader Army officer who has plans to enter Rabbinical school came to Naray to lead a Seder service. It was a bit unnerving to hear over the loud speaker here, "a Jewish service will now be held in the chapel." Haha, it might have been a good thing that I arrived to the chapel armed, because we have just about as many Muslim workers on this base as we do U.S. soldiers at times—and the enemy's spy network is vast. Other than having to occasionally raise our prayer voices over the sounds of mortar rounds and helicopter blades, the service felt like a little slice of home. I even managed to corral the 4 other Jewish soldiers on FOB Naray to attend.

Our sister-unit out here, 1-32 Infantry, has had a rough couple of weeks. They lost 2 soldiers from the same platoon in two separate incidents . . . hard to accept sometimes when you consider that we should have all redeployed home 2 months ago. I recently heard a statistic that made my heart sink: our brigade has lost 40 Soldiers and sustained over 300 wounded during the course of our deployment, so far. Please god, let there be no more.

I am so sick of seeing new people come through FOB Naray. Since I arrived at Naray last year, I have seen three different Special Forces detachments, I'm on my third Afghan Army unit here, my third Provincial Reconstruction team, my second cohort of National Guard-ANA Trainers, and countless numbers of other people that come and go, or have just been assigned to Naray and come prancing up to my desk all excited to be here. Well good for them, but all we want to do is get outta here. I read in the news today that all soldiers forward-deployed had their tours extended 3 months in both theaters. I just don't know how the higher ups ever expect their numbers to retain if they keep along this path. The news won't affect me, since I was already extended 4 months—which is seemingly the biggest turd you can eat while deployed in the Army today. It just solidifies my disgust with our Army leadership and my confidence in my choice for a new profession.

We only have about four weeks left of deliberate operations, before we welcome our replacements in country and begin handing off the torch to them. If you plan to send me anymore mail, please do so before the beginning of May—any later and I might not get it. I have daily internet contact now, except here and there when I leave the wire.

Ross

8 May 2007. Letter Home. FOB Naray.

Hey everyone,

There is finally some light at the end of this 16-month long tunnel. Our replacements have begun to arrive (for real, this time), and although we are still busy as ever conducting operations up to the end, it still feels good to see the patch of the 173rd Airborne walking around FOB Naray.

A quiet moment underground. 3-71 Cavalry Trooper reads in solitude inside a bunker at COP Keating, far from home. *Jeb Ridgeway*

I've been running around non-stop these past few weeks. I made a couple trips across the border into Pakistan again. It always surprises me (or embarrasses) how professional and well-educated the Pakistani officers are compared to their Afghan army officer counterparts, who we are supposed to be mentoring. The meetings laid the groundwork for the beginning of real communication between U.S. forces operating along the Afghan border and the Pak military on the other side. Now, whenever I get intel of bad guys crossing the border, I can call them up directly and give them a grid—and vice versa. It's pretty amazing progress from when I first got up here.

I also just recently returned from an operation in an area called Barge Matal—it's the northern most Afghan district along the Pak border, that's under U.S. control. It was stunningly remote, but so serene and beautiful that if it were in the U.S., it would already be a rec-resort for the rich and famous. I attached a pic that I took during a march into the district's main village. It is so isolated that not even the Soviets were able to breach its borders. The elders recalled that the last westerners they had seen were the British (early 1900s I think) . . . and many must have bred with their foreign guests back then because I never saw so many red and blonde beards before. We pitched to them our plans to come back with more soldiers, more humanitarian goods, a permanent base, and more money for reconstruction projects, but I think these people were smart enough to see right through all that. They realize that wherever U.S. forces make camp in this country, the Al Qaeda and Taliban inevitably emerge to target them. Right now, they say they enjoy peace and prosperity without the Coalition's help, and "when we build it, they will come" is the unspoken sentiment. Unfortunately, they are probably right. But such is our never-ending appetite for "progress" in this country. From an intelligence standpoint, there is much more to it. Whether or not the Barge Matal people believe it, pretty senior bad guys flock to their mountains because it's so isolated from U.S. presence. That's the real reason why we want to expand there. Ok, that's the end of my country lesson for today.

The Chief London correspondent for CNN, Nic Robertson, came to Naray to interview a few of the officers here. He was finishing up a 2-month tour and actually filmed me giving an intelligence update. I doubt, however, it will ever make its way on the air. I remember watching him on the news as a kid—he was always the first face on CNN inside some 3rd world country's conflict. On 5 May, I flew south to Jalalabad airfield to speak at the dedication ceremony that renamed it Forward Operating Base (FOB) Fenty. It's hard to believe it's been a year since our first commander, and three other 3-71 soldiers, died in that crash. They say time heals all wounds, but one year later, I don't think I've healed all that much. Business continues out here, without much time to really mourn anyone. I think seeing his wife Kristen and meeting his baby daughter Lauren next month, along with visiting his Arlington grave will give me some closure.

Love, Ross

CHAPTER 20

FOB FENTY

13 May 2007. FOB Naray.

I suppose with the extension and some of my letters home I've grown tired of logging entries into this journal, but I wanted to make another contribution before this deployment finally ends.

On 19 February, I flew to Bagram to attend a meeting with my New Jersey district Congressman, Rep. Steve Rothman. Unfortunately, he was weathered-in somewhere and he could not attend. So I got to enjoy a few days of relaxation on that large airfield. It might as well be Nebraska compared to our life here at Naray. The same day I left for Bagram, Alpha Troop got into a big firefight near Kamu village. Sergeant Buddy Hughie was shot down by enemy fire, trying to rescue a wounded ANA soldier. SGT Hughie was not part of 3-71 CAV organically, but he was attached to Alpha Troop from a national guard unit and he served as a security force soldier that travels with and helps mentor the ANA. He was the ninth and hopefully the last soldier to die in combat in our Task Force Titan.

On 23 February, my 27th birthday, I flew back to Naray and I returned to my daily duties and responsibilities. March and April were a continuation of combat operations. We set up a small outpost in Kamu village, in that police compound that I mentioned back in October. Alpha Troop—already strung out and broken—was ordered to keep a platoon of Troopers at the Kamu Outpost to keep up relations with locals in that area and step-up security patrols.

In early March we got into a big gun fight near Nishigam, a village along the road a little south of Naray. Probably no big coincidence, but we recently built a new outpost near there too, named Camp Monti after SFC Jared Monti.

Bravo Troop basically lives at Camp Monti now. We captured a Taliban fighter and we killed about three or four others. This was the first instance of a captured enemy fighter during my deployment. As the S2, I play a critical role in "PUC operations" or Persons Under Custody. He was brought to our holding cell and HUMINTers from my own S2 team, in addition to ODA here, all contributed to the interrogation. The PUC told us he was paid to shoot at Americans. He says he's poor and he just needed the money. And that's probably all true. Still though, we had to send him by helicopter to the main detention center at Bagram. It was a strange feeling to actually talk to a Taliban fighter. Up close and personal. For all these years, I've only seen them operate in the shadows, from a great distance, through night vision goggles or drone imagery. They were not people, they were "the enemy." Listening to this boy tell his story changed me. It made me think of what the Army Cavalry character LT John Dunbar said: maybe they are not the bogeymen they are made out to be. I'm not really sure if that's true, but I felt wholly disoriented by the encounter.

In late March, and then again in late April, we flew north into Barge Matal District. This district is the last unchartered area in Nuristan along the Pakistani border and is due north of Kamdesh. Barge Matal is like the new Kamdesh. With lots of new brass in country, it's the "next cool place" we need to go and set up an outpost. Well, they can have it. We're so tired of setting up outposts. The locals in Barge Matal were surprised to see us as we may have been the first Westerners to breach their borders since the British.

On 30 April I flew north into Barge Matal for a brief reconnaissance. I landed a few kilometers short of the village and hiked in with LTC Howard, and parts of Alpha Troop. Some of the CIA case officers came with us too . . . looking for any hints of intel on Bin Laden in these parts. Once in Barge Matal, we held a village shura with several score of village elders and prominent local politicians, but we began to receive news that an assassination had just occurred nearby. A famous warlord who had turned into a very vocal pro-U.S. and pro-Afghan Government leader was killed by the Taliban or other thugs near Kamu. His name was Mullah Fazal Ahad, and for while his name was associated with radical Salafist-based Islam and anti-Coalition propaganda. In fact, over the past few months, I had been receiving intelligence reports that he was playing both sides quite adeptly, and I was careful to ensure my intelligence assessments (sent up higher) included those nuances. LTC Howard was quick to bring down his wrath upon me for it. Howard was trying his best to show his higher ups that he's got a grip on the security situation here. In truth, no one does.

In December, Fazal Ahad apparently turned a leaf and began his tenure as the chief of the Security Shura for Eastern Nuristan. We obviously needed his

CPT Berkoff patrols through Barge Matal to meet with the Governor of Nuristan. *Ross Berkoff*

help. The reports say he was pulled out of his truck near Kamu and executed by the local HIG, but I tend to believe only outsiders could have done this, or more likely foreign fighters, would be so bold to murder this popular local mullah. Or maybe, the local insurgents just hated him that much for turning? His death has caused an uproar among the masses and 3-71 CAV has been called into action once again, this time to find and capture the Taliban fighters responsible for his killing and turn them over to Afghan security forces to handle punishment. Easy right? Despite the fact that we're in the middle of a RIP to get out of this damned country, we now have orders to deploy an assault force into Kamdesh and Barge Matal tomorrow for our last major operation to find those responsible for killing Ahad. Tomorrow, I will be moving north to Camp Keating by Blackhawk helicopter and leading the Squadron Intelligence Node[1] from there—closer to the fight. I hope and pray that everyone returns safely, and we make no serious

1 Refers to the full range of intelligence apparatus that I had arrayed at Camp Keating including all-source analysts, human intelligence collectors and signals intelligence platforms to support our area of operations.

contact. I am tired of fighting and would be more content if this entire operation turns out to be a dry hole, without finding or killing anyone.

In late April and again on 3 May, I went on a few more patrols across the border into Arandu, Pakistan. This time, we were accompanied by OGA intelligence officers who hoped to meet the Pakistani Intelligence Security Directorate or ISI, as their agents were known to be at or near the meeting. However, the ISI guys failed to show up. The meetings with the Pakistani military were informative nevertheless and they served us a nice fine spread of local Pakistani food, coffee, and chai.

The preponderance of our replacement unit 1-91 Cavalry (RSTA—just like us) of the 173rd Airborne has arrived in country and will begin their piecemeal movements to our many FOBs over the course of the next three or four days. By the time I return from this major operation, I will begin handing my tasks over to the new S2. I'm supposed to leave Naray in 12 days and begin my homeward bound travels. I hope to arrive in the U.S. on or around June 1. I've been at this firebase so long I just saw the third ODA detachment rotate in. Three different ODA units have come and gone over the past 12 months, but I am still here.

On 3 May I flew to Jalalabad Airfield so I could help dedicate the airfield's newly name FOB Fenty. On 5 May, on the one-year anniversary, we had a very solemn and moving naming ceremony, with the presentation of the FOB Fenty sign. COL Nicholson approached me when I arrived and he asked me if I'd like to say a few words at the dedication. At a podium, the next day, I was allowed to speak for a couple of minutes about what LTC Fenty meant to me. Other speakers included CSM Byers, COL Nicholson, and LTG Lloyd Austin, who used to be our Division Commander, but is now leading the 18th Airborne Corps. It's hard to believe it's been a year since that terrible crash. I remember that night vividly.

These were my words at the podium at the newly named FOB Fenty, which I had written out in advance, the day prior:

> LTG Austin, MG Rodriguez, COL Nicholson, Distinguished Guests and Fellow Spartans,
>
> I remember the events of May 5, 2006, very well. It was Operation Mountain Lion, D-Day +25. I was here at JAF, conducting intelligence liaison between our brigade staff and my squadron who was forward deployed in central Konar. LTC Joe Fenty had just flown into the airfield during twilight morning, and after a few hours of sleep, he was the first one into the office to start the day's work. For anyone familiar with his work ethic back at Fort Drum, this

(Top) CPT Berkoff patrols through Barge Matal to meet with the Governor of Nuristan. (Bottom) Afghan National Army soldier hovers for warmth during the winter of 2007 in Kamdesh. *Jeb Ridgeway*

CPT Berkoff (right) with CPT Roy Chiquitucto at the FOB Fenty dedication, May 5, 2007. Roy assumed platoon leadership for 2nd Platoon/Apache Troop when Ross returned home from Afghanistan in April 2004. *Author Collection*

was no surprise. The man had been humping the mountains with his soldiers for the better part of the month and he rushed back to Jbad to conduct final coordination before Commanding/Controlling the nighttime extraction of 3-71 Cav from the Chalas Ghar mountains.

When I saw him, he looked more tired than I've never seen him before. His hair was longer than usual, his ACUs had that now very familiar tarnish and stench. And one would think he was bearing the weight of the world on his shoulders. After all, only a few weeks earlier, his wife Kristen had given birth to their first child Lauren. Also the previous week, our Task Force sustained our first casualties when four ANA soldiers were killed by an IED. I know he personally felt the grief that went along with that. But despite all that going on in his mind, he first saw me and said "Ross did you ever get a chance to see that Jewish chaplain I had sent over for Passover?" That one question taken with everything else going on at the time, just summarizes everything I've known or believed about Joe Fenty. That his love for his Soldiers supersedes everything.

No matter what he always made time to sincerely ask you about your well-being, or your child's illness, or if you enjoyed your weekend. I first met Joe Fenty when I interviewed to be the first S1 of 3-71 Cav about three years ago. He struck me as a soft spoken, yet omnipotent commander. But over the years he became much more than just my boss. He became a mentor, a friend and a father figure. His life and his death will change me forever.

I'm honored to be here to dedicate this airfield, but in my opinion, there's no monument monumental enough to bear his name in commemoration. On the contrary, it was his life that will serve as the real monument with the thousands of people that he touched over the 41 years of his life. They will help carry on his legacy to include his young daughter Lauren, who as far as I'm concerned about two dozen surrogate fathers here in 3-71 Cav that can't wait to meet her. In closing, I want to say it's been my honor to serve in this fine brigade. I have had the opportunity to watch this unit grow from our formative years on Old Post, to now this hard fighting force on our 16th month in Regional Command-East. I will forever stand in awe of what we accomplished. Climb To Glory! Spartans!

Special Note: I had no idea when I wrote these words, that almost four years later to the day, FOB Fenty would be used as the staging area for Seal Team 6 to launch into Pakistan to conduct the raid that killed Osama Bin Laden. Some reports suggest the body of Bin Laden was secured on the CIA compound at FOB Fenty before being dumped into the Indian Ocean. Thinking back, I believe Joe Fenty would be proud to have his name memorialized in support of the U.S. operation that killed the planner of September 11th and the leader of Al Qaeda.

CHAPTER 21

WHISKEY FOR MY MEN, BEER FOR MY HORSES

30 May 2007. Letter Home. Bishkek, Kyrgyzstan.

Hey Family,

Well after a 2-hour nap on a cold cement floor along the airfield at Bagram, I finally heard my social security number called which meant I could board a C-17 Jet bound for Manas, Kyrgyzstan. We finally took off at 8am this morning for a very queasy 2-hour plane ride. I overheard the pilots bragging afterwards of their stunt exploits with the jet which caused most on board to feel immediately ill . . . including myself. Once I got off and had a good meal and shower, I felt better.

The transient living conditions for the soldiers passing through here have somehow declined—I remember this being a cush base, but I suppose that's only for the Air Force who have to deal with their arduous 4-month long tours. They make me sick. For those of us who've been roughing it for over a year, we were welcomed to another circus tent, again with no working a/c, and filled to the max occupancy of—wait for it—250 soldiers. Sorry if I sound bitter and tired, but I am. I know that home is so close, so I'm making the best of the situation, despite the gross living disparity so ubiquitous here. They even have a 2-beer limit bar open for all Air Force soldiers on this base—real beer too, not the fake stuff. Off limits for Army Soldiers passing through, of course. How I long for freedom again?! I've spent the last 16 months worried about everyone else's freedom except my own. One more leg of this journey, and a few more days of waiting.

Love and miss you, Ross

2 June 2007. Letter Home. Bishkek, Kyrgyzstan.

Hey Everyone,

Well, this will be my last mass email during what turned out to be Operation Enduring Freedom VII and VIII. I left FOB Naray about a week ago and after spending a few days at Bagram Airbase near Kabul, I flew to Manas Air Base in Bishkek, Kyrgyzstan which is where I currently sit in limbo.

The month of May seemed to fly by. Ya know, my deployments have always been filled with difficult, monotonous, routines, punctuated with periods of great excitement and adrenalin. Somehow, the latter summed up the month of May for me, more than the former. In early May, every one of our firebases were attacked in what looked like some kind of massive enemy coordination. I was playing soccer on the heli-pad when I heard what sounded like a train whistle, I looked to my left and watched a volley of 3 rockets impact outside the outer wall of our base. Luckily, they were set on timers and the enemy didn't have a chance to zero their mark.

Then, on May 14th, as our unit was in Nuristan on a manhunt mission for an insurgent cell responsible for assassinating a local government leader, the Taliban must have been waiting for us because they conducted a very effective ambush as some of our platoons traversed along the floor of the river canyon. We were traveling with a fresh crop of Afghan National Army soldiers who had just been relocated from the arid deserts of Kandahar. Out of the 40-man Afghan company moving with our convoy, 14 of them were killed outright in the ensuing fire-fight—they just were not ready or trained to handle a fight in the Nuristan mountains. The local Nuristani elders that I talked to after the battle were visibly disturbed with the news. It's mostly their own hothead sons doing all the shooting from the mountains in the name of "jihad" . . . but the local elders averred that there is no jihad, they repeat over their loudspeakers that the Americans are here to build, not to fight. This is not propaganda, it's the truth . . . we've done very few offensive operations, every time we have to fight, it's purely self-defense. The local elders were so sad that so many of their own Afghans were killed, by fellow Afghans. It seems to me to be the emerging alloy of Civil War here.

Anyways, five of our own soldiers were wounded on that day, but thank god all will recover. One of our gunners had an angel on his shoulder . . . a 7.62mm round passed right through his mouth and neck but somehow missed every major artery. Even our embedded photographic journalist (from Ireland) received some serious gunshot wounds but I hear he will pull through too . . . all of this and we were trying to find the insurgent/assassins and conduct a relief-in-place with the 173rd who was trickling into our area.

My replacement from the new unit had a rocky start which actually delayed my scheduled departure by a few days, but he took the reins after about a week of coaching and I got the green light to leave. It was a great feeling to step off the Chinook helicopter that safely carried me to Bagram last week . . . my last helo ride in Afghanistan. For all intents and purposes, I was out of harms way. So now, I've been trying to pass the time here as best as I can. On Monday morning, I'll begin the 18-hour journey back to Fort Drum.

This last year and a half have been the hardest of my life and I want to thank all of you for making it just a little bit more bearable with all your emails, letters, care packages. They all went a really long way at making our lives and jobs a little bit easier. I am SO excited to finally return to the U.S. and begin my transition out of the Army and don civilian suits again. People here are shocked when I tell them I am leaving, the common response is always "you seem like you love this stuff." Well, I do love what I do and I know my service in Afghanistan will serve as this immeasurable space of time for the rest of my life . . . but I feel like I've given 110 percent of all that I am for the past 5 years and there is no way I can keep up that pace. Since the soldiers deserve nothing less, this means it's time for me to move on. So exactly 478 days after I left Sackets Harbor, NY on a cold wintry morning, I will be returning there again to begin a new chapter. Thanks again for all your love and support. Please stay in touch.

Love, Ross

3 June 2007. Manas Air Base. My Last Entry. Bishkek, Kyrgyzstan.

It's hard to describe my feelings right now. It's such a potent combination of overwhelming joy, overlayed with despair and sorrow that not everyone is coming home.

The day after my last entry was another significant date for this deployment: 14 May 2007. On that morning, I air-assaulted[1] into Kamdesh, to Camp Keating, onto its river-logged landing zone. I set up an S2 Node and intelligence collection point, from a position closer to the front. We were pursuing the insurgents who had executed Mullah Fazal Ahad, a famous Mujaheddin fighter during the Soviet era, and an outspoken radical fundamentalist during the Taliban era,

1 To deploy ground-based military forces by rotary-wing aircraft (typically Blackhawk or Chinook) to seize and hold key terrain or conduct other offensive, defensive, or stability operations.

and someone who, most recently, was one of the more influential pro-Afghan government leaders in this part of Nuristan. The man certainly knew how to pick sides, but it caught up with him at the end. Our manhunt in the Kamdesh mountains was unsuccessful in finding the killers, but we got into a much larger pickle down the road.

A platoon of mounted troopers from Alpha Troop, along with a company of ANA, were moving towards the Kamu outpost when they were ambushed. This was probably the most well-coordinated, planned-out attack against our convoys that we have seen yet. In the ensuing melee, 14 ANA soldiers were killed several more wounded, and five Troopers from Alpha and Bravo Troop were wounded. Our battle drills were dialed in at this point: once ambushed, drive through the kill zone as fast as possible. Easier for us to do in our armored trucks. The ANA, however, with their men crammed and exposed riding in the open beds of their Ford pick-up trucks, they naturally jumped out and sought cover. This chaos was their death knell. Our trucks pushed through but the ANA had no where to run or hide. Many of the dead ANA soldiers were dumped into the river by local fighters. I was told some of their bodies washed up over 100 miles away south of Naray. We made one attempt to go back and retrieve their bodies but we were ambushed a second time when we tried. During this fight, SGT Steele—one of the original Cav scouts from when we were still under Captain Barnes in 2004, was shot in the face manning his .50 caliber machine gun. The round passed right through his mouth and cheeks and exited his neck, somehow missing every major artery. He was relocated to the U.S., along with PFC Kittle, who had a gunshot wound to the shoulder blade. Both will recover.

I said goodbye to Kamdesh once and for all, and returned to FOB Naray on 17 May and I made ready for my replacement, CPT George Hughbanks, of 1-91 CAV. He finally arrived to take the reins on 19 May. I was slotted to leave Naray on May 23 and move back to the U.S. on the 31st. LTC Howard, however, wanted to ensure that my S2 replacement received enough coaching time with me. So I was ordered to remain a few extra days. I briefed CPT Hughbanks and his intelligence section on the many lessons that we've learned over the course of 16 months of hard fighting.

On 25 May, the day before I left Naray, CPT Tom Bostick—one of the newly arrived Troop Commanders from 1-91 CAV, asked me if I could brief him and his leaders on "enemy threats in this area." He and his guys are going to replace Matt Gooding and Able Troop out in Kamu and Kamdesh. I took out my maps and showed Bostick's team all of the icons indicating the enemy's preference to launch ambushes from the same general locations, time and time again. Bostick asked me why we continue to drive through those death traps? I tried to explain, the terrain doesn't offer many options. He was cool about it, and he thanked me profusely, and he said he'll make sure his platoons are made aware of the Named Areas of Interest (NAIs) and will do everything he could to avoid them, even if it meant dismounting and taking to the hills. I wished him luck with that. I provided similar threat briefing to LTC Chris Kolenda, the 1-91 CAV commander, and some of his staff officers.[2]

In the middle of our relief-in-place and right after the disastrous 14 May operation, some really good news finally came in to boost our morale . . . Toby Keith was traveling with the USO and decided at the last minute to see the "outer bases". . . which he isn't supposed to do. So, he flew to Naray (with almost no entourage) and sat underneath our howitzers with nothing but a wooden bench and a guitar. My 2nd Platoon soldiers from my first deployment to Afghanistan introduced me to Toby Kieth. Despite my admonishments, they'd blast the song *Whiskey for My Men, Beer for my Horses* through a little boom box hooked up to their discman, while we drove through the Kandahari deserts. It continues to be the unofficial anthem of the Army Cavalry. . .our generation's Garryowen. Toby played that song for us at FOB Naray and it gave me chills. We all sung along with him during the chorus. Everyone knew the words. The lyrics couldn't have been more appropriate considering what we had all just experienced. "When the gun smoke settles we'll sing a victory tune and we'll all meet back at the local saloon . . . we'll raise up our glasses against evil forces. . . whiskey for my men, beer for my horses!" I enjoyed it immensely, no sound dubbing or glimmer or lights. He played a few other songs too but we knew he'd only be with us briefly and no one wanted the moment to end. He sounded like home . . . and that's where we knew we were finally heading.

On 26 May, during strong lunar illumination of the late night, I boarded a final ride out of Naray, onto a CH-47 Chinook bound for Bagram. Elements of 3-71 CAV vacated their positions from across five different outposts and FOBs, and they all consolidated at BAF. We were corralled like sheep into a giant, hot tent with old Army green cots. We call them circus tents. With about 200 guys per tent, they're hot and crowded and smelly. I complained to KBR about it. He said there is not enough electrical power to run the A/C into the transient tents. Bull shit. They just don't want to take any power away from the nice little hotel rooms that are all over this place for the FOBBITS. That's a play on Lord of the

2 Thomas G. Bostick Jr. was killed in action two months later, on July 27, 2007, during an ambush at one these same NAIs. He was posthumously promoted to Major and received the Distinguish Service Cross for his bravery and valor.

Toby Keith jams at FOB Naray next to 10th Mountain Division howitzer guns. *Author Collection*

3-71 Cav Trooper silhouetted against the sky near Kamdesh village. *Jeb Ridgeway*

Rings Hobbits, a term we've been using for the plump and jolly soldiers and airmen that never leave their cushy FOBs.

I found an internet café on the airfield and sat in the A/C lounge with some coffee and internet, and TV. It was nice. I tried to stay out of that horrid circus tent, except to sleep. BAF is so big and we are so spread out that I couldn't even find my friends.

On the morning of 30 May I flew on a C-17 jet to Manas Air Force Base where I currently wait, patiently. Tomorrow is the big day. I have been dreaming about tomorrow for 16 months and it's finally here. At 12 PM local time I will lift off on a commercial airliner, westward bound. I hope to arrive at Ft Drum around 11 PM local time on June 4, 2007. I'm told that our plane will have to refuel in Turkey at the Incirlik Air Force Base, then again in Shannon, Ireland, and then again somewhere at a Canadian Base (Gander) in Newfoundland.

Tomorrow's arrival and reunion is a huge landmark day for me. It signifies the beginning of a new chapter in my life. For all intents and purposes, my active-duty Army career is over. For the next 60 days of what's left of it, I will conduct a reverse SRC (Army term for getting re-acclimated to being a stateside Soldier again). I'll have 30 days of leave followed by a couple of weeks of clearing the installation, turning in my gear. Sometime around August, I should be out completely. I've talked before about my Army career being synonymous with my college years. I'm currently a 5th year senior, going into a summer semester in order to graduate in August. Haha.

The homecoming will be bittersweet and I'm sure we will be crying and laughing in turns. I still see the faces of the men 3-71 Cavalry has lost during the last 16 months. I see their faces everywhere . . . such good men that should still be alive today, but for this war. I have seen enough of it for a lifetime.

I'm very proud of 3-71 CAV and the 3rd Infantry Brigade Combat Team. I watched us grow from 10 men on Fort Drum's Old Post, to now a formidable fighting force, who have played a significant role in this war, and with unit colors now draped in banners representing honor and valor. I will always stand in awe of what we accomplished here.

I've now been an officer in the U.S. Army for 5 years and 17 days. 25 months of that time was spent on the front lines of Afghanistan. I remember towns and districts and names of provinces where I did things that will seem impossible to my older self, reading this 10 or 50 years from now . . . Places like Kandahar city, Musa Qaleh in Helmand, Dichopin district, Oruzgan City, the castle built by Alexander the Great in Qalat City, Zabul Province, Khowst, Gardez, Kabul, Jalalabad, Chalas, Asadabad, Naray, Gowardesh and Kamdesh. Nuristan Province. I've tramped almost every corner of this poor, rugged, contested, plagued, yet resilient country during my two tours. And I watched the Afghan government mature, all the while I've also seen the enemy grow more resolute, and his tactics evolve with greater precision and lethality.

We came here in response, and I know that I made a small difference while I served here. I've seen too many men die for there not to be a reason, for there not to be a positive result. There must be a change going on here for the better. I've seen it. I can sense it. But I guess it will take many more generations to fully realize it.

Well, 478 days later I'm finally coming home. My parents are currently waiting for me in New York. And that's all there is.

Signed
Captain Ross A. Berkoff
Military Intelligence, U.S. Army
3-71 Cavalry, 3rd IBCT
10th Mountain Division (Light Infantry)

EPILOGUE

Four months after I redeployed home to Fort Drum, and after my fair share of tear-filled farewells with my 3-71 CAV comrades, I finally got my wish: I started civilian employment with the Intelligence Community. More specifically, I joined the Defense Intelligence Agency (DIA) in Washington, D.C., as a contractor intelligence officer. I was more than ready to trade in my boots for brogues, and my uniform for a business suit. Maybe too eager, as I took one of the first job-offers I received. I was assigned to the DIA Balkans Branch and spent the next nine months tracking the disposition and strength of the Albanian Navy and Croatian Coast Guard. It was utterly boring. In my head, I was still in Afghanistan. I had all this knowledge built up in my memory store: the different insurgent groups, which ones worked together, and which ones didn't; their motives; their tactics, techniques, and procedures; their geographic and tribal affiliations. But I couldn't do anything about it. I tried desperately to be reassigned to the DIA Afghanistan Intelligence Cell, applying for several government positions there.

Finally, in July 2008, I got the chance I was waiting for. I moved to a new DIA Afghanistan Intelligence Analysis Services contract that specialized in providing strategic, all-source analysis on the Taliban insurgency (i.e. blending intelligence received from human sources with that of signals and imagery). Our analytic products were delivered to general officers, senior Defense policy makers, and intelligence executives. It was not long before I found myself briefing the highest-ranking intelligence officer in the armed forces—the J2 to the chairman of the Joint Chiefs of Staff. At that time, his name was Major General Mike Flynn. He was not quite the lunatic he became later, and I worked hard to make sure that my strategic level intelligence assessments, on topics ranging from Taliban shadow governments to Iranian Quds Force lethal aid to Taliban, subtlety integrated my 25 months of tactical intelligence reporting on Afghanistan's battlefields.[1] Several of my intelligence products were placed on the desk of both Presidents Bush and Obama. I had found my new calling.

In September 2009, I received an invitation from the White House to attend the Medal of Honor ceremony for SFC Jared Monti. His father, Paul Monti, and his family, received the medal on behalf of Jared. I had known, since mere days after Jared Monti was killed in June 2006, that LTC Howard and COL Nicholson were working hard to submit Jared for the Medal of Honor for his actions on "Hilltop 2610," near Gowardesh village. In the East Room of the White House on September 17th, 2009, I sat alongside Jared's boys who fought like hell on that hill three years earlier. Most of them now wore civilian clothes—like me—eager to reenter the civilian world. 15 years later, I still remember hearing President Obama's words. It was surreal. "Duty. Honor. Country. Service. Sacrifice. Heroism. These are words of weight," the President told us.

> But as people—as a people and as a culture, we often invoke them lightly. We toss them around freely. But do we really grasp the meaning of these values? Do we truly understand the nature of these virtues? To serve, and to sacrifice. Jared Monti knew. The Monti family knows. And they know that the actions we honor today were *not a passing moment of courage*. They were the culmination of a life of character and commitment. And so, as Jared would have wanted, we also pay tribute to those who fell alongside him: Staff Sergeant Patrick Lybert. Private First Class Brian Bradbury. Staff Sergeant Heathe Craig. And we honor all the soldiers he loved and who loved him back—among them noncommissioned officers who remind us why the Army has designated this "The Year of the NCO" in honor of all those sergeants who are the backbone of America's Army. They are Jared's friends and fellow soldiers watching this ceremony today in Afghanistan. They are the soldiers who this morning held their own ceremony on an Afghan mountain at the post that now bears his name—Combat Outpost Monti. And they are his "boys"—surviving members of Jared's patrol, from the 10th Mountain Division—who are here with us today. And I would ask them all to please stand.

1 Iran's special operations unit responsible for clandestine military and intelligence operations outside Iran.

In that moment, the veterans from 3-71 Cavalry in the East Room stood and received applause from the President of the United States, from our nation's top generals and lawmakers, and from the country. For a moment in time, those feelings that we were forgotten on those mountaintops, that our deployment to Nuristan was pointless—it was all eclipsed by a surreal, wonderful instant that our sacrifices were appreciated, worthy even of national gratitude. It sent chills down my spine and still does today as I write this. It was one of the most moving moments of my life.

The Army Special Forces ODA team that had just finished its FOB Naray deployment during the spring of 2007 included SSG Robert J. Miller, of the 3rd Special Forces Group. I conversed with SSG Miller on a few occasions at Naray, and I remember seeing his team off as it prepared to re-deploy back to the States, just a few months before I finally did. His team didn't get much rest. In October 2007, SSG Miller joined a new team for another FOB Naray rotation. I later learned, just a few months into that deployment, that his team was ambushed near the village of Bari Kowt, a few kilometers north of FOB Naray and just opposite the Pakistani border village of Arandu that I often visited. SSG Miller was killed in the ensuing firefight, but not before displaying uncommon valor. In October 2010, President Obama presented Miller's parents with their son's Medal of Honor. SSG Miller's Medal of Honor citation reads: "After killing at least 10 insurgents, wounding dozens more, and repeatedly exposing himself to withering enemy fire while moving from position to position, Staff Sergeant Miller was mortally wounded by enemy fire. His extraordinary valor ultimately saved the lives of seven members of his own team and 15 Afghanistan National Army soldiers."

SFC Jared Monti, SSG Robert J. Miller, and Navy Seal LT Mike Murphy: names of some of the American heroes that did extraordinary things in this ghastly corner of Afghanistan. They make up three of the five total posthumous Medals of Honor awarded during the 20-year War in Afghanistan. Not by coincidence, all three fought and died within a fifty-mile radius of each other, within the turbulent borders of northern Konar and Nuristan Province. In fact, out of the 20 total Medals of Honor awarded during America's Longest War, 13 of those medals were awarded for actions in or very near this same fifty-mile radius. To magnify this statistic, I would submit that this same deadly region saw many fewer "boots on the ground" than the rest of the country, and much less density of troops per square kilometer compared to places like Kandahar and Helmand. Fewer boots, but more intense fighting, which was often the result of the severe terrain-disadvantage our troops faced here. This statistic reveals some notion of the bond felt by U.S. Cavalry Troopers that rotated through this treacherous region. It was a place deceptively malleable yet unforgivably impenetrable. But it wasn't just the terrain that made it so daunting. We also faced a formidable adversary of stern resolution. The enemy in this region possessed the unique faculty for exhibiting unyielding resilience, agility, and bravery, layered with a deep-rooted ideological and xenophobic persistence. In the face of their tenacious nature, the valor and courage displayed by so many Americans who served here remains a testament to our unwavering commitment in opposing such a tough foe.

As a DIA intelligence analyst with a top-secret security clearance, I kept close track of the deteriorating security situation in Konar and Nuristan, the place that I had called home for 16 months. The July 13, 2008, battle at Combat Outpost Wanat, in western Nuristan Province and only about 20 miles from Kamdesh, was a terrible day for the U.S. Army. Nine American soldiers lost their lives, and more than two dozen were wounded in the type of coordinated attack, using overwhelming numbers, that we feared would eventually come.

In 2009, I was working in the Pentagon's National Military Command Center (NMCC), and I was assigned to a special DoD task force assembled to monitor and analyze daily security and governance successes and failures in Afghanistan; to keep members of Congress, the chairman of the Joint Chiefs of Staff, and the secretary of defense well informed. Ironically, our task force director was newly promoted Brigadier General John "Mick" Nicholson—my old Spartan 3rd Brigade Combat Team Commander.

October 3, 2009, started like any other day in the NMCC. After my twenty-minute metro ride to the Pentagon, I stopped in the courtyard for a coffee and then descended through several concrete layers, and multiple badge-swipes, to the underground SCIF that housed the NMCC's 24/7 watch floor. As I started compiling the overnight intelligence reports, one of my coworkers walked up to my desk and said: "Hey, Ross, weren't you in Kamdesh? Did you hear our guys got whacked there last night? Reports are coming in that COP Keating was overrun." I started digging through the raw reports, while watching the news for the story to break. That morning, a force of approximately 300 Afghan and foreign fighters conducted an early morning surprise attack from all directions. They came down hard on the troopers from 3-61 Cavalry. Eight American Cavalrymen were killed that day and 27 wounded. COP Keating was completely destroyed. 3-61 CAV withdrew its forces from that part of Nuristan. Soon after, all the small, remote outposts in the region were closed. Not unlike the chapters opened and closed by the Greeks, the Mongols, the British, and the Soviets, the story of the American military forces in Nuristan had come to an end.

In 2011, I read a press release that an *ABC Nightly News* reporter named Jake Tapper was going to write a book about the battle of Kamdesh and about COP Keating. My first reaction was "what does this White House Lawn-correspondent know about Kamdesh? What gives this guy the right to tell *our* story, or more than likely, to screw-up telling our story?" I decided to write a letter to his publisher and introduce myself as the Army intelligence officer who was assigned the unglamorous task of selecting the site and establishing what became known as COP Keating, three years before the final battle there. My letter went on to say that if Mr. Tapper is going to write a book about this battle, I want to make sure he understands the full depth and breadth of the situation there; the full scope of why the Army was there to begin with. In a nutshell, I didn't want this book to be about just the battle, without telling the whole story—our story. To his credit, Mr. Tapper contacted me almost immediately.

Over the coming months and years, Jake and I met up in various Georgetown diners and hotel bars near Lafayette Square to talk about 3-71 CAV's small role in the Army's larger strategy to drive a wedge between the insurgents and the civilian population of Nuristan province. It became clear to me that Mr. Tapper was genuinely inspired to tell the *whole* story, and he was committed to getting it done right, fully vetted by the men and women who served there. *The Outpost: An Untold Story of American Valor* was eventually published in 2011, and it chronicles not only 3-71 CAV in Nuristan, but also the three Army RSTA Squadrons that came after us during the following two and half years. I was honored when Jake decided to integrate several excerpts from my war journal into the final version of *The Outpost*. In addition to the fact that it's truly an all-encompassing, authentic account of U.S. Army Cavalry Operations in Konar and Nuristan, I know the veterans of 3-71 CAV remain very proud that the book is filled with the names of brave and good men with whom we fought and remember fondly—men like Jared Monti, Ben Keating, and Joe Fenty.

By 2013, the Afghan government had quit Nuristan. The province had become saturated and overpowered by Taliban and Islamic militants. Around that time, I recall viewing a Taliban propaganda video taken from inside our former outpost near Gowardesh, Camp Lybert. Taliban fighters were parading through the camp's main street, many showing off their U.S.-made M-4 carbine assault rifles, while others were trying to figure out how to use our treadmills and elliptical machines in our old fitness center. I began asking myself: "What was it all for?"

Watching Afghanistan's security and government infrastructure collapse in 2021, in real-time, followed by the chaotic and deadly withdrawal of American forces from our last remaining bases, left me, and many of my fellow veterans, grappling with profound feelings of frustration and a sense of betrayal. After two decades of sacrifice, loss, and commitment, the abrupt and seemingly futile conclusion to the conflict left us with a bitter taste of defeat. For those who served on the front lines, like the men and women of the 10th Mountain Division with whom I served, the scenes of Taliban resurgence and the rapid fall of provincial capitals triggered a mix of emotions: anger at the perceived failure of leadership, sorrow for the Afghan people left behind, and deep questions about the purpose and validity of our sacrifices. I personally invested years of my life, witnessed the untimely death of good men, and endured the physical and psychological toll of combat, all under the belief that I was contributing to a greater cause—destroying those that attacked us on 9/11 while also bringing stability and security to the people of Afghanistan.

To witness the unraveling of those efforts in such a swift and chaotic manner evokes feelings of betrayal and abandonment. I remember the sight of our Afghan allies desperately seeking refuge, clinging to the wings and landing gears of an American C-17 before falling to their deaths against the flawless blue Kabul sky. Watching the collapse of Afghan institutions we painstakingly helped build, and the uncertainty of what lay ahead intensifies the collective sense of disillusionment among my friends and fellow vets who had once believed in the mission.

In July 2021, when Afghanistan's future seemed increasingly bleak and uncertain, I tuned in to NPR radio during my drive home from work and caught a very moving story about SPC Justin O'Donohoe, one of the Alpha Troopers killed in that terrible helicopter crash on May 5th, 2006, alongside Joe Fenty. Justin was from the San Diego, California area and with so much media coverage of Afghanistan that summer, a local NPR reporter, Steven Walsh, wanted to do a story on San Diego Gold Star families—families who've lost loved ones in the war. Listening to Justin's father speak over the radio about the devasting loss of his son, his voice crackling and choking back tears all these years later, brought on a surge of unexpected emotion for me.

But I was also jolted with a sense of joy to hear the familiar voice on the radio broadcast of a former Alpha Trooper and 3-71 CAV scout, Nick Pilozzi. Nick was one of the troopers on the mountaintop that terrible night. I remembered Nick as one of the first cavalry scouts assigned to Alpha Troop as I helped stand up the organization in 2004. During this radio tribute to Justin, Nick talked about the dangers of that nighttime landing zone on May 5th, and how the Chinook tumbled and exploded down the cliff. The radio report mentioned the fact that Nick had actually boarded the Chinook during its first landing attempt, but he was jettisoned back to the ground during the aircraft's turbulence. He sustained leg and head wounds as a result. He was forced to watch the helicopter, only seconds later, crash and burn, carrying his buddies down the mountain who were not as lucky as he. He talked about the futile attempts to contact possible survivors or reach the 3000-degree Fahrenheit crash site.

Nick said something during the broadcast that really stood out to me, referring to the broader conflict. He said: "It was about 9/11, but at this point, I don't really know what it's about." I could sense the anguish in his voice when he uttered those words. Very simply, he summed up what most of us were feeling at the time. "The damage that comes from this stuff is unbelievable. None of these families will ever be the same, after this," were his final words in that NPR segment.

The NPR report said Nick was living peacefully on a farm near where he grew up outside Buffalo, New York. Nick was a Facebook friend and after the radio report, I decided to reconnect and check in on him. I told him I was proud of him for speaking up, and that he did well. I told him to hang in there. I got the sense that he was dealing with traumatic survivor's guilt. Whatever comfort I was trying to offer him, it was not nearly enough. I did not know at the time that Nick had recently lost his leg during a lawnmowing accident, likely related to muscular deterioration stemming from his war wounds. I certainly had no idea that Nick was in, or was heading into, a very dark mental and emotional cave. Six months later, I heard from a fellow veteran that Nick took his own life. His family said that Nick, during that summer of 2021, was addicted to news outlets relating to the final collapse and withdrawal in Afghanistan. They also said he fixated on the idea that the sacrifices he and his friends in 3-71 CAV made were meaningless. He was the fourth soldier with whom I served in Afghanistan to take his own life. Nick Pilozzi, certainly, was the 11th and hopefully the last casualty stemming from that terrible crash.

In the fall of 2020, as the security situation was crumbling across Afghanistan, I lost my stepfather to a very aggressive cancer that he contracted while breathing in Ground Zero's toxic dust. While he was very lucky to have avoided the WTC on September 11th, a location he often frequented for early morning work meetings, he had no idea what he was about to sign up for. In the months that followed the attack, my stepdad slept on his Weehawken, New Jersey, office couch by night so that by day he could help the Port Authority of New Jersey and New York re-build the train systems underneath the ashes of where the WTC once stood. Bill Czirjak married my mother when I was 11 years old, four years after my father, Steven Berkoff, died of cancer. An Army veteran from the Vietnam War era, Bill's passion for adventure combined with his highly disciplined work ethic was part of my own inspiration for a career in military service. After he passed, my family was contacted by the World Trade Center Health Program and the 9/11 Victim Compensation Fund. They confirmed an awful truth, and I was once again reminded of the costs of our response to that terrible day. Suddenly my Afghanistan deployments, the men that I lost and their families who continue to mourn "The Vacant Chair," formed for me a symbiotic relationship with my own dad's passing. All these years later, re-reading my words "I came here in response" held a whole new meaning for me. Reflecting on the notion that my service in Afghanistan is somehow intrinsically linked to my own stepdad's sacrifice is difficult to bring into focus, yet I'm hoping it might become clearer if examined from an unexpected vantage point. In time, perhaps I'll gain the clarity.

In the aftermath of 2021, many of us were gripped with existential questions about the meaning and legacy of our service. We struggle with—and continue to unpack—feelings of guilt or regret, wondering if our sacrifices were really in vain. I have talked to some veterans that harbor strong resentment towards policymakers whose actions led to such a futile end. However, amid the disillusionment, I have also seen positive moments of reflection and solidarity among our veterans, as we lean on each other for support and understanding. Despite the chaotic nature of the 2021 withdrawal, I think many of us feel a strange sense of peace that we can finally close that chapter of our lives. I believe that we, the veterans of the Afghanistan War, can finally find some solace in using the past tense to refer to the Global War on Terror (GWOT). It's now a *former* military campaign and not unlike other American wars, GWOT veterans deserve their own national memorial. Over the past couple of years, I've been privileged to support the GWOT Memorial Foundation, a non-profit organization designated by Congress in 2017 as the entity to plan, fund, and build our memorial. The National GWOT Memorial is planning to open to the public in 2028 in Washington, D.C., adjacent to the Vietnam Memorial, once its construction is completed. We will finally have our own lasting tribute to those who served and sacrificed—honoring the heroes of *this* century's Greatest Generation.

I never expected my journal entries to become the basis for my own book more than 20 years later. In some ways this book was born from the collision of two tragedies: the Army's withdrawal from Afghanistan in 2021 (including the national debate that followed) and my stepfather's untimely passing, which made September 11th and my combat deployments even more personal. This motivated me to publish my accounts for posterity, so that the public would better understand the perspectives of common soldiers who served there. This has been a cathartic experience for me, personally. The mental task of recalling and putting to paper some of the more painful thoughts, memories, and images that have been stored away for two decades oddly engendered a cathartic healing effect that I was subconsciously craving.

As we navigate the aftermath of the Afghanistan conflict, I hope this book—my journal entries and letters home—will help carry some of the weight of our collective experiences. The feelings of our Afghanistan veterans related to the troop withdrawal are complex and deeply personal, perhaps reflecting the difficulties and contradictions of the Longest War itself. Despite some feelings of betrayal with the war's outcome, I am confident the bonds I forged with the servicemen and women of the 10th Mountain Division will endure and offer a glimmer of hope and resilience. I hope, in the end, my stories help our veterans combat the feeling that while it may have felt like it was all for nothing, we can honestly say that we left that country a better place than we found it—at least for the period of time we were there. And of course, for those of us who remember where we were and how we felt on September 11th, 2001, with pride and certainty, we will continue to say: "We're here in response."

INDEX

About the Author

Ross Berkoff served on active duty as an Armor and Military Intelligence officer from 2002 to 2009. After his service with the 10th Mountain Division, he joined the District of Columbia Army National Guard before transitioning to the private sector, where he became an industry executive in the federal government contracting, defense, and intelligence communities. His combat deployments earned him two Bronze Stars, two Army Commendation Medals, and two Afghanistan Campaign Ribbons. He takes great pride in the 3-71 Cavalry's Meritorious Unit Commendation for conducting "highly successful counterinsurgency operations against determined opponents in the most austere and rugged conditions in the world." Ross and his wife Rebekah reside in Virginia, with their two children, Eliana and Aaron.